RUNNING SCARED

RUNNING SCARED

The Life
and
Treacherous
Times of
Las Vegas
Casino King
Steve Wynn

JOHN L. SMITH

Four Walls Eight Windows

New York

Published in the United States by:
Four Walls Eight Windows
39 West 14th Street, Room 503
New York, N.Y., 10011

Originally published by Barricade Books, Fort Lee, N.J.

Visit our website at http://www.4W8W.com

First printing January 2001.

Library of Congress Cataloging-in-Publication Data:
Smith, John L., 1960-
Running scared: the life and treacherous times of Las Vegas casino king Steve Wynn.

p. cm.
Includes bibliographical references and index.
ISBN: 1-56858-190-4
1. Wynn, Steve. 2. Casinos—Nevada—Las Vegas. 3. Organized crime—Nevada—Las Vegas. 4. Nineteen twenties. I. Title.
HV6711.S64   1995
364.172 092—dc20   [B] 95-15251
                                                              CIP

Book design by Cindy LaBreacht Design

10 9 8 7 6 5 4 3 2 1

Printed in Canada

For my stand-up wife, Patty. For my parents, Prince and Janet, desert people who taught me the difference between an oasis and a mirage.

And for the good people of Las Vegas, because there is no such thing as a benevolent dictator.

TABLE OF CONTENTS

PART III

Preface by Lyle Stuart, publisher of Barricade Books, the original hardcover publisher of *RUNNING SCARED*

This book gave birth to the most important First Amendment court case in America at the beginning of the new millennium.

Las Vegas *Review-Journal* columnist John L. Smith submitted his proposal for a Steve Wynn biography. Wynn, the reputed "most powerful man in Nevada" had managed to discourage any book about himself from being published.

As you will learn in these pages, he had reasons.

No sooner was *Running Scared* announced than Wynn called the *Review-Journal* four times in a single week to demand that the newspaper, in which his casinos were major advertisers, "do something" about Smith.

The clear implication was, "Fire him!"

Smith wasn't fired, but he was told to not mention *Running Scared* or its publisher in his column, and to avoid references to Steve Wynn.

Two days later, Smith was sued for libel by Steve Wynn. Not for this book, which he'd written but which hadn't been published yet, but rather for the description of the forthcoming book in a Barricade Books wholesale catalog.

Wynn's action was an obvious move to delay the book. Or better still, to scuttle it.

I immediately wrote to Wynn's attorney to tell him that it was I, and not John Smith, who had written the catalog description. I added that Smith hadn't seen my words until the catalogs had been produced.

An agreement was reached, thanks to noted Philadelphia attorney and dear friend Albert B. Gerber. Gerber persuaded me to agree to do something that I hadn't done in forty years of publishing books: I would show the manuscript to Steve Wynn so that he could point out any factual inaccuracies.

In return, Wynn would withdraw his lawsuit against John L. Smith.

Steve Wynn obviously misunderstood my motive. By allowing him to read the script, I hoped to make the book as accurate as possible.

A few days later, he spoke to a radio interviewer about our forthcoming meeting. He declared, "There won't be any book. I've cowed the publisher."

He didn't know his man.

When Albert B. Gerber, John L. Smith, my wife Carole and I appeared at Wynn's executive office at the Mirage for our scheduled meeting with him, we were met instead by two attorneys who told us, "We don't expect you to publish this book."

I set them straight. "Listen carefully. No matter what, we're publishing this book."

The conference, scheduled for a day or maybe two, ended in about thirty minutes when the four of us walked out.

A top Mirage executive later told me, "Nobody wants to bring bad news to Steve Wynn. He's got a legendary bad temper."

Until that morning, I'd been a Mirage high-roller. I had a $100,000 line of casino credit. Wynn's failure to appear as agreed, changed this. I never gamble in any casino where the owner breaks his word.

Two days later, on learning that Barricade was going forward with the book despite his lawyer's menacings, Wynn sued again.

This time he sued Barricade Books and myself as well as John L. Smith. Suing Smith was obviously mean-spirited and vindictive. Barry Langberg, Wynn's sleazy attorney, would eventually lose his case against Smith.

Wynn has the allegiance of many of Nevada's judges because he has made regular contributions to their election campaigns. It's all legal in Nevada, but he has often acted as if it placed him above the law. And in the minds of others, it gave the impression of corruption.

My agreement to meet with Wynn contained a confidentiality clause. Neither I nor Wynn were to discuss it. In violation, Wynn spoke about in on a radio discussion program as well as in an interview with the New York *Times*.

Nevertheless, when *Running Scared* appeared, he sued to have my introduction torn out of every copy because, he claimed, I had violated our confidentiality agreement.

My attorneys easily proved that Wynn had clearly violated the agreement first. The judge had no choice but to rule in my favor. Langberg lost another lawsuit.

A trial took place in August, 1997, in Las Vegas before a state judge. Twelve other judges had recused themselves from the case because they had accepted campaign contributions from Wynn. The thirteenth, a judge by the name of Sally Loehrer, had taken Wynn's money, and accepted the case. So much for ethical considerations.

The jury that was selected contained a man who admitted he'd like to get a job at a Wynn casino, and a woman who said she'd socialized with one of Wynn's attorneys. Several others said in their questionnaires that they hated the press.

The jury trial lasted almost two weeks. It was a charade. When one of Wynn's attorneys stood up, the judge smiled. When one of my attorneys stood up, she scowled.

Judge Loehrer wouldn't allow us to present critical evidence linking Wynn to famous underworld figures. She allowed all of Wynn's evidence in.

Even in her final instructions to the jury, she weighted things to favor Wynn. For example, the state law requires a defendant to have "serious doubts" about the accuracy of his words. She removed the word "serious."

She allowed Langberg in his summation to erroneously tell the jury that "Stuart has done this twice before." He implored the panel, "Give me millions...to show him he can't continue to do this."

Langberg knew otherwise, because I had explained to him in detail when he took my deposition, that the two other libel suits had nothing to do with me, and that one case had nothing to do with Barricade Books either.

Nor would Judge Sally allow us to inform the jury that we didn't carry libel insurance.

The jury returned a decision for Steve Wynn. Following the judge's instructions, it decided that when I cited the New Scotland Yard investigation report, I committed libel.

Thus the critical First Amendment issue. It is widely accepted that a writer or reporter may quote from an official document and be protected against libel even if the material is inaccurate.

My statement was accurate. The 100-page New Scotland Yard report ended by saying that "Wynn is under the aegis of the Genovese crime family."

I simplified this by promising that "This book would detail why a New Scotland Yard report said Wynn was a front man for the Genovese crime family."

The book does just that.

The judge wouldn't allow *Running Scared* as evidence. Nor would she allow as evidence a confidential Atlantic City report considerably stronger in associating Wynn with mob figures. Or allow a CBS television documentary to be shown to the jury which charged Wynn with mob associations. (He walked off the set when questioned on this.)

Wynn isn't innocent Joe College. He got his first loan from the Teamsters Central States Pension Fund which was then controlled by the Genovese capo Anthony Provenzano.

Wynn said the damage he'd felt from the catalog copy was that it caused him to lose sleep and to lose interest in going to work.

For this, the jury awarded him $3,100,000.

We had been home-towned.

We didn't have $3,100,000. So Langberg obtained a court order that stopped our warehouse from shipping not only *Running Scared* but all Barricade titles as well. In short, we were out of business. To release our books and stay in business, we applied for and were given Chapter 11 bankruptcy protection.

Meanwhile, Wynn filed a libel action against *Running Scared* in Kentucky. Why Kentucky? I'll never know. Sleazy Langberg may have been unaware that years before, the Governor of Kentucky had appointed me a Kentucky Colonel. That would have played well with a Kentucky jury, but Wynn was too smart to let it come to this.

In order to sue in Kentucky, Wynn had to show that people he knew had read this book. That was a tough one, since we had shipped maybe three copies of *Running Scared* into the entire state... And the chances of his knowing anyone who'd bought one of those three copies were millions-to-one.

At this point, someone suborned perjury. An agent was asked to get five people who didn't know Wynn to swear that they did.

The book you hold in your hands is so accurate that Wynn was forced to withdraw his Kentucky libel suit. Before we would allow him to do that, he had to agree to never sue on *Running Scared* anywhere in the world.

We needed a competent lawyer to handle our appeal before the Nevada Supreme Court.

We got lucky. Brilliant New York attorney David Blasband agreed to handle our appeal.

The entire publishing industry rallied behind us. An amicus (friend of the court) brief supporting us was filed by such publishers as the Washington *Post*, *Time*, the New York *Times*, *Playboy*, Rupert Murdoch, the Nevada Press Association, the American Book Publishers Association, P.E.N. and twenty others.

Several book publishers wanted to help. John Oakes of Four Walls Eight Windows is a principled fellow who offered to publish this trade paperback edition as a statement in support of the First Amendment. Thus, no matter how Barricade Books fared in the courts, the public could continue to have access to the truth about Steve Wynn.

We could have settled this matter several times if we agreed to withdraw *Running Scared* from circulation.

As a First Amendment fanatic, there was no way I would agree to do that.

Lyle Stuart
Fort Lee, NJ 07024
September 2000

Postscript:

Just before this edition of Running Scared went to press, a story by A. O. Hopkins appeared in the Las Vegas *Review Journal*.

Hopkins, an investigative reporter on that paper, revealed that shortly after the trial, the judge's husband was given a high-paying executive position in Steve Wynn's Bellagio.

Judge Loehrer was quoted as saying this revelation was "demeaning" to her. Steve Wynn never promised her any reward for the way she favored him in conducting the case and her husband got the job all by himself.

This prompted JoNell Thomas, our Las Vegas attorney in the case, to respond, "Under the Judicial Code, the judge had an obligation to make disclosures involving any issue that raises even the appearance of impropriety.

"This was a very high-profile case. The judge could have sent a letter to the parties in the case saying, 'My husband now works at the Bellagio and I had nothing to do with getting him the job.'

"It is something I have just learned that I would have liked to have known almost two years ago when it happened," Thomas said.

ACKNOWLEDGMENTS

No one walks the streets of Las Vegas without his share of sources and allies. In my time, I have been blessed to become acquainted with some of the greatest characters to ever escape from the pages of a Damon Runyon short story. From cops to bookmakers, cornermen to casino men, dozens of Las Vegans not only provided encouragement for this project but plenty of anecdotes as well. I'll see you on the street, fellas.

This book would not have been possible without the assistance of nearly 100 people who generously shared their documents, stories, and perspectives on Steve Wynn. The fact so many of them wish to remain anonymous only proves they are as prudent as they are cooperative.

The work and insight of dozens of newspaper, magazine, and television journalists also was a tremendous help. Among many: George Anastasia, Lolita C. Baldor, Warren Bates, John Bebow, Myram Borders, Jeff Burbank, John G. Carlton, Monica Caruso, Bill Cummings, Tim Dahlberg, the late Ned Day, John Edwards, Roger D. Friedman, John Gallant, Bill Gang, Carri Geer, Jeff German, Marian Green, Daniel Heneghan, Boyd Hagen, Mary

Hausch, Carmel Hopkins, Mary Hynes, Patrick Jenkins, W.F. Keough, George Knapp, Wayne C. Kodey, Sergio Lalli, Bob Macy, Jane Ann Morrison, Peter O'Neil, Dave Palermo, Marcia Pledger, Jeff Scheid, Stanley Tromp, Lynn Waddell, Pat Wechsler, Charles Zobell.

The support of members of the *Las Vegas Review-Journal* staff in general and Editor Thomas Mitchell particularly cannot be overstated. I especially would like to thank Al Tobin, Jim Laurie, and Ed Becker for their steadfast friendship.

Attorneys Dominic Gentile and Al Gerber helped usher the manuscript through tumultuous legal waters, and Howard Schwartz of Gamblers Book Club proved an invaluable source.

A special note of thanks to my agent, Frank Weimann, for his encouragement. Frank had the good sense to seek out Lyle and Carole Stuart, who never have backed away from a fight and never gave up on this manuscript. They were wise enough to have Sandra Lee Stuart edit the story. Nor can I overlook the valuable contributions made to my script by Anthony Winkler and Arnold Bruce Levy. Of course, my first editors remain my wife, Patty, and my big sister, Cath Cassidy.

My parents taught me to speak my mind and stand my ground, which isn't always easy in Las Vegas. The rest of my family, Christy, Jim, Margaret, Marie, and Grandma Emma, have backed my play for years. To them I owe my love and respect.

"Can I be as I believe myself or as others believe me to be? Here is where these lines become a confession. ...Here is where I create the legend wherein I must bury myself."

—MIGUEL DE UNAMUNO

"I'm dying to take as much credit as I can get, just like everybody else. But, honestly, the longer this goes on and the more I get a chance to look at it, the more convinced I am in the overwhelming impact of timing in all of our lives."

—STEVE WYNN

"It's a very difficult thing to deny or say: 'You've been living in Las Vegas. Surely you must have met or been involved with those kinds of people, the underworld, the unsavory element.' First of all you're asking a fellow, if it were true, he would had to have lied about it all these years. If he were to admit it, he would immediately lose his status as a gaming executive. He would be out with shame and disgrace....The fact of the matter is, though, it was never even close. I never even got approached."

—STEVE WYNN

PIRATES IN THE DESERT

October 27, 1993—a night for pirates, pyrotechnics, and sleight-of-hand of unprecedented proportion; a night for carving out one legend while reducing another to the rubble and the fine dust of the past.

More than 200,000 gawking revelers flood the Las Vegas Strip and press against police barriers. It is the kind of crowd that assembles in the street on New Year's Eve or to watch a ten-car pileup on the Interstate. Through the tangle of teenagers and tourists, a few gawkers have elbowed in to pay their final respects to the last great symbol of the old Las Vegas, the Dunes Hotel and Casino. The rest are here for the apocalyptic spectacle brought to them by the king of the new Las Vegas, Mirage Resorts Chairman Steve Wynn.

"Blow it up! Blow it up! Blow it up!" the crowd chants.

The implosion of the twenty-three-story Dunes tower and destruction of its eighteen-story neon sign with "No Vacancy" on the marquee is being covered by more than 300 members of the world media, and by every major television network. For months, national magazines and newspapers have hyped the arrival of the new, family-safe Las Vegas. The big bang marks the opening of the pirate-themed Treasure Island next to the Mirage, Wynn's formidable entry into the multibillion-dollar casino industry's burgeoning family market.

In a city built on hyperbole, illusion, and endless hucksterism, the implosion ranks as the biggest commotion on the Strip since a super-radiated mutant five stories high stole the Silver Slipper's Buick-sized shoe in the fifties science-fiction movie, *The Super Colossal Man*. This moment seems almost as surreal, with Steve Wynn playing the role of the fifty-foot giant.

"Blow it up! Blow it up! Blow it up!"

With a single command, and $1.5 million in explosives, Wynn will do in thirty seconds what his wiseguy predecessors failed to accomplish in two generations: erase from the skyline and the public's mind the memory of the old mobbed-up Las Vegas.

Its scandalous thirty-seven-year run of luck marked by everything from the mob-dominated Teamsters Central States Pension Fund to hidden ownership by some of America's most infamous members of organized crime, the Dunes is a particularly notorious reminder of the dark heart of the city.

"Blow it up! Blow it up! Blow it up!"

In a moment, it will be reduced to a thirty-foot-high mound of rubble and twisted iron by the explosives experts of Controlled Demolition International.

The evening's festivities, total tab nearly three million dollars, are being filmed as part of the one-hour infomercial called "Treasure Island, the Adventure Begins," featuring thirteen-year-old *Young Indiana Jones* star, Corey Carrier. The night belongs to Steve Wynn. Television stations interrupt their regularly scheduled programs to go live from ground zero.

"Ready," Wynn shouts over the public-address system, "aim...fire!"

The one-million-dollar fireworks display fills the sky with bright colors and choking smoke, rousting a flock of pigeons from its roost and scattering them through the violent scene like tiny warplanes darting through antiaircraft fire. On the street, the chaos is crushing. Half the crowd cheers, the other half flinches from the booming reports of the fireworks.

Explosion after explosion tears the night sky: Disney meets Desert Storm.

Showers of sparks shoot from the roof of the Dunes, its neon sign throbbing as if it were not its last night on the Strip. The John Williamsian "Treasure Island" theme music blaring in the background is overwhelmed by thunderous booms. The movie dialogue is drowned out by the rapid-fire pounding of the fireworks.

Suddenly, a fire in the sky. White pompoms and silver plumes splash the night like a Jackson Pollock painting.

A red wave of fire lights up the rooftop.

At the given signal, a series of explosions appear to batter the property like incoming bombs from an unseen source. They coincide with the pirate battle one-half mile up the Strip at the Treasure Island.

Yet another blast rocks the Dunes sign, and the eighteen-story icon topples like a neon Christmas tree. Seconds later, flames climb the tower, setting off a death rumble.

The twenty-three-story tower collapses like an accordion in a 100-foot wall of dust and the black smoke of Vegas past. Rooftop cameras capture the collapse of the old Las Vegas through the choking smoke. More than two tons of dust billows into the atmosphere—a small price for such a grand illusion. Not even Wynn's own house magicians, Siegfried and Roy, could have made the notorious Dunes vanish so completely.

"Oh, my God," one breathless spectator gasps. "It's like the end of the world."

Not quite. Armageddon wouldn't be this well conceived.

This moment marks not the end, but the beginning of a new world based on a generations-old theme.

It is a world under the reign of Steve Wynn.

Steve Wynn is perennially voted the most interesting Las Vegan by newspaper readers. He is the person locals say they want to know more about.

Backed by a powerful political machine of his own making, he employs more than eighteen thousand workers—most of them registered voters—and has curried favor at the highest levels of the Republican Party. He commands the helm of a $1.5 billion corporation he crafted out of a tawdry downtown Las Vegas grind joint and isn't shy about spending money to impress the right people. He has been called America's casino don, and behind the expensive Cheshire-Cat grin is said to be the man who made the mob vanish in Las Vegas.

Wynn claims the presence of the mob has been a "nonevent" in his life. Yet a look into the files amassed over the years by law enforcement agencies, ranging from New Scotland Yard to downtown Las Vegas, suggests otherwise. Whether by nature of the casino business or his own aggressive nature, Wynn's monumental business climb has remained disturbingly close to the mob.

Wynn combines the creative brilliance of Caesars Palace and Circus Circus developer Jay Sarno with a flamboyant knack for self-promotion never before seen in the legalized gambling racket. Compared to Wynn, Benjamin "Bugsy" Siegel—incorrectly portrayed as the father of modern Las Vegas—was a bug-eyed thug with short pockets. Compared to Wynn, eccentric industrialist Howard Hughes was little more than a neurotic landlord.

The Wynn who can laugh at himself after accidentally shooting off his index finger is the same fellow who is capable of throwing an epithet-laced tantrum over a single burned-out light bulb in his hotel, or smashing a table lamp onto the floor because a reporter's question triggered his anger. Bugsy and Hughes had nothing on the latest Vegas king.

Wynn belies the classic Las Vegas stereotypes, being adorned with no loud sport coats, no white shoes, no pinky rings. He shuns the company of craps dealers and pit bosses, preferring such diverse characters as Michael Milken and Michael Jackson. He has an Ivy League education, impeccable taste in clothes, and a command of the English language. And he is handsome, thanks to a power coif, capped teeth, a facelift, and a daily fitness regimen under the guidance of a personal trainer. Now past fifty, Wynn continues to cut an image of a young, up-and-coming entrepreneur out to shake up the world.

It is a legend as carefully sculpted as the man.

Among many accolades: He is a patron and member of the advisory council of the prestigious American Academy of Achievement, which brings together promising students with some of the nation's greatest minds.

As a victim of retinitis pigmentosa, a degenerative eye disease, Wynn is a multimillion-dollar contributor and chairman of the Moran Eye Institute at the University of Utah.

He is an advisory board member at the Center for Strategic and International Studies in Washington, has given generously to the University of Nevada–Las Vegas, and has used that relationship to promote himself and his company in other gaming jurisdictions.

He has emerged as the self-appointed spokesman for the casino industry, in part because so few others can get a word in edgewise. But only a fool would doubt his intellect and articulate rhetoric.

Wynn's apostles are legion.

"Everyone knows about Steve Wynn. And I take it to start with as a given fact that Steve Wynn is the most creative personality in modern gaming," British journalist and author David Spanier reported to an audience of casino executives at the ninth International Gaming Conference in Las Vegas in 1994. "I went to the opening of the Mirage in November 1989, and it was an incredible event. The Mirage did not happen overnight, although it looked like that when it hit the Strip running at full tilt. I couldn't believe it when I saw the amazing setup there. Not just the volcanoes and the tigers and then the dolphins, and the light and dark interior, but the marvelous way this huge place was scaled down to give a human dimension of warmth and intimacy and fun."

Steve Wynn has truly rocked the industry to its foundations with his formidable casino resorts and outspoken political stands. The nation's press has responded with hosannas: He is the Great Casino Salesman; He is the Vegas King; He is Mr. Lucky; He is the man whose image and message is helping spread legalized gambling throughout the nation.

"He is demanding, he is energetic, and he can run through people very easily," his wife, Elaine Wynn said.

———

Just who is this guy?

And what role, if any, has the underworld played in his rise to power?

The son of a wiseguy gambler with bingo hall operations in seven states, Wynn entered the Las Vegas casino market at the Frontier in 1967 among the company of Detroit mobsters and their front men.

The series of stepladder business deals that enabled him to bankroll the takeover of the Golden Nugget were carefully planned by a Las Vegas banking pioneer who facilitated the millions in mob-tainted Teamsters Central States Pension Fund loans used to fuel the first great casino construction boom on the Strip.

Allegations of drug abuse and cocaine trafficking have plagued Wynn throughout his career, and he has invited federal scrutiny by refusing to sever himself from a suspected narcotics trafficker and mob associate.

His foray into Atlantic City was reported to be riddled with links to the Genovese crime family, not the least of which was his insistence on hiring a longtime friend who had met at least twice with La Cosa Nostra boss Anthony "Fat Tony" Salerno.

While the effects of Michael Milken's junk bonds were causing the demise of at least fifty-five savings and loans nationwide, Steve Wynn used his relationship with the securities wizard to raise untold millions to build the Golden Nugget in Atlantic City and the Mirage on the Strip. His domination of the Las Vegas casino and political scene has made him the most intimidating force in Nevada.

But over time, like a silent-movie queen, his youthful charm and endearing cockiness have turned into bullying and arrogance. His inability to control his volatile ego has helped sabotage the impressive casino proposals of Mirage Resorts in gaming jurisdictions from British Columbia to Miami Beach. Steve Wynn has spent millions in corporate assets attempting to rewrite laws and his own portfolio. In the end, it is Wynn's volcanic personality—not stubborn legislators, angry voters or negative press reports—which has proved to be his own worst enemy.

That and a daunting mound of documents raising troubling questions about his relationship with organized crime.

Steve Wynn has long said he wants his epitaph to read "Running Scared, Straight Ahead," but his words provide a puzzle in two parts:

How has this golden boy of legalized gambling run so far?

And what has he had to fear?

PART
I

YOUNG STEPHEN

Like a tale from an American mythology, the Steve Wynn legend begins in youth with a vision of Las Vegas shimmering in the middle of the Mojave Desert.

It was 1952, and the city of Las Vegas held all the architectural appeal of a pop-up set from a Hollywood back lot. Steve was ten years old when, on a two-week visit with his father, Mike, he caught his first glimpse of the place he one day would reshape, dominate, and battle to control.

Their short trip to the Wild West of Las Vegas transcended glitter and pony rides. It altered the young boy's world view and left him forever changed. Young Stephen was a grownup in kids' clothing with brown eyes that took in everything around him— the intoxicating lights, noise, and action. Even in 1952, there was much for a boy to see in Las Vegas.

"There was magic in this place. It was like stepping back into the frontier," Steve Wynn would recall years later. "Casino owners were king: they owned the town. They were glamorous; they had beautiful women and lots of money."

Las Vegas was a crude cow-town, but dapper Mike Wynn—a bingo parlor operator—was drawn to the desert from Utica, New York, like a gypsy moth to neon. He was determined to open a bingo hall on the second floor of the Silver Slipper, and his son jumped at the opportunity to play the role of trusty valet.

Migrating from bingo halls to Las Vegas casinos was almost a natural and expected move for any ambitious operator, and Nevada gambling history is replete with examples of others who, unlike Mike, successfully followed that path. They range from Sam Boyd, patriarch of the Boyd Group which operates the Stardust, Fremont, and California Hotel in Las Vegas, to Bill Harrah of Reno who is recognized as one of the founders of the modern, image-conscious casino industry.

On that magical holiday, father and son spent their days riding horses not far from the Strip. They crossed wide stretches of desert real estate that today are covered by asphalt, shopping centers, and housing tracts. They chased cows, tried to rope a wild burro, passed the skeletons of cattle.

Like a couple of actors from a Hollywood western, they rode to the back door of the Sands and tied up their ponies. The desert began a few feet behind the Frontier, and silent-screen cowboy star Hoot Gibson's ranch was a short jaunt away.

For young Stephen, the two weeks in Las Vegas provided a rare chance to enjoy his father's exclusive attention without the interruption of sudden business trips to Pennsylvania, Connecticut, or Florida. For a son who worshiped his father, it was an idyllic interlude.

For Mike Wynn, Las Vegas had all the alluring glitter of a rare opportunity. But as an inveterate gambler, the city that never closed also exploited his every weakness. "He used to go to bed with me and then sneak out at night and shoot dice at the Flamingo and the Sands," Steve Wynn recalled years later.

One night after awaking alone, as the tale goes, young Stephen dressed and slipped out into the streets in search of his father.

There were plenty of sights to see.

Stripper-deluxe Tempest Storm was headlining at the Embassy Club. Abbott and Costello were at El Rancho Vegas, Red Skelton was at the Sands, and at the Silver Slipper Saloon, the Parisienne Follies were just finishing their risqué run. Along the way, the kid blundered into an adult fantasy world filled with boozy laughter and the irresistible scent of vice. Mike Wynn wasn't hard to find, the number of clubs and dice tables being then limited. The father was reveling in a gambling world that would break a man's heart faster than a bad woman.

And how Mike Wynn loved to gamble. If it moved, he would bet on it—cards, dice, horses, sports, and especially baseball. Mike Wynn bet with and befriended some of the biggest bookmakers in New York, including baseball "specialists" Charlie Meyerson and Herbie Liebert. Other bookmakers and loans harks, including mob bookmaker and money lender Gaspare "Jasper" Speciale, were well acquainted with Mike Wynn, who would himself be suspected of booking bets out of his bingo operations.

"I remember thinking, 'What a place to live,'" Steve Wynn recalled. "'What an incredible, outrageous environment. What a glamorous, colorful, totally bizarre environment this is. The fellows who control this must be having a ball.' They were, in those days, having a ball."

But after two weeks in Las Vegas, Mike Wynn was just another loser. The tables had not been kind.

He was broke again.

———

Las Vegas of that era was not merely a desert oasis where people carried on, drank, smoked, and gambled. It was almost as much a state of mind as a speck on the map. In 1952, the Strip, which eventually would emerge as the largest hotel corridor in the world, was still known by most locals as U.S. Highway 91. Although the town was booming, there was more sagebrush than sin.

Mike Wynn's acquaintances were in on the ground floor and stood to make a fortune as America warmed up to the Vegas idea. Estes Kefauver's U.S. Senate Special Committee to Investigate Organized Crime in Interstate Commerce hearings had played out months earlier, and illegal gamblers and back-room casino bosses had begun migrating from every region of the United States to take a shot at the nation's only state with legalized gambling.

Transplanted Cleveland liquor and gambling racketeer Moe Dalitz had moved the center of his operations to Las Vegas a few years earlier and by 1952 had staked his claim with the Desert Inn.

Meyer Lansky associates Edward Levinson and Joseph "Doc" Stacher led a collective of characters investing—in part on behalf of Eastern mob interests—in the sparkling new Sands Hotel.

Dallas cowboy gambling czar Benny Binion rode into downtown ahead of the sheriff and set up the Horseshoe Club on Fremont Street.

Bookmaker and race-wire operator Gus Greenbaum arrived at the back door of the Flamingo in the summer of 1947 only hours after a hit man in Beverly Hills had unceremoniously retired Benjamin "Bugsy" Siegel with several .30-caliber slugs courtesy of the Syndicate's Las Vegas corporation. (Greenbaum would operate the Flamingo and the Riviera before permanently falling from grace with his benefactors. In 1958 the throats of gregarious Gus and his wife, Bess, were cut from ear to ear.)

It was in this milieu that Mike Wynn found himself, and he was comfortable enough to open a bingo parlor at the Silver Slipper, a smoky grind joint dolled-up in Gay Nineties whorehouse decor on the grounds of the Last Frontier. (His pal, Frontier president Maurice Friedman, who also controlled a piece of the Silver Slipper Saloon, had gotten him the spot.)

Now all Mike Wynn needed was a license, for which he had duly applied, to make his dream of a score of a lifetime in the gambling business come true—a legal score, at that. And getting a license didn't appear to be a problem since the state of Nevada was handing them out practically for the asking.

But Mike Wynn's dream of legalized bingo crumbled when in April 1953, after a background check, the Nevada Tax Commission—precursor to today's State Gaming Control Tax Commission—found him unacceptable.

On the same agenda, Frank Sinatra negotiated to be approved for a piece of the mob-connected Sands Hotel, and Chicago mob bookmaker Lou Lederer was cleared as a 5-percent owner of the Sands.

Adding insult to this injury, Mike Wynn's Silver Slipper bingo parlor, which he had been operating without a license, went belly up. Some would argue that nearby better-run bingo parlors drove Wynn out of business and out of Las Vegas. But that doesn't change the fact that he was rejected by the tax commission even when it was approving ex-bookmakers, moneylenders, and racket bosses who had decided to come to the desert to cleanse themselves of their notorious pasts like a bunch of biblical characters in baggy pants.

After that rejection, even though the Silver Slipper eventually opened a bingo hall under the supervision of former Golden Nugget operator Bill Adams, Mike Wynn never again attempted to buy a piece of legalized salvation in Las Vegas.

His base of operations would remain in the East—three thousand miles from the desert in cold, colorless Utica, New York.

Mike Wynn was a handsome, dark-haired fellow who was fond of custom-made suits and never traveled without a substantial cash bankroll. He always had money, but time would reveal that he lived on a dangerous margin. He was a silver-tongued speaker with a line of endless patter.

The son of a traveling vaudevillian, Mike was in constant motion throughout his life. Born Michael M. Weinberg, he is said to have changed his name after applying for a job at a soft drink company whose bosses were suspected of being anti-Semitic. He later had his name legally changed. His mother died when Mike was an infant, and he was packed off, along with his brother and sister, to a foster home.

As a boy growing up in Revere, Massachusetts, at the outset of the Great Depression, Mike Wynn first worked at a bottling plant, then at a sign company to help support his family. Between shifts he noticed something odd through the Massachusetts gray: People might work like dogs for almost no pay, but few were so poor that they failed to visit the church or synagogue on Bingo Night. Although illegal, bingo was tolerated by local police, many of whom were not above extracting their percentage from the proceeds.

As a kid, Mike Wynn hung around bingo halls. By the time he was seventeen, he was managing one.

He would eventually become a big-time bingo operator.

———

Bingo was one of the country's early lotteries. Whether operating under the sanction of a priest's collar, a rabbi's yarmulke, or a set of Elks Lodge antlers, bingo's early association with religion and its image as a game played by the elderly for a few nickels helped it survive law enforcement scrutiny and political reform — even after it had become a multimillion-dollar racket linked time and again to New York organized crime figures.

Bingo first surfaced in the United States shortly after World War I and spread rapidly during the Great Depression as a featured back-room attraction at vaudeville shows and carnivals. The game itself probably originated in the 1500s in Italy as an activity called lotto. Whether called Housey-Housey, beano, or the corn game, bingo became popular and developed huge followings in beachfront tourist centers such as Atlantic City, Venice and Long Beach, California, and Miami.

Beyond its image as a cottage industry frequented by blue-haired grandmothers, bingo was a big business. Two years after charity bingo was legalized in New York by constitutional amendment in 1957, the reported gross income of games in the state was more than $80 million. As the chief counsel of the lottery control commission said at the time, "The real income is much larger than that. Promoters took their percentage off the top, and the amount not reported amounted to a considerable figure."

By June 1958, more than 200 New York cities and towns were on the verge of legalizing bingo as a means of charitable fund-raising. But the laughable level of regulation of the game proved such an embarrassment that in April and May 1961 Governor Nelson Rockefeller's Moreland Act Commission and the State Commission of Investigation conducted a series of public hearings in New York City, Utica, and Syracuse into the "abuses, corruption and violations of the law. [Bingo] had become perverted by professional gamblers for selfish gain." One of the key players: Michael M. Wynn.

In six months, the Moreland Commission reexamined the state's bingo law and compiled a small mountain of evidence linking charity bingo to professional gamblers, swindlers, and criminals of every stripe.

In his March 1962 report to Rockefeller, Moreland Act Commissioner Thomas Gilchrist, Jr., presented an inch-thick summary of the investigation's findings. The profits of Mike Wynn's seven Utica bingo operations amounted to as little as 7 percent of their receipts. There was evidence of skimming, fraud, and corruption throughout the Utica and Syracuse bingo halls.

The licensing process was a sham. No background investigation was conducted. Laws supposedly designed to keep out the professional operators had had just the opposite effect. Mike Wynn's associates, upstate New York swindlers William Buckner and

Eugene "Buddy" Keane, were suspected of fixing license applications and bribing officials.

Corruption was as much a part of the process as the calling of the numbers. Lottery officials and city councilmen often were paid to look the other way, and church and civic groups were exposed as little more than fronts for the bingo racketeers. In Utica, licenses often were issued even before operators filled out the proper applications. Investigations were not conducted; officials seemed to know with whom they were dealing. In some instances, false financial records were filed, and men such as Buckner and Keane were at the heart of it. Wynn's business partner, Sidney Franklin, of the bingo-card maker Metro Manufacturing Company, testified before the bingo rackets commission that he paid Buckner $3,000 to assist in hiring the right people to keep the bingo halls operating. It was the same Sidney Franklin who years later would join Steve Wynn in investing in their friend Maury Friedman's mob-tainted Frontier casino deal.

Witnesses testified that Mike Wynn fronted giant bingo games in Utica, Syracuse, and Binghamton before the activity was legalized in 1958 for churches, service organizations, and charities. Outside New York, Wynn had operated bingo halls in Scranton, Pennsylvania; Baltimore and Anne Arundel County, Maryland; Waterbury, Connecticut; Savannah, Georgia; and Dayton, Ohio, as well as the brief stint in Las Vegas. In all, his bingo network stretched over seven states. In the estimation of witnesses, Wynn was a ruthless force in the illegal bingo racket. Wynn had been indicted in Syracuse in 1947 on charges of violating three state gambling laws. He eventually was acquitted. In Utica, Wynn quickly drove his nearest competitors, Milo Merrill and Stanley Philo of P and M Amusement Company, to their knees but occasionally used both to front his heavily skimmed operations.

Although he often has been described as a simple bingo parlor operator, Mike Wynn was a little giant in his industry. And while he was mainly known to investigators as a New York bingo operator, he managed halls that ranged in description from cramped buildings to expansive and highly profitable. Several featured bars and restaurants. In later years, some of the bingo halls added slot machines.

The report to Rockefeller described Wynn's activity as a series of "wholesale abuses" of the law.

In June 1961, Mike Wynn shut down his Utica operations and moved his base to Anne Arundel County in Maryland, leaving behind in New York a jumbled mess of scandal and corruption.

———

But there was also a paternal side to the wiseguy charmer.

At the outset of World War II, Mike and his bride, the former Zelma Kutner, moved into a public housing project near the Marlin Firearms factory in New Haven, Connecticut. Mike operated a bingo parlor in neighboring New Britain, and he performed his part for the war effort by putting in shifts at the Marlin factory. It was also the best location to book and bet baseball and buy and sell lottery tickets.

The couple longed for children, so there was much joy when Zelma Wynn gave birth to Stephen Alan Wynn on January 27, 1942, in New Haven. Having lost her previous pregnancy, Zelma felt especially blessed. Kenneth Wynn was born a decade later. To his parents who had longed for a child, Stephen Wynn was a golden boy.

Young Stephen was spoiled from birth. From an early age, he emulated the man who provided so well for his family right down to the natty hats and custom suits. Even if business kept Mike Wynn on the road, the homecomings were filled with gifts, games of catch, train trips to Yankee Stadium and Coney Island, excursions to watch the diving horses on the piers in Atlantic City, first-class vacations in Miami, skiing in winter, outings to the summer home in Old Forge, New York, as well as that fateful trip in 1952 to Las Vegas. Mike and Steve's relationship has been described as more of a friendship than the usual father-son kinship. After all, how many sons feel comfortable calling their dad by his first name?

Where Mike Wynn was a suspected bookmaker and successful bingo hall operator, Steve Wynn would receive an education at a top-notch university. Where the father operated on the edge of the law, the son would be a solid citizen—a doctor, lawyer, or perhaps even a fighter pilot. Michael and Zelma Wynn would see to it that their son wanted for nothing and went to the best schools.

"There was a stigma back then," Zelma Wynn said. "If you ran a bingo parlor, some people looked at you as if you were a bookie. Steve was going to be a doctor."

He was handed everything, but the lack of supervision by his father was telling. "Steve ruled the roost," his wife Elaine said years later. "Mike was not home, meaning that there was no paternal supervision. Zelma was a pussycat. She didn't have the—I don't want to say the knowledge or instincts—but maybe not the patience to deal with Steve."

Mothers are biased by nature, but Zelma Wynn from the outset doted on her firstborn. "He was a mensch [a person of integrity and honor, a stand-up guy] from age three months," she once said.

In fact, he was more of a mischief-maker, something of a devil in short pants. Stephen was a spoiled kid on whom gifts were lavished. At the family's Old Forge summer home, young Stephen had his own motorboat that he used to devilish effect, spraying docks lined with sunbathers and playing the big man on the water for his summer pals. One summer, proud Mike Wynn used multiple cameras to film his beloved son ski jumping. It was a home movie Steve Wynn would play for friends and casino executives more than three decades later.

"He was a guy who couldn't say no to his family. Whatever we wanted we got," Steve Wynn said. "I had cars, the best education, everything. But it was borrowed money. It's a funny kind of thing. You've got all these good things, but you're always afraid."

The Wynn family lived in a second-floor apartment above Graham Sales, a Whitesboro store. As Mike Wynn's business improved, he moved his family to 12 Parkway in Utica.

Throughout the Wynn residence, opinions were always vehemently expressed in shouting matches that alarmed friends and neighbors. John Meagher, one of Steve Wynn's childhood friends, was frightened after a short stay at the 12 Parkway house.

"They were screaming at each other," Meagher recalled. "I told my parents and they said, 'That's the way they are. They scream at each other. It doesn't mean anything.'"

Their friends, Frank and Estelle Goldman, had been Utica residents since the 1920s and lived at 10 Tarbell Terrace. By the end of World War II, Goldman's Bakery at 233 Whitesboro had become a city institution. Founded by Louis and Sarah Goldman, the business came to be called the Pershing Bake Shop. Later, a second store, Allan's Pastry Shop, was added at 228 Columbia near Mike Wynn's bingo business. Mike Wynn often would borrow from Goldman to pay gambling debts. Steve Wynn would call the relationship between the Goldmans and his family innocent; at least one law enforcement authority has surmised that Frank Goldman was associated with the mob.

———

Steve Wynn attended Kemble School and John F. Hughes School then was shipped off to Manlius Academy, a West Point preparatory school, from the eighth through twelfth grades. If young Stephen was a wild-eyed rich boy given to hyperactive pranks and two-bit delinquency, a kid no mother could control, then there was only one place for him: military school. But Steve Wynn insists his attendance at Manlius near Syracuse was part of an educational plan to make him someone special. Despite rebelling against the crewcut authoritarianism at Manlius, Steve advanced by his senior year to battalion adjutant.

At first Steve entertained thoughts of becoming a fighter pilot in the years following the Korean war and prior to the American military build up in Vietnam. But he did not enter military service. Instead, he enrolled at the University of Pennsylvania as a chemistry major and was on track to become a doctor, a career path sure to please his mother and father. He pledged a fraternity and was on his way. At freshman orientation, as the story goes, Mike took Steve to a clothing store near campus for some new outfits. The salesman confused the father and son for brothers. Michael Wynn was then forty-three.

Max C's Corned Beef Junction on Spruce Street across from the Penn dorms was one of young Wynn's many haunts.

"You could see Steve was a very bright kid. He was easy to remember. He was a big talker," the deli's proprietor Max Corsun recalled. "He wasn't as much of a dresser in those days."

Although Corsun served only sandwiches, another neighborhood hangout, the Samson Street Restaurant, offered the latest odds on boxing, baseball, basketball, and football and was operated by Philadelphia mob lieutenant Frank "Blinky" Palermo and his pal Sam Margolis. Both men would manage heavyweight champion Charles "Sonny" Liston, a classic mob fighter who was suspected of throwing his second title fight against the then-Cassius Clay. Liston died mysteriously in 1971 in Las Vegas.

The fraternity brothers would pool their money and send a lone "beard" to the Samson Street Restaurant for a slice of the action. Wynn was a regular at the Samson, where he gave Liston lessons in effective public speaking. "We hung out at the same delicatessen in Philly," Wynn once told a reporter. "Sonny had just won the belt and needed help. He was the most baleful-looking man I ever met. Everyone thought Sonny was invincible, the way everyone thought Mike Tyson was invincible."

Even after Steve had gone off to college, father Mike continued to keep in close contact with his son.

On trips to Philadelphia, Mike would mingle at the best restaurants and nightclubs in the city, including Pep's Lounge, a famous Black nightclub owned by his friend "Wild Bill" Gerson. Vacations were spent in Miami. Beginning in 1960, Steve Wynn would go home on the weekends to assist in the operation of a popular Sunday-only bingo hall at Wayson's Corner in Anne Arundel County, not far from Washington, D.C. As Steve Wynn moved closer to the family business, he changed his major to English literature and in his final years at the university took classes at the Wharton School of Business. Wharton had one of the nation's best MBA programs, but young Steve Wynn's life, thanks to his father, would take another turn.

━━━━━━

Mike Wynn and his Florida pal, Michael Pascal, had been busy bragging about their children between games of gin rummy and pinochle at the Jockey Club in Miami Beach when the two cooked up a scheme. They would bring their kids, Steve and coed Elaine Pascal, together on a first date at a Miami jai-alai fronton during the college Christmas break.

Both men were gamblers by nature and compulsion who knew more about fixing thoroughbred races than arranging dates for their children. Nevertheless, they devised their matchmaking plan.

And it worked, even though one of Steve Wynn's friends told him that he didn't stand a chance with the young beauty queen.

"If it weren't for your father fixing you up, turkey, you'd never get a date with this girl. And you're lucky to get the date," one of Wynn's Florida pals told him.

"Hmm, that good, huh?"

"She won't even look at you after the first twenty minutes."

But she did. Even as a brash twenty-year-old, Steve Wynn had a way with the ladies, and he had stumbled onto a classy one in Elaine Pascal.

As a high-school girl, Elaine had been named most likely to succeed, best looking, and most popular. She was voted Miss Miami Beach. "This is going to sound horrible," she told an interviewer years later. "They only allowed a kid to receive two things in the 'Who's Who' [yearbook]—and I got three! So they had to drop one of them! They gave 'Most Likely to Succeed' to somebody else, which was all right because they told me at least that I was voted that...They didn't let me choose, and I think the reason was that they figured that the second runner-up really wasn't that good looking!"

Then at UCLA, where she was named Southern Campus Spring Queen, Elaine was studying political science but also entertaining careers in acting, psychiatry, and law.

After about an hour of watching their fathers bet at the jai-alai fronton, Steve and Elaine sneaked out into the Miami night, borrowed a car, and ended up at the Boom Boom Room of the Fontainebleau on the ocean at Forty-fourth Street. The Fontainebleau's motto: "In all the world...In any season...one of the most beautiful resort hotels, anywhere."

The two danced the cha-cha, mambo, and the meringue across the crowded dance floor. After ninety minutes, they caught a glimpse of probing eyes from across the room.

It was their parents, smiling and waving at the kids.

———

Elaine Pascal was swept away by the cocky young suitor.

"I wasn't sure what he was going to do, but on the first date I knew that we were going to do it together," Elaine said in an interview with her husband present. "There was something about Steve. He had, I don't know, I call him the flimflam man. And he flimflammed me. He's got great enthusiasm. And I thought he was extremely intelligent. I mean, I couldn't have gone for him if I felt there was no substance.

"I believe there was substance. He overwhelmed me. And I thought that, 'Here's a guy that I'm going to latch onto because it's going to be an exciting ride.'"

"Is that [flimflam] the same as snake-oil salesman?" Steve Wynn asked.

"Slim difference," Elaine deadpanned.

To be closer to Steve, Elaine transferred from UCLA to George Washington University where she earned a political science degree.

They planned to marry after college, but in the spring of 1963, a few weeks before Steve was scheduled to graduate from the University of Pennsylvania with an English literature degree, Mike Wynn checked into the University of Minnesota Hospital.

He had been diagnosed with a congenital heart ailment brought on by rheumatic fever.

Only open-heart surgery could save his life.

———

Ever the gambler, Mike Wynn knew long odds when he saw them.

Although commonplace today, in the early 1960s open-heart surgery was highly risky. Mike called Steve to his hospital bed and attempted to allay his son's fears by assuring him the operation was sure to succeed. Nevertheless, the elder Wynn still wanted to set his worldly affairs in order.

"I'll be all right," Mike Wynn told his son. "But just in case, I want you to write a few things down."

The elder Wynn had played on margin throughout his life and had no intention of welshing on his debts. In 1963, he was more than $200,000 down.

"He asked me to record some debts that he owed that he wanted me to pay in case the surgery was unsuccessful," Steve Wynn said, adding, "He thought he was going to be all right."

Zelma and Steve paced more than three hours in the waiting room, only to have a surgeon enter and whisper, "I'm sorry."

Mike Wynn, who had lived so wildly and well, was dead at age forty-six.

Steve Wynn was devastated, but he didn't show it. At the funeral, he didn't cry. "Steve was stoic," Elaine recalled. "He didn't express any grief at all. Even when we were alone together, there was no crying. At the funeral, he gritted his teeth. He became the dad of the family, and he was only twenty-one."

Wynn's former professional companion, Ron Tucky, said, "It was hard for Steve because, what was he to Kenny? He was ten years older. Steve was a father, a brother, someone to look after this ten year old. He had a lot of different hats with Kenny. It's pretty tough."

———

Mike Wynn died on the operating table March 29, 1963. One of the debts he left behind was a $5,000 marker owed to Charlie Meyerson, owner of New York City taxicab companies and a major bookmaker in the Big Apple. Attempting to carry out his father's wishes, Steve contacted and eventually met with Meyerson.

"I offered to give him $5,000 and he laughed at me," Wynn remembered. "He was sitting in this three-bedroom apartment we had [in Washington, D.C.], and he said, 'Don't you know that a gambler's debts die with him?' He thought it was very comical. I said, 'Well, you've got to take this money because if you owed it to my father, I'd ask you to pay it.' And he got almost hysterical. He said, 'If I had ever owed your father any money, he'd have collected it from me before dinner.'…Well, that was the beginning of a friendship. I didn't know Charlie when my dad was alive. As I say, I met him a year or so, or within a year, of my father's death, and I was so taken and thought he was such a fetching guy. I've always loved colorful people. Then he said, 'If you're ever in New York, I'll take you out to lunch or dinner. Give a call.'"

Although he left his son with a hefty tab, in the process Mike Wynn also left him with a lengthy registry of longtime friends, acquaintances, and reliable outs.

One of those men, wiseguy bookmaker Herbie Liebert, in 1965 introduced Wynn to a rotund Las Vegas gambler, mob conduit, and all-around con artist named Maurice Friedman. Through Friedman, and backed by a loan from family friend, baker and gambling supplier Frank Goldman, Wynn was able to make his first investment in a Las Vegas casino, buying 3 percent of the Frontier in 1967 for $45,000.

As Wynn tells it, it took nearly five years for Zelma and Steve to pay off the various bookmakers and friends to whom Mike had died owing money. In the ensuing years investigators have repeatedly tried to determine whether Steve Wynn continues to pay debts incurred a long time ago to the mob.

———

Mike Wynn had shared a partnership in the sprawling Anne Arundel County, Maryland, bingo center with longtime friend Edward Wayson. Wayson's Corner, as it was known, was one of five legal bingo operations in the county.

After Mike Wynn's death, Wayson's Amusements Company was incorporated, its stock in 1965 divided thus: Zelma Wynn, 30 percent; Stephen Wynn, 20 percent; Kenneth Wynn, 10 percent; Edward Wayson, 20 percent, and Daniel Wayson, 20 percent. In years to come "Boom" Wayson's son, Daniel Boone Wayson, would go to work as an executive for Steve Wynn at the Golden Nugget in Atlantic City.

Two months after his father's death, Stephen Alan Wynn married Elaine Farrell Pascal on June 29, 1963 in New York. Their first daughter, Kevin, was born in 1966, their second, Gillian, in 1969.

Steve and Elaine immediately set to work at Wayson's Corner in Maryland, where he managed and called the bingo numbers while she counted the money.

The bingo hall may have carried Edward Wayson's name, but the operation was run by twenty-one-year-old Steve Wynn. Like his father, Steve had been observing bingo games for years and appreciated the nuances of customer relations.

One of the greatest lessons young Steve Wynn learned from his father was taught all those years ago in Las Vegas. "When you see a person crumble and lose his self-confidence, it's a very, very horrible experience," Wynn said. "But one thing my father's gambling did was that it showed me at a very early age that if you wanted to make money in a casino, the answer was to own one."

And so he did. Several, in fact.

More than three decades after his father's death, Steve Wynn still invokes his father's name in interview after interview. A photograph on the wall is as close as the adoring son will get to ever seeing his best friend again.

"I'd give up everything for fifteen minutes with my father," the golden boy said. "To have him walk through this hotel and see what happened. Now you're talking something more than a big number. I miss the thrill of showing my dad that it worked out OK. He would have been awful proud."

Where the father had failed, the son had succeeded. But not even the resourceful Mike Wynn could have predicted this success or how it would happen.

CHAPTER 2

FRONTIER DAYS

In 1964 Steve Wynn found himself at a crossroads in Anne Arundel County, Maryland.

Flamboyant Mike Wynn was gone. The Sunday bingo he had left behind at Wayson's Corner provided Steve with a gambling apprenticeship and his family with a comfortable living, but it was three thousand miles away from the real action. For Mike Wynn's oldest son, Maryland bingo didn't move nearly fast enough.

But father Mike had left son Steve more than a pocketful of sports-betting debts. He also had supplied him with plenty of gambling contacts, associations which led to Steve Wynn's 1967 purchase of 5 percent of the Frontier Hotel, landed him a heartbeat from the mob, and nearly mired him in a federal racketeering indictment that netted three Detroit La Cosa Nostra figures and their frontmen. Wynn enjoyed a discount on his purchase other investors did not receive and was made a working officer in the Frontier. Although Wynn was not accused of wrongdoing, his Frontier days serve to illustrate a recurring theme in his career: Wherever he has been, the mob has been close by.

To hear Wynn tell it, fate was a wild card in a deck full of aces: One day he was a simple Maryland bingo operator with big dreams, and the next he was loading up his family and moving to Las Vegas to seek his fortune in gambling's big-time town. He had borrowed enough money to take a seat at a high-stakes game, initially purchasing 3 percent of the Frontier and acquiring another 2 percent only days before Hughes purchased it.

It is a pretty story, but in recalling it Wynn often leaves out the dark, tangled underside of the Frontier deal.

With his father gone, a new bride, a widowed mother and younger brother to watch out for, by 1964, Steve Wynn had grown restless with Wayson's Corner. He had been spending time in New York City and had taken classes at Georgetown University Law School. And he was itching for something bigger than his small slice of Maryland.

He began studying the real-estate market and thought he had scored a coup with a twenty-seven-acre piece of raw real estate located on the edge of Baltimore International Airport. The land would have made an ideal site for a light industrial park, he thought. The cost, $1.1 million, would have intimidated most young dreamers but not Wynn.

In hopes of landing a loan, Wynn has said he arranged an appointment with John D. MacArthur, president of Bankers Life and Casualty, at the Plaza Hotel in New York. MacArthur, who also was the owner of record of the Breakers in Palm Beach, turned Wynn down but was impressed with the confident young second-generation bingo operator with the Ivy League education.

Weeks later, Steve Wynn received a call from MacArthur. It just so happened that the insurance executive's friend and associate, Maurice Friedman, was attempting to gather investors to finance and expand the Hotel Last Frontier in Las Vegas. MacArthur wasn't sure how far the deal would progress, but he already had his company's money tied up in the transaction.

And he had recommended Wynn as an ideal investor to Maurice Friedman.

———

Maurice Friedman, principal player in the Frontier purchase, was an obese fast-buck artist, casino operator, and mob conduit who had talked his way into the good graces of some of the toughest organized crime figures of his day. Friedman was well acquainted with Wynn's father and with bingo-card supplier Sidney Franklin, also an investor in the Las Vegas project. It was Friedman who had gotten Mike Wynn's foot in the door at the Silver Slipper when he unsuccessfully tried to open a bingo parlor there.

Friedman was a flamboyant thief, a fellow who never was far from a dice scam or a crooked card deck. He also had a talent for making connections and using them to best advantage. Among his more notorious business contacts were dapper Johnny Rosselli, the Chicago Outfit's man in Las Vegas, and Anthony Zerilli and Michael Polizzi, rising young executives in Detroit's powerful Cosa Nostra clan. Friedman's Detroit connection would acquire 30 percent of the Frontier for $500,000.

To comprehend the scope of Friedman's contacts and the Frontier deal, it is essential to understand the kind of mobsters with whom he dealt.

It also helps to know a little about Friedman and the Frontier casino.

———

The Hotel Last Frontier, built on the site of the Boulder Dam-era Pair-o-Dice nightclub, predated Ben Siegel's Flamingo by four years.

The idea of a casino resort wrapped in a frontier village theme was the brainchild of R.E. Griffith, who died of a heart attack two years after it opened, leaving his nephew, William J. Moore, to become its operator.

Under Moore, the general manager of the Last Frontier in 1955 was Jake Kozloff, whose casino career included partnerships with associates of Meyer Lansky. Before separating himself from the casino in 1955, Kozloff and two other men were accused of funneling casino profits to hidden interests. They also would be suspected of conspiring to cheat the owner of record, German actress Vera Krupp, one-time holder of the Hope diamond.

Friedman's association with the Frontier long preceded the 1967 purchase offer involving Wynn. More than a decade earlier, Friedman had been an inside man when the Last Frontier made way for the New Frontier. When Kozloff departed in 1955, Friedman became hotel president. T. W. Richardson, who later would be indicted in the Beverly Hills Friars Club scam, was appointed his vice-president and casino manager.

The joint was packed, but the profits were illogically low. By 1957, the Frontier was mired in bankruptcy and riddled with rumors of skimming and hidden ownership. Friedman then tried to land a loan from the Vegas-friendly Teamsters Central States Pension Fund to acquire the property on behalf of himself and his friends from Detroit.

In April 1964, Friedman, Zerilli, and Polizzi traveled to Palm Springs to meet secretly with Teamsters President Jimmy Hoffa to arrange a $6-million loan for the Frontier. Although they agreed in principle, the deal collapsed after Hoffa went on trial and was convicted in Chicago for stealing from the Central States Pension Fund. It was the beginning of the end of his career as the czar of America's trucking union. Hoffa disappeared July 30, 1975 after arranging a meeting at a Detroit restaurant with Zerilli family capo Tony Giacalone.

By 1967, the indefatigable Friedman and his cast of characters were back at the Frontier. But Friedman couldn't stroll up to the Nevada Gaming Commission and admit the Detroit mob was the driving force behind the casino takeover. So he lied, rather obviously, according to the commission's transcripts, throughout his testimony. He lied about his previous difficulties with the commission. He lied about his business relationship with Chicago mob lieutenant Johnny Rosselli.

Friedman assured the commissioners that the mob had nothing to do with the Frontier when he knew that Johnny Rosselli secretly held a percentage of the lucrative gift-shop concessions and that Mike Polizzi's Detroit company had installed plumbing fixtures at the hotel. Rosselli had also received a $25,000 payment for assisting the Hotel Last Frontier Corporation to find a suitable casino lessee.

Rosselli's contacts ranged from Chicago mob boss Sam Giancana to Howard Hughes's Las Vegas business adviser Robert Maheu, from Frank Sinatra to CIA operatives. Through Rosselli, Friedman gained access to Zerilli and Polizzi and the potential financing from the Teamsters' pension fund. After testifying three times before a U.S. Senate committee investigating the CIA's failed plots to assassinate Fidel Castro and other Cuban political leaders, Rosselli was murdered, his corpse stuffed into a fifty-five-gallon oil drum found floating off the Florida coast near Miami.

In happier days, it was Friedman who had introduced Rosselli to the Friars Club, where the fat man had worked his way into what would become known as one of the most notorious card-cheating operations in the country. Regulars at the Friars included Phil Silvers, Zeppo Marx, nightclub singer Tony Martin, and comedian George Jessel. Gin games on the third floor weren't for the timid. It was common for $40,000 and more to cross the table in a single evening.

With operatives peeping through holes drilled in the ceiling, and a sophisticated radio transmitter relay system connected to the card mechanics, Friedman and his cast of cheats—Albert "Slick" Snyder and Manuel "Ricky" Jacobs among them—couldn't lose.

Friedman, Rosselli, and three others were convicted in the scam. Friedman was slapped with a six-year prison sentence and ordered to pay a $100,000 fine. The indictment surfaced just weeks after Friedman and his friends were licensed for the Frontier; the group managed to sell out to Howard Hughes in record time—just days before investigators closed in on Friedman and his unsavory associates.

About his relationship with Rosselli—who was, incidentally, godfather of Friedman's son—Friedman told the Gaming Control Board, "Well, my association with him is merely one of knowing a person for a long, long time. I have no business ties with him. I do see him because we are members of the same club that I've been a member of for twenty-two years and when I'm at the club, inevitably I'm bound to run into him. When he comes to Las Vegas, he does phone me and ask me how the family is doing. Once in a great while, we'll have dinner together, and if I see him in one of the hotels, I certainly won't avoid him, and I don't know how else to tell you that I think I'd be hypocritical if I said if I'd get a license I'll never talk to the man again."

Friedman received his license.

So did Anthony Zerilli's puppets.

———

Anthony Zerilli was the son of Detroit Mafia boss Joseph Zerilli, who masterfully ruled the Motor City's rackets for half a century. For many years Joseph Zerilli was one of only two non-New York crime bosses to gain a seat on the mob's national commission. He became as much an institution as Ford in Detroit, and by the mid-1960s, his son was being groomed to take over. Father Zerilli later would be implicated but not charged in the 1975 disappearance of Teamsters czar Jimmy Hoffa.

Years before the 1967 Frontier deal was made, Friedman, looking for investors in the adjacent Silver Slipper, had offered Zerilli and Polizzi a $500,000 buy-in at the Silver Slipper, but the mobsters declined.

The offer was too small for their gluttonous appetites. They were looking for a larger score, and, sure enough, one materialized in the form of the Frontier.

To make the Frontier deal palatable to the Gaming Control Board, Friedman assembled a twenty-four-carat crew of frontmen investors including attorney Peter J. Bellanca, a director of Hazel Park racetrack (of which Anthony Zerilli was president); Arthur Rooks, a former municipal judge in Hamtramck, Michigan; and Jack Shapiro, a former Detroit jeweler who would become the resort's casino manager. All bought into the Frontier on behalf of their Zerilli mob benefactors.

In April 1972, all would be convicted on conspiracy and hidden ownership charges. Bellanca, who handled all the hiring at the hotel, received a five-year suspended sentence, five-years probation, and a $10,000 fine. Rooks got off relatively lightly with a five-year suspended sentence and $10,000 fine. Shapiro got three years in prison and a $30,000 fine.

Jack Shapiro's work history was typically compelling and mob related.

A longtime jeweler and gambler, he divided his time between Detroit, Miami, and Las Vegas. He was a former partner in the Silver Slipper at the time Mike Wynn attempted to operate a bingo parlor there. Shapiro's business and personal connection to Polizzi were undeniable. Yet somehow it did not prevent him from being licensed as a stockholder at the Frontier in 1967.

Polizzi, Zerilli, Dominic "Fats" Corrado, and Anthony Tocco were four of the most powerful mobsters in America. Shapiro admitted he was close to all of them but said he had no knowledge as to their alleged organized crime ties. Shapiro received 10½ percentage points in the Frontier for a heavily discounted $157,500. The percentage was worth $472,500, and it was up to Shapiro to sell the points at full face value. He considered the transaction a perk for his past part-ownership in the Silver Slipper. He purchased his points for $15,000 each and sold them for $45,000 apiece. It was a sweet deal, but then Shapiro was an insider and accustomed to sweet deals.

Nevertheless, Gaming Commission Chairman George Dickerson was understandably curious.

"Was anyone else given this discount?" he asked during a commission hearing.

"... Oh yes," Shapiro said. "Mr. Mel Clark, I believe, first had this deal and couldn't move the points to anybody. Mr. Richardson had this deal and did move his points and wound up with his percentage, whatever he had. Now, Mr. Steve Wynn was given free points on this basis and wound up with his percentage, although he was given a much better deal than anybody else. The only deal in here that you'll find inequitable as far as distribution is Steve Wynn—three of these $15,000 points against two regular points. I sold far, far, far in excess of two for one of my points."

In June 1967, around the time of the Frontier deal, Steve Wynn was twenty-five years old. He might not have been a frontman—although years later gaming regulators maintained their suspicions—but there were plenty around him.

Wynn paid $45,000 for a 3-percent ownership in the Frontier, $30,000 of which had come from his family friend, Frank Goldman. He held so-called working points—given to an investor who also takes a position within the company, in this case as slot and keno manager—from February through October 1967, then borrowed $30,000 from Valley Bank to purchase 2 percent more just days before billionaire Howard Hughes paid a sucker's price of $24 million. By the time the deal was struck, the Frontier's problems were well publicized, and even the reclusive Hughes had to know that the Detroit mob had infiltrated the hotel.

Wynn later claimed he didn't make a profit on the deal.

———

Robert Maheu, Hughes's aide, recalled Wynn as being a cocky, handsome young man who may have lacked financial resources but was flush with confidence.

"I was very, very impressed," Maheu said. "But when Steve talked about his plans for the future, I thought, 'My God, this young man is tired. There's no way in God's creation he'll do everything he wants to do.'

"We were scheduled to close the deal at midnight on a given day, and we were waiting for the Gaming Control Board and the gaming commission. My son, Peter, and I happened to end up in a room talking to Steve. All of a sudden he starts telling us what his ambitions are, and when he gets through, after he left, I said, 'Poor Steve. He's been so anxious for this to close. It's obvious he's been working too hard.'

"When he opened the Mirage, I realized that it was I who had been working too hard. He did what he said he would do."

At 5 percent, Wynn was the sixth largest shareholder in a deal that included thirty-four investors. The Friars Club cheating case broke that same month, and Clark County Sheriff Ralph Lamb already had booted Zerilli from the Frontier. Big changes were coming. It was time to sell and sell quickly.

If Wynn realized he had fallen in with a dangerous crowd weeks before the Frontier opened, why did he borrow $30,000 from Valley Bank on October 11, 1967, to acquire 2 percent more of the company?

It was a question New Jersey gaming regulators would ask two decades later.

———

Four years after the Frontier was sold to Hughes for what then was considered the staggering sum of $24 million ($16 million cash and the assumption of $8 million in liabilities), the government finally caught up to Friedman and his associates.

In March 1971, Zerilli, Polizzi, and Anthony Giordano—the latter with a police record dating back to 1933 and undoubtedly the toughest among the hidden owners—Peter J. Bellanca, Jack Shapiro, Arthur Rooks, and giant sports concessionaire Emprise Corporation were indicted by a federal grand jury in Los Angeles for concealing hidden ownership in the Frontier.

The trial lasted nine weeks. The jury deliberated four days before finding all the defendants guilty. Unindicted coconspirators included Emprise patriarch Louis M. Jacobs, who had died three years earlier; Emprise officer Max Jacobs, Louis Jacobs's son; mobster Irving "Slick" Shapiro; as well as Friedman, Richardson, and Frontier investor Alex Kachinko.

True to his deal-making nature, Friedman had become a government informant and helped convict his former partners. He spent two weeks on the stand outlining the operation as the prosecution's leading witness. Although Friedman had managed to avoid prosecution, his betrayal would not be easily forgotten: Detroit mobsters let out the word Friedman had made their hit list, but the threat never was carried out.

Wynn was summoned before the grand jury, which must have wondered how such a nice young man with Ivy League credentials had become so intimately involved with a thoroughly mobbed-up casino takeover.

Assistant U.S. Attorney Thomas Kotoske, who prosecuted Zerilli, Polizzi, Giordano, and the Frontier frontmen, later would play an integral role in helping salvage Wynn's credibility in the case. Years after the trial, Kotoske wrote a special report on behalf of the Golden Nugget clearing Wynn of any wrongdoing. When he went hunting for a casino license in New Jersey, Wynn produced the report, which was submitted into evidence, but did not recall whether he had paid Kotoske for writing it.

Wynn admitted later that he'd been less than forthcoming with the grand jury. He said he felt intimidated because he was seated next to Chicago crime boss Anthony Accardo just before being called to give testimony.

Others fell all around him, but Steve Wynn kept smiling and running. He was not publicly accused of playing the role of frontman for the mob. He had survived his first leap into the hostile sea of casino ownership, but he still was seeking his big break.

Some who met Wynn during this time had no doubts he would get that break.

Claudine Williams, a longtime executive and member of the board of directors of Harrah's, was impressed with Wynn from the start. So was her husband, Las Vegas gambling pioneer Shelby Williams.

"Steve was young, excited, and wanted to do a lot of things," Williams said. "He was excited to talk to everyone. Steve had a tremendous curiosity about the gambling business. He had a tremendous thirst for knowledge and would listen to any of them who would talk to him about the business. I think Shelby was a very knowledgeable man, and he said, 'Someday that kid's going to be big. He's not going to quit until he gets to the top. He's going to learn it all. He asks the right questions, and he doesn't leave you alone until he gets answers.'"

———

Of the many mysteries in the background of Steve Wynn's rise to power in the casino industry, none can match the tale of the lady in the lake for tragic intrigue.

The grisly death of the thirty-one-year-old divorcée, who was nearly cut in half by the propeller of the forty-five-foot Caesars Galley yacht, is riddled with unanswered questions thanks to an incomplete investigation, no autopsy, and witnesses who "prefabricated" their stories for officials.

On the morning of August 2, 1967, Nancy Mottola had been drinking for hours. She was down to $5.43 in her purse, but on that day she wouldn't be needing money. She'd accepted an invitation to a party and had jammed a beach bag with a bathing suit, suntan lotion, a toothbrush.

It wasn't just any party.

It was a day cruise aboard the posh Caesars Galley yacht, then the longest vessel on Lake Mead. The Caesars Galley was captained by Boulder City-based licensed skipper Paul Chandler, owned by Tracy Leasing Corporation, and under contract to Caesars Palace. On board were party girls Bonnie K. Lee, Randi Jones, Beverly Erickson, and a woman the other passengers said they knew only as Nancy. Notable passengers included Maury Friedman, meat company owner and Meyer Lansky bagman Irving "Niggy" Devine, and young casino boss Steve Wynn.

In the legitimate world, Devine was a part-owner of the Silver Slipper and Fremont casinos, as well as New York Meats and Provisions, the company which supplied beef to hotel restaurants on the Strip and downtown.

But there was a substantially darker side to Niggy Devine that included allegations ranging from gunrunning to acting as a Lansky courier. With his wife, Ida, known to FBI agents as "the lady in mink," Devine carried hundreds of thousands of dollars in skimmed Las Vegas casino profits to Lansky and other hidden owners throughout the nation. After 1961, Devine filtered some of his money through the Bank of World Commerce of Nassau, an offshore institution recognized as one of the earliest money-laundering facilities.

What was Wynn doing on a yacht in Lake Mead with Devine, Meyer Lansky's trusted courier, and Friedman, the veteran mob frontman?

Having one helluva party.

Wynn had plenty to celebrate. The twenty-five-year-old was obviously headed for big things in the Las Vegas gambling community. Wynn had bought his way into a mob takeover of the Frontier. He had his points and the job of slot and keno manager. His position at the resort and his bingo experience in Maryland qualified him for the coveted casino job.

The Caesars people may have courted him because he was a comer.

How the lady in the lake wound up taking that fateful yacht cruise is far less clear. In their official reports, none of the seven other people on board admitted ever having seen her before she joined them on the yacht. They knew her as Nancy but didn't catch her last name.

Her purse wasn't much help to authorities, either. It contained a few dollars but not a single piece of identification—no driver's license, social security card, credit cards, or family photos. All forms of identification were conspicuously absent from the dead woman's personal effects. She left behind nothing but the usual female paraphernalia in her purse along with a cryptic note to see Dunes casino boss Sherlock Feldman regarding a winning black-jack strategy.

Beverly Erickson later recalled that Nancy mentioned leaving an automobile in the parking lot of the Club Black Magic. It was from that vehicle Clark County sheriff's deputies recovered a vehicle registration for a Nancy Roberts and a laundry slip with the name Nancy Mottola.

But Nancy Mottola didn't just surface in Southern Nevada in time to be butchered by a yacht prop.

Born in Bronxville, New York, in 1936, she had lived in Las Vegas for several years and had been picked up by sheriff's deputies in 1962 for displaying erratic behavior in public. In March 1966 she was registered as a solicitor for the International Album Company. Mottola and Gary Gene Roberts took out a marriage license on June 6, 1962, and stayed together until December 7, 1966, when Nancy Roberts filed for divorce, taking from the couple's community property at the house at 2259 McCarran Street in

North Las Vegas only her personal belongings, two paintings, and the family German shepherd.

By August 1967 Nancy Mottola had been divorced several months and was living with Rick Krantz, who the day after her death submitted a statement to Mohave County Sheriff's Deputy Charles Crane.

Krantz said Mottola left their apartment at 5:30 on the morning of the accident to go on a boating trip. He said he was unaware with whom his live-in girlfriend would be spending the day and did not ask.

The dark-haired, brown-eyed Mottola was a tall, attractive sun-worshipper. Her boyfriend said she loved swimming at the lake. On the too-warm Wednesday afternoon of August 2, in the company of people who didn't even know her full name, she died.

Chandler had maneuvered the Caesars Galley to a spot just off Sandy Point about fifteen miles from the Temple Bar marina. Once there, he let the engine idle then shifted the boat into reverse.

It was then the nude Mottola would have decided to jump from the aft of the yacht directly in front of the reversing engines. The forty-five-foot cabin cruiser backed over her, its propeller nearly chewing her in half. Although everyone on board heard the noise, by the time the skipper reacted, the craft had traveled at least forty-five feet. Mottola had surfaced at the front end of the boat.

"No one seemed to see her jump, but it is thought she might have jumped directly over the rear end of the boat," Mohave Sheriff's Deputy Charles Crane reported.

Nancy Mottola died of shock and blood loss at approximately 6:40 p.m. as the yacht party returned to the Temple Bar boat dock. The aft deck, where she laid under bloody sheets, was awash in crimson. Two National Park Service rangers met the group, and police officials from Nevada and Arizona began an investigation into events surrounding the tragedy and the precise cause of death.

Less than forty-eight hours after Mottola plunged into the warm water off Sandy Point, her death was ruled accidental. A spokesman for the Mohave County Sheriff's Office said that no coroner's inquest would be conducted. The body was removed to a Kingman mortuary, where it was claimed two days later by her father, Anthony Mottola, Sr., and brother, Anthony, Jr.

"The cause of death is immediately apparent, even to non-professional eyes," Mohave County coroner Clyde McCune reported in his visual examination of the body. "Damage to the body in the vicinity of the thighs is massive. Both legs are nearly severed in the thigh just below the area of the crotch. The right leg has suffered a compound fracture midway between the knee and ankle. Bleeding would have been of massive proportions..."

A shapely, 5-foot-8-inch woman was walking naked around a forty-five-foot yacht, and seven people were on board, but no one saw her jump into the water. No one knew her name. It must have been some party.

"Nancy dove over the side without me knowing anything about it," Irving Devine wrote in an official statement. "The next thing I knew he was hauling her in with my captain."

"He" was Wynn.

Friedman said, "I was asleep in the rear cabin of the boat when I was awakened by someone yelling that there was an accident. I dashed up to the rear deck and saw two men dragging a woman to the rear ladder of the boat in the water. We all helped take her aboard and covered her with sheets. We also applied cold towels to her forehead. The boat returned to Temple Bar."

Paul Chandler, the skipper, wasn't the first on the scene. He was, however, the only one of the seven on board to jump in after the dying woman. Chandler: "I was idling the boat into the beach at Sandy Point when it felt like the boat hit a log. Someone on the boat yelled, and I stopped and turned off the engines and went into the water after the girl and brought her back on board and headed for Temple Bar."

Like Friedman, Wynn said he also was asleep below deck when he heard and felt the boat bump into something.

"Immediately there was shouting for help outside," Wynn told Deputy Crane. "I went up the steps out to the rear deck where I could see the captain struggling in the water with the lady. I jumped over the rear rail onto the lower catwalk and helped get her into the boat. Thereafter we tried to administer first aid, stop the bleeding with a tourniquet and came back."

The women on board added little to the picture.

"I was sitting on deck and heard a bump," Bonnie Lee said. "Thought someone fell down or ran over a log. Next minute, Mr. Devine called for help. She was cut up in the water. They got her on deck. Next tried to do everything we could. She died as we pulled up to dock."

Her roommate, Randi Jones, offered even less information.

"I was sitting on deck and heard a funny noise in the engine then I heard them saying that Nancy had got caught in the propeller."

Beverly Erickson, who listed her residence as room 137 of the Colonial House Motel, echoed everyone else: "The boat was idling and Nancy jumped in. There was a loud noise, and everyone ran to see what it was. Then we saw one of the men aboard bringing her in. After she was brought on deck, we immediately came to shore, and within one minute before we got to the dock, she was dead."

Deputy Crane might not have been the most literate fellow, and he might have been stationed at the rural outpost of Chloride, Arizona, but he was not so far out in the country that he couldn't tell a series of too-neat stories when he heard them.

"It was also learned by the [officer] that the passengers other than the pilot were drinking prior to the accident, just how drunk they were at the time we could not determine, as each one covered up for the other," Crane wrote in his official report. "It is this officer's opinion that they had their stories prefabricated before any officers arrived at the scene."

The newspapers responded immediately.

"Yacht Party Tragedy" the *Las Vegas Review-Journal*'s August 3 edition declared on page one.

A gala swimming party aboard the plush Caesars Palace yacht on Lake Mead ended in tragedy Wednesday when a 31-year-old divorcee fell from the boat and died from injuries suffered when she was chopped to pieces by the propeller, the story began.

After a four-paragraph follow-up, the memory of Nancy Mottola diluted as fast as her blood in Lake Mead. There would be no investigation into the exact cause of Mottola's death or the events that led to her demise.

The grisly accident remained a mystery in Wynn's life for several reasons.

First, the press failed to scrutinize the incident. Only the most perfunctory accident investigation and autopsy were conducted: It was ruled an accident. Although a woman was nearly cut in half, the leader of the yacht party—a businessman with connections to organized crime, an extensive arrest record and several aliases— got away with making a vague, two-line statement.

Second, no one asked Steve Wynn what he was doing that day aboard the Caesars Galley yacht.

CHAPTER 3

A BOTTLE OF WINE, AN ACRE OF LUCK, A FRIEND FOR LIFE

Steve Wynn's media apologists rush to call him a genius businessman, but he concedes that his rise in gaming would not have been possible without E. Parry Thomas.

The gray-haired Thomas is the single most important banking figure in the history of Las Vegas. In an era in which respectable lending institutions scoffed at the notion of financing the legalized gambling industry, his Valley Bank was the conduit for millions in financing to select casino operators. In some circles, he was considered Mr. Las Vegas; in others, a hoodlum banker.

———

Shortly after World War II, in which he served as a paratrooper, Thomas returned to Salt Lake City to complete his education at the University of Utah. Thomas helped design his own degree in business, then went to work for Walter Cosgriff's Continental Bank, which sent him to Las Vegas, a city perceived as having both a world of potential as well as a problem with its image as a mob town.

Thomas's posting to Las Vegas made sense. He had begun studying Southern Nevada's real-estate market shortly after World War II, and his obvious familiarity with the market and the men who ran the town were two reasons Cosgriff tapped him to represent civilized lending in the notorious gambling city.

Thomas wasted no time exercising his bank's casino-friendly philosophy. An early remodeling loan to the original Sahara set the tone.

At the time, the Sahara's hidden owners included brothers Meyer and Jake Lansky. As money became available to the bank, Thomas was prudent but generous with local casino operators. The downtown Fremont Street casinos benefited from Thomas's belief in the future of the industry; as did such Strip casinos as the Riviera, Desert Inn, Sands, Dunes, Thunderbird, and the Hacienda.

With the banking conduit in place, funding from Morris Shenker's Galveston, Texas-based American National Insurance Company (ANICO) flowed into Las Vegas. Shenker's ANICO transferred $20 million through the Bank of Las Vegas (its name was later changed to Valley Bank)—nearly $14 million of it going to Shenker himself. Loans from Jimmy Hoffa's Teamsters Central States Pension Fund began pouring in—nearly $230 million was processed through Thomas's Valley Bank before federal investigators shut down the corrupt Teamsters source of casino construction loans.

Valley Bank, with Parry Thomas as its president in 1961, grew along with the town. Although it was founded with a modest $375,000, by 1988 the bank's assets exceeded $2.2 billion. Thomas eventually handed the leadership of his bank to his son, Peter, a Georgetown graduate. Valley Bank later merged with Bank of America.

Years after Thomas had reduced his day-to-day role in Valley Bank's activities, he remained a formidable and respected figure. In 1983, for example, Thomas single-handedly gathered warring factions at the scandal-riddled Aladdin Hotel for a summit meeting to settle a protracted dispute.

The participants included veteran casino operator Edward Torres, who cut his teeth in Meyer Lansky's Riviera in Havana, and former Aladdin attorney and reputed mob associate Sorkis Webbe. Thomas moved as easily among casino industry tough guys as he did with the well-heeled at the Las Vegas Country Club.

"Okay, fellas, you've got two hours," Thomas said. "Put together a deal. I'm leaving the room, and when I come back, I want it done."

Two hours later, the deal was done.

"Thomas is to casino industry entrepreneurs what the Big Bang was to the Universe," Las Vegas columnist Ned Day once wrote. "If it weren't for Parry Thomas, Steve Wynn might still be hustling wholesale hootch."

———

With the Frontier deal blown apart, Steve Wynn was itching to get back into the game. Wynn did not stray far from the action while waiting for his next deal. Then as now, there was more than enough action to keep a handsome, glib young hustler busy.

For a few months, Wynn produced lounge shows for several Las Vegas casinos in partnership with promoter-director Matt Gregory. He bounced around from lounge to lounge for a year, but according to a report compiled years later by New Jersey gaming investigators, still managed to make nearly $70,000 from his partnership with Gregory in Cassandra Limited, an excellent salary in 1969.

Like many people who knew the young Wynn, Gregory was taken by the energetic fellow's charm and unabashed assertiveness. But, Gregory said, if Wynn earned $70,000, then it didn't come from Cassandra. In the heart of the psychedelic sixties, Gregory received less than $1,000 a week for producing Mod Squad Marmalade at the Sahara Hotel. The lounge production show featured saxophone player Lee Greenwood, who went on to become a popular country and western performer. Gregory recalled Wynn's take of their partnership in Cassandra was about $140 a week.

"He got his money every week. He was thrilled. He was now in show biz," Gregory said, laughing.

It was clear to those around Wynn then that he was attracted to the dancers and the nightlife. But instead of crafting a career booking no-name house bands or has-been crooners wrapped in polyester and dripping in gold chains, Wynn would become the biggest name in a city high on hyperbole.

Wynn was thousands of miles from Wayson's Corner, where he intimately understood the terrain, and still was on the outside looking in at the Las Vegas that for years had filled his dreams.

So, he did what anyone with his rare contacts would do: He approached E. Parry Thomas, his new mentor and one of the most powerful men in the city.

"Pop, I gotta get something to do," Wynn said. "I gotta go to work."

"I could see his brightness and quickness and ability as a young man," Thomas recalled. "The friendship grew into a very strong friendship. It might even be considered a father-son relationship."

"Parry Thomas was the most significant banker in gaming's growth," Wynn said. "His sponsorship was the equivalent of having Bernard Baruch guiding you on Wall Street."

Thomas, the ultimate parts man in a city flush with facilitators, crafted a deal that not only revealed his business acumen but also gave a glimpse into the evolution of organized crime from felonious racket to legitimate business.

━━━━━

On Jan. 1, 1969, Thomas put Wynn to work as the Nevada distributor for Schenley Industries liquor products after arranging the purchase of one of its many subsidiaries, Best Brands, for approximately $65,000. Wynn became the exclusive Nevada distributor for Schenley, best known for its Dewar's Scotch.

Thomas, whose Valley Bank had not previously had a liquor company as a customer, secured a loan to cover the purchase. He had the contacts necessary to do the deal quickly, and he sent Steve Wynn to see Bob Maxey, a senior vice-president at First Western Financial.

Maxey, who served as the president of the Golden Nugget in Atlantic City and later was the president of the 5,005-room MGM Grand Hotel and Theme Park on the Strip, smiled as he recalled the fresh-faced fellow wearing shorts who charmed his way past a secretary and stormed his inner office.

Maxey, a systems engineer raised in a straight-talking Missouri household, wasn't interested in a career change, but with Wynn using E. Parry Thomas as a calling card, Maxey was impressed enough to listen to the kid's sales pitch.

Wynn had just taken ownership of Best Brands and was looking for an inside man to operate the liquor distributorship in an exceedingly competitive Las Vegas market. But Maxey was not as easily charmed as his secretary.

"When he's trying to sell something, he knows how to do it. We had just met, and he said how much he needed me. He said the company needed me," Maxey said years later of Wynn's ability to paint a promising picture. "The fact that it never works out that way is secondary. He's one of the world's greatest salesmen and always has been. Basically I was trying to refuse, but he wouldn't listen. His salesmanship wore me down."

Maxey was courted over the course of two months and believed he had made his final decision to reject Wynn's offer when the two met for breakfast at the Dunes Hotel. After they had finished eating, Maxey delivered the bad news. But Wynn still wasn't through.

Under the Dunes porte-cochere, a driver wheeled up a brand new blue Cadillac Eldorado convertible. Maxey, an articulate fellow whose conservative dress and lifestyle more closely resembles a banker than a casino boss, was staggered.

In a few days, Maxey was driving his Eldorado to the Best Brands warehouse, where he served as vice-president and financial paramedic for the flamboyant, free-spending Wynn.

———

Schenley, which like many liquor distilleries had its beginnings in the Prohibition era, recently had been purchased by Meshulam Riklis, who, at the time, also owned Revlon cosmetics, the Riviera Hotel, and a thick portfolio of other companies. Riklis, perhaps best known by the general public as the one-time husband of Pia Zadora, is considered the godfather of the form of high-interest, high-risk funding that later became commonly known as junk bonds.

Before Riklis, however, Schenley was owned by Lewis Solon Rosenstiel, whom liquor made into one of America's wealthiest men. Although the cigar-smoking behemoth in a business suit would groom a reputation as a philanthropist, his heart was as dark as any mobster's. Like Las Vegas legends Moe Dalitz and Meyer Lansky, Rosenstiel was a Prohibition-era bootlegger. But the fat man possessed a particular vision Lansky lacked: He realized Prohibition wouldn't last forever and that few outlaws live to a ripe old age.

Rosenstiel and Samuel Bronfman (founder of Seagrams) cut lucrative illegal liquor deals with Meyer Lansky. During a hearing of the New York State Joint Legislative Committee on Crime, Rosenstiel was named as one of a collective of bootleggers who purchased cases of Canadian liquor and smuggled the goods in the United States for resale. But where Rosenstiel cleaned up his illegal business activities after Prohibition, paid his taxes, groomed his political contacts, and became known as a mainstream capitalist, Lansky chose to remain an outlaw. Years after Repeal, Lansky wondered aloud about the phenomenon.

"Why is Lansky a 'gangster' and not the Bronfman and Rosenstiel families?"

But Lansky knew the answer. Rosenstiel juiced the system and made himself an indispensable part of the political process. In his time, Rosenstiel became closely associated with FBI Director J. Edgar Hoover through a charitable institution into which more than $1 million was pumped to be used at Hoover's discretion.

"Rosenstiel cultivated Hoover assiduously," Anthony Summers wrote in *Official and Confidential: The Secret Life of J. Edgar Hoover.* "In the '60s, he would contribute...to the J. Edgar Hoover Foundation, a fund established to 'safeguard the heritage and freedom of the United States of America...to perpetuate the ideals and purposes to which the Honorable J. Edgar Hoover has dedicated his life...[and] to combat Communism.'"

But in 1968, Schenley was just another Riklis acquisition. With Thomas in the background, Wynn was introduced to the liquor offer through Jake Gottlieb, a trucking executive and board member of Continental Connector who had owned a piece of the Dunes. Gottlieb's early career in Chicago had been sponsored by the Capone mob and was punctuated by a friendship with future Teamsters President Jimmy Hoffa. With men such as Gottlieb and Thomas to open doors, Wynn had few worries.

━━━━━

In the three years he held Best Brands, Wynn sold liquor to major hotels and restaurants in Las Vegas and Reno. He compiled wine lists and used the influence of Thomas to persuade people to buy his products.

"I got a call one day from Moe Dalitz. It was about Steve Wynn," one longtime Las Vegas casino operator told a reporter. "Moe said Parry Thomas had asked him to ask me, as a favor, to give the kid some of my liquor business. So, I did. For a while he was fine. The deliveries were made on time, but it wasn't long before he lost interest. Casinos go through a tremendous amount of liquor. You could see he didn't want to be there. He was biding his time. He was a kid, and he was irresponsible.

"Steve was rarely around. I was never sure who ran the place. When [Schenley] forgave his debt, I think they were just glad to get their distributorship back."

In interviews, Wynn remembers his experience in playful terms. "I wrote almost every wine list on the Strip," he often has said.

He also came up with a idea for marketing Boodles gin to their local clients. He and Bob Maxey were having trouble finding something new to say about the product. Gin, after all, was gin. Then Wynn was inspired.

"This gin is so fine," he said, "that nine out of ten of the bottles it comes in are smashed."

"I can't remember whether we sold any or not," Maxey recalled, laughing. But bar owners and liquor managers sure were impressed with the quality control.

Wynn's expansion was intense. On May 15, 1970, Wynn (not Best Brands) bought ten acres of real estate off the Strip near Flamingo Road for $154,000. Less than two weeks later, he tapped Valley Bank for a $400,000 construction loan to build a liquor warehouse and lay a rail spur to the back door of the new Best Brands building. It took another $200,000 of Valley Bank's money to complete the project. That placed Wynn some $600,000 in debt to Thomas.

By December, Wynn had become not only the president of the company but its landlord as well. He rented the building to the company for $7,500 per month and extracted a security deposit— just in case the tenant decided to skip out, perhaps—for $87,000.

Wynn kept the warehouse for a little more than a year before selling it to L.E. Jung and Wulff, a real-estate subsidiary of Schenley Industries for $700,000. He owed Schenley approximately $360,000, but for some reason the distillery forgave much of the debt and arranged a nearly pain-free buyout. Wynn netted $121,000 from the warehouse sale alone. He netted $51,000 from the sale of his foundering liquor company. He had run the company deep into the red but was, nevertheless, handed a bankroll for future investment.

Such corporate kindness was not the rule, but, after all, Steve Wynn was a protégé of Parry Thomas.

"It was an extreme amount of hard work, for a relatively marginal return," Bob Maxey said, "which is not a situation calculated to hold the interest of Steve Wynn for long. Steve's life requires almost constant challenges. He needs challenges. He thrives on them."

If Wynn's early financial maneuvering appeared a bit confusing to a layperson, it was understandable. It had the same effect on the Internal Revenue Service, when they conducted an investigation of the young entrepreneur that spanned five years. The agency's audit discovered he had underreported his income by approximately $37,000 for 1971-72. Investigators also surmised that another $12,000 in Best Brand business expenses actually were personal expenses. Wynn quietly paid the government what he owed, and no charges were filed.

The audit came at a time the IRS was investigating reports of citywide kickbacks in the food and liquor supply industries servicing Las Vegas casinos. Such practices were accepted in Southern Nevada, and stories of food and beverage managers doubling their salaries with cash kickbacks from suppliers were common. The IRS wasn't interested so much in the ethics of a distributor slipping a manager a few hundred bucks to push one brand of tomato sauce over another; investigators wanted to know whether Uncle Sam was receiving his annual tribute.

In 1978, a federal grand jury convened to investigate alleged extortion, bribery, and racketeering in Las Vegas. By the time investigators interrogated the owners of Best Brands, later named Southern Wine and Spirits of Nevada, for rumored kickbacks related to mob front Allen Glick's Argent Corporation casinos, Wynn was off on other business.

———

Las Vegas lore has it that Wynn gathered his bankroll from his Best Brand venture and in November 1971 gambled it on the next improbable but immensely profitable venture: a 1.1-acre slice of real estate squeezed between Caesars Palace and the corner of Flamingo Road and the Strip—one of the four busiest corners in Las Vegas. In reality, although Wynn's investment in Best Brands had been protected by the loans and influence of Thomas and his associates, he possessed nowhere near the land's $1.1 million sale price.

The property, at the time used as a Caesars Palace parking lot, was owned by Howard Hughes, who was in the habit of buying— not selling—his sizable chunks of Las Vegas. Although separated by a wide financial gulf, Hughes and Wynn had something in common: Parry Thomas. It was Thomas who brokered Hughes's $24 million Frontier acquisition. It was Thomas who jump-started Wynn's stalled young career. It was Thomas who would separate Hughes from his real estate on Wynn's behalf for approximately 50 percent of the real estate's worth, only to have the land purchased by Caesars Palace after what qualifies as a little gentlemanly extortion.

Although he lacked the cash necessary to make the deal, Wynn already had a credit history at Valley Bank. But he needed an even more credit-rich partner. He found one in J&B Scotch executive Abraham Rosenberg. With the help of Thomas, and the signatory guarantee of Rosenberg, Wynn secured a $1.2 million loan and made his intention clear: They were interested in acquiring a valuable slice of the Strip. The land fronted the Strip little more than 100 feet and extended 1500 feet to the back of the property.

Wynn and Rosenberg faced one small problem. Caesars Palace President and Chief Executive Officer Bill Weinberger believed the Hughes Tool Company had promised him a first right of refusal on the land. Others involved in the brief negotiations were Hughes aide Robert Maheu, casino executive Al Benedict, and retired Army General Ed Nigro. Obviously, if Hughes ever wanted to sell his property, the logical buyer would be Caesars Palace. Before Weinberger could act—he said he planned to offer Wynn a quick $250,000 to back off—Hughes Tool sold the land. Clifford Perlman, who ran Caesars Palace and eventually would be ushered out of the gaming industry because of his organized crime associations, informed Weinberger of the done deal.

On Oct. 27, 1972, Wynn and Rosenberg sold their acre of pure gold to Caesars Palace for $2.25 million. Their free $1.2 million loan from Valley Bank was repaid, and they divided a cool $1 million.

Wynn's share of the transaction was approximately $687,000.

———

As if scripted, word of the land sale leaked to the local newspapers. Wynn was described as a brilliant young entrepreneur with an uncanny sense of timing.

"Among Las Vegas' brightest business luminaries, one on a rapid rise to fame and power is also the youngest," the *Las Vegas Sun* gushed. "At age 30, Steve Wynn, Thursday closed a deal many men his senior would give their eye-teeth to have."

He was depicted as a Las Vegas *wunderkind* who had almost magically burst onto the local casino scene.

His foray into the Frontier was alluded to without mention of the mob.

His debt-riddled liquor distributorship was described as a past success.

It was only natural, then, that he would outwit the wily old operators of Caesars Palace and purchase from the Hughes Tool Company the slender but valuable piece of real estate.

A legend was being born, and Wynn did little to set the record straight.

"Well, first of all, at the time we were short of legends," Wynn told an interviewer on a local PBS program. "You can't really bluff in a good game without any cards. You've got to be prepared to do it. So we were going to build one of those smallish kind of hotel-casinos, for example, the Barbary Coast [across the street from Caesars Palace] is a perfect example. The Barbary Coast is sort of a takeoff on what we wanted to do.

"I don't think we wanted to do it. It was the kind of site that didn't give you a chance to fix it if you made a mistake. So the whole thing worked out well. Clifford Perlman decided that it'd be better if they had the land on the corner, and I think he was right. He paid a fair price. It seemed like a lot at the time, but since then the prices have gone up for that location, for that corner."

Wynn was a genius, all right. But his genius was not always found in what he knew but in whom.

Although Wynn acknowledges Thomas's guidance, the banker was characterized as little more than a minimally involved mentor to the brilliant young fellow with the perfect hair and Colgate smile.

But if Thomas received less credit than he deserved for Wynn's arrival, Rosenberg received none at all. It was Rosenberg who, at least technically, had performed an act of great trust by guaranteeing a $1.2 million loan for one-third of the profits.

It makes one wonder why he didn't make the deal himself. It also prompts other questions: If Thomas, who represented Hughes, wanted to sell a slender slice of real estate, why not sell it to Caesars Palace? Or, better still, why not allow a little friendly competition and bidding for the property?

The answer appears clear to critics: The land deal was meant to build Wynn's viability as an entrepreneur. With Hughes in his pocket, Parry Thomas had complex plans for Steve Wynn. If Wynn had a genuine intention of constructing a 500-room hotel and slot joint on the site—like the scale model he proudly displayed to the media—then it would have to be a long and narrow one financed by a man who possessed more debts than dollars. Building a small casino was his threat, but not his intention.

"Caesars Palace wanted the corner [parking lot] more than I wanted the hotel," Wynn said in 1972.

How much was the land worth? Rosenberg didn't know. Although the aging gentleman signed on for more than $1 million in debt, he did not have the property independently appraised. According to a New Jersey Division of Gaming report on Wynn: "Rosenberg stated that he agreed to the partnership mostly because of his friendship with Wynn and also because of his [Rosenberg's] belief that the property was much more valuable to Caesars Palace than 1.2 million dollars....Rosenberg related that it was his understanding that the purchase of the property was for the sole purpose of selling back to Caesars because he [Rosenberg] would not be involved in owning a casino."

If the sale of Best Brands, the warehouse, and remaining acreage gave Wynn financial credibility, then the Caesars shuffle—as choreographed by E. Parry Thomas—added viability.

CHAPTER 4

GRABBING THE GOLDEN NUGGET

Las Vegas is built on a thick foundation of legend and fantasy, and one of the greatest stories ever told is the tale of Steve Wynn's takeover at the Golden Nugget.

It is the story of how a gifted young entrepreneur traveled west at substantial risk, bounced around a few jobs, built his bankroll, and, in one daring move, swept into the front office of a downtown casino. As the years have passed, the legend has grown into a myth of the bingo man's son who, with hard work, dedication, and a touch of stealth, prevails.

But it was Parry Thomas, not Wynn, who scripted the Golden Nugget takeover, and not for altruistic reasons.

Business was the motive, and business at Thomas's Continental Connector was being nagged by the pesky Securities and Exchange Commission.

Wynn had been buying shares of Golden Nugget since 1969, when Thomas led an unsuccessful attempt to acquire the company through his role on the board of directors of the Continental Connector Corporation. The Securities and Exchange Commission halted the takeover because of alleged violations ranging from a false and misleading proxy statement to inappropriate accounting practices. The American Stock Exchange, on which Continental Connector was listed, froze the stock. Continental Connector signed a consent degree, admitting no guilt, and agreed to halt its bid to acquire the Golden Nugget.

That created not only the opportunity for Wynn but also the need for a viable entrepreneur with an acceptable financial statement to grab the casino. Wynn admitted he bought 14,000 shares of the casino company's stock in 1969 "on the basis that he thought it had been announced that Continental Connector was going to buy the Golden Nugget." Price of the stock: $115,694.45.

On the advice of Thomas and in part with loans from Valley Bank, Wynn continued buying Golden Nugget stock on the open market.

In 1971, he paid $23,372.87 for 4,000 shares. A year later, he spent $503,305.23 for 92,000 shares, and from September 11 through October 26, bought another 53,500 shares. On October 24, he submitted to the Nevada Gaming Control Board his licensing application, signaling his intention to become a major stockholder. The lucky acreage at Caesars Palace was sold October 27, and with that bankroll, Wynn picked up another 38,000 shares before the end of 1972.

By January 1972 Wynn held about 5.8 percent of available Golden Nugget stock. Although Continental Connector wouldn't get the Golden Nugget, the casino would be owned by a protégé of Parry Thomas.

———

Wynn was buying into a casino with a fascinating history.

Located at 129 Fremont Street in downtown Las Vegas, the Golden Nugget originally had been incorporated in 1949 by Artemus Ham, making it, in a city incorporated only four decades earlier, one of the more venerable operations. More than twenty-five years after Bugsy Siegel was murdered in Beverly Hills, the Golden Nugget remained a bustling joint.

It was small by Strip standards but possessed several features that made it ripe for a takeover. Although it had no hotel rooms, the casino had once been the largest downtown, and there was plenty of real estate for future expansion. Moreover, the Golden Nugget was a public company at a time when casinos were almost never publicly owned. It was traded on the Pacific Stock Exchange. That is part of what made it so attractive to Continental Connector.

Wynn inherited more than Continental's role when he began buying up blocks of Golden Nugget stock. He also inherited a problem with the mob in the form of dapper Jerome Zarowitz, whose link to organized crime figures had been well established by federal law enforcement years before he was bought out of the casino industry. A takeover of the Golden Nugget would go a long way toward cleaning up that casino's image, not to mention the town's.

Zarowitz owned 92,000 shares of Golden Nugget stock, making him the third largest stockholder behind Wynn and El Cortez casino owner Jackie Gaughan. But Zarowitz's stock portfolio was healthier than his reputation. The former Caesars Palace credit manager, who owned 4.85 percent of the Golden Nugget, was as well connected as anyone in a city dominated by racketeers-turned-solid citizens.

Zarowitz was an organized crime associate in partnership with Genovese crime family member Anthony "Fat Tony" Salerno and New England La Cosa Nostra leader Raymond Patriarca. During a November 1971 Gaming Control Board hearing Zarowitz was described by member Shannon Bybee as "a man whose connection, directly or indirectly, with gaming would be harmful to the best interests of the state and the gaming industry." Translated, Wynn's staunch advocate Bybee—a friend and fellow church member of Parry Thomas's—meant Zarowitz's veneer of legitimacy had been cracked to pieces even by Gaming Control Board standards. Sensing another embarrassing moment in legalized gaming history, Control Board Chairman Phil Hannifin attempted to persuade Wynn to buy out Zarowitz.

From his main office in Miami, Zarowitz had gained a nationwide reputation in the illegal gambling business long before Caesars Palace was built.

Zarowitz and three accomplices—New Jersey bookmaker Alvin Paris, David Kraukauer, and veteran fixer Harvey Stemmer—set out to beat the point spread by fixing the 1946 National Football League championship game between the Chicago Bears and the New York Giants. The plan, however, was shattered by a government wiretap on the phone of Paris, who, along with Kraukauer and Zarowitz, was convicted for conspiring to rig a sporting event. Zarowitz served just short of two years for his role; Giants players Frank Filchock and Merle Hapes were banished from the league for life. (Trivia buffs can rest easy: The point spread was 10, and the game was won by the Bears, 24-14.)

Nevertheless, the sports-fixing conviction didn't keep Zarowitz from becoming the credit manager of Jay Sarno's Caesars Palace, a key position for which he went unlicensed and minimally scrutinized by state authorities even after it was established that he took part in an October 1965 mob summit at Palm Springs. Known as the Little Apalachin, after the infamous gathering of America's mob bosses 1957 in upstate New York, the Palm Springs meeting was held—or so federal prosecutors believed—for the purposes of relocating the outlaw betting line from Miami to Las Vegas and to straighten out the mob's investments, including its stake in Caesars Palace.

When word of the Little Apalachin broke in the *Los Angeles Times* more than a year later, Zarowitz had some explaining to do.

His days working in an official capacity at Caesars Palace appeared to be numbered. But instead of being branded a mob frontman and unceremoniously exiled from the industry, Zarowitz continued his lucrative association with Caesars Palace for years until it was sold in 1969 to Lum's, a Florida-based restaurant chain. Zarowitz received $3.5 million for his interest in the resort even though he held no official interest.

Zarowitz eventually retreated in style to Palm Springs but not before removing his name from his Las Vegas holdings—which included 92,000 shares of Golden Nugget stock—after laughing at Nevada authorities. He would force the Gaming Control Board to make one last concession before slipping out of town. His son, Lonny, would have to be taken care of after initially being denied a slot-route operator's license.

On March 23, 1973, the commission crafted a deal with Zarowitz to approve his son Lonny as a percentage owner in the tiny Red Garter Casino. After being granted that concession for his son, Papa Zarowitz agreed to sell his 92,000 shares directly to Wynn.

———

With Zarowitz out of the way, Wynn now held a high enough percentage of stock to enter the Golden Nugget in style. Of course, that was not his stated intention to Nevada casino authorities. In a gaming commission meeting, with plenty of assistance from its chairman, future Golden Nugget counsel Frank Schreck, Wynn painted a picture of himself as little more than a benevolent helpmate for Golden Nugget President Buck Blaine.

Mr. Schreck: "You stated that at this time you're not in a management position of the Golden Nugget and that that's obviously not your expectation in the future relative to your own stock."

Mr. Wynn: "Good point though there's been a lot of talk about that and it's a good point and I'll be happy to tell you about what's going on because I was with Bucky Blaine yesterday. Naturally anybody—I have more at stake than any other single person—and naturally I would like to be a member of that family, but I'm convinced of the integrity of the management of the Golden Nugget. I think the things that will make that the biggest success around are things that you and I can see here today that can be done by building and things like that. We got the keno back April 1; I want to be a member of that family but as a family invitational thing only.

"...But I don't intend to start a proxy fight nor do I intend to go for a tender offer of a stock; this is not a takeover in that sense and the relationship between me and the men who are there now is great. I don't know Mr. Boyd, for example; I don't know Mr. Green, but I know Charlie King and Buck Blaine, and I know Jackie Gaughan, and there's enough ability and experience there to get the job done if they get some help, and that's how I see myself helping if possible. I might be a bingo consultant there; I might be able to do something about that, but that's it, Mr. Schreck, that's the relationship today."

Wynn's license application was approved by the Nevada Gaming Commission on March 22, 1973.

Less than a month later, Wynn pitched Golden Nugget President Buck Blaine from a position on the corporation's board of directors.

Theft was common at the casino, and without hotel rooms, the place never would be more than a grind joint. Blaine was to be eased out if possible, tossed into the street if necessary. Thomas met with Blaine and helped arrange his departure.

Wynn had documented substantial evidence of theft on the casino floor. He went to Blaine's office and approached the boss.

"We can do it easy, or we can do it hard," Wynn said. "What do you say?"

Blaine, seated behind his desk, just caved in.

"It was my situation as a businessman to rough up Bucky Blaine," Wynn said years later. "I was real glad when he said he wanted to work something out."

Blaine's hurt feelings were assuaged by an agreement that he'd be paid $30,000 a year as a consultant.

Although Wynn remained the majority stockholder, he was not the biggest player in the August 1973 tender offer. The group included Jackie Gaughan, Mel Wolzinger, Earl Wilson, brothers Edward and Fred Doumani, and, most significantly, Albert Parvin. Of 225,000 shares acquired in the bid to assume control of the company, Parry Thomas's friend Parvin picked up the most, 75,000. After the August takeover, the Wynn group controlled in excess of 25 percent of the stock.

Of note in the original takeover group were the two Doumani brothers, who in years to come not only would cause Wynn headaches as he fought to become licensed in New Jersey and Great Britain but also would prove problematic for the industry as a whole after they were linked to a mob-skimming operation at the Tropicana Hotel. Ed Doumani eventually would be fined $50,000 for violating Nevada gaming regulations and would pull out of Golden Nugget's Atlantic City foray—at Wynn's request—after his friendships with mob associates Joey Cusumano and Frank "Lefty" Rosenthal were revealed.

But Al Parvin, whom Wynn had met through Maurice Friedman, was by far the biggest name in the group. If Parvin's presence on the board spoke to the influence of Parry Thomas in Steve Wynn's life, it also attracted suspicion in law enforcement circles. Parvin's stock in trade was interior design—he was responsible for the wild carpeting seen at many Las Vegas casinos, including the original Flamingo—but it was common knowledge that he was closely aligned with the Teamsters, the mob, and the friends of Meyer Lansky.

When Wynn bought three points (3 percent) of the Frontier in 1967, he became the first Nevada licensee to simultaneously hold an interest in a gambling concern in another jurisdiction. (He placed his 20 percent bingo interest in a trust held by his family in Maryland.)

When he completed the Golden Nugget takeover, he became the first operator to be allowed to maintain outside holdings.

When he pushed into Atlantic City in the late 1970s, he became the first Nevada operator approved for a casino on the Boardwalk.

At his licensing hearing, Wynn complained that carrying out his big plans for the Golden Nugget would not be possible without the few thousand in income he derived from the Maryland bingo hall, which back in 1967 he called an insubstantial enterprise but by 1973 depicted it as "by far the largest bingo operation on earth." The argument was persuasive but not consistent with the facts.

Wynn's pitch that his $1-million investment in the Golden Nugget would not be possible unless state casino regulators allowed him to maintain a form of interest in the bingo hall ought to have produced laughter at the April 11, 1973, Gaming Control Board meeting. After all, it was easy to see Wynn's rise at the downtown casino had been sponsored by E. Parry Thomas. Instead of finding humor in Wynn's rhetorical soft shoe, the control board found his situation suitable and in so doing set a precedent that eventually would help open the door to the proliferation of casinos in the majority of states.

"It is a wonderful thing to be able to invest $1 million in anything. And I'm very proud of it. The reason that I'm in a position to be involved in a financial transaction of that size is because of the background—because of the earnings—and because of the success of Wayson's bingo. When my dad died in 1963...his entire estate was zero. My dad had no other income. I graduated from the University of Pennsylvania and then thirty days later went to work for Wayson's Corner. My wife counted the money, and I called the numbers. I moved to Nevada because my business was successful enough and because I had an interest in investing in the Frontier in 1967. But, like most men who make investments, we all need sustenance. We need that regular steady income that allows us to take the time and the energy to look into business deals, to explore possibilities, to manage whatever money you may have been able to accumulate.

"To afford expensive legal help. Wayson's affords me the opportunity. Without Wayson's I would not have been able to pay for the $8,246.37 investigation fee yesterday of the Gaming Control Board. So, whereas I choose to live in Nevada and I chose to invest my money here, or I will choose to invest my money here if you see fit. I would not be able to do it were I prohibited from owning Wayson's. As a matter of fact, I mentioned that to Mr. Bybee in December. I said: 'If it's impossible for me to participate here although I live here without maintaining the dividend income that I realize from Wayson's I don't think that I'll be able to do it.'"

Wynn conjured images of his poor mother scuffling for a few bucks if he were unable to look after Wayson's. Bybee, who was well aware that Thomas was the applicant's mentor, guided Wynn through the interrogation by Chairman Hannifin.

"I would have to say that, under the circumstances, Mr. Wynn comes close to that line of there being no visible substantial benefit to the state of Nevada," Bybee said. "I do think perhaps there is some tangible benefit from his being permitted to be involved in Nevada gaming without surrendering his interest in foreign gaming. For one thing, he's not an outsider who's coming in for the first time now and seeking to have the benefit of involvement in foreign gaming in conjunction with Nevada gaming. He's been a resident of some six years."

Bybee's gushing endorsement practically made Wynn a Las Vegas pioneer. Hannifin's mild protests aside, the vote to recommend Wynn for licensing was unanimous.

———

Wynn, young and brash, began to exude power. He developed a violent temper, which he unleashed at the slightest provocation.

A man named Milton Stone was owed $6,000 by Wynn and was having trouble collecting the money. He flew from his New Jersey home and met a friend connected to several Las Vegas casinos. The friend was Sicilian.

Stone was concerned over his meeting with Wynn because it was said that Wynn surrounded himself with Sicilian bodyguards.

The friend agreed to accompany him.

The two men met at the small original Golden Nugget. The casino lacked a hotel at that time.

Wynn himself confirmed the fact that "the gentlemen" standing nearby were Sicilians.

Milton Stone was uncomfortable, to the amusement of his Sicilian friend. At this point the companion looked at the three men standing about fifteen feet away. He spoke to them with a few very private words in Sicilian dialect. Then he focused his eyes on them and repeated his words.

Steve Wynn's head and eyes turned back and forth as though he was watching a tennis match. It was obvious the little speech in Sicilian was causing the bodyguards concern.

The bodyguards backed away, showing respect.

Suddenly Wynn seemed to soften. He asked: "You fellows like porterhouse steaks?"

When Stone nodded, Wynn picked up a casino phone and called in an order for three porterhouse steaks and three large glasses of cold milk.

"I like my milk very cold," he said.

The three men went on to enjoy a pleasant lunch. Wynn related stories from his youth and described how he got to Vegas. He spoke of his friendship with the Binion brothers.

As the two men prepared to depart, Wynn handed Stone his money. Then he handed Stone's companion a large box of Golden Nugget western belt buckles to be given to his children.

Stone's escort thanked Steve Wynn and wished him great success, with "*buona fortuna*."

As for the Sicilian bodyguards, they were tripping over their feet to shake hands with Stone and his companion as the two men departed.

The companion, speaking in 1995, reported, "My impression of Wynn was that he was a very nice, well-spoken guy, an honorable gentleman who really liked Italians."

———

In short order, fortified by millions in financing from Valley Bank, Wynn embarked on a remodeling and expansion of the Golden Nugget. The old 1890s bawdy house interior design Wynn once claimed to love so much was ripped out and replaced by brass and marble.

If his path had been cleared and funded by Parry Thomas, no one could deny the intense energy with which Wynn himself attacked a project. The Golden Nugget Rooming House, with its 579 rooms, was completed in 1977. By then, Golden Nugget's pre-tax earnings had increased to $12 million. Wynn was getting everything out of his casino horse, which was developing as nothing less than a thoroughbred. Wynn, gifted with an eye for managerial talent, brought in the hard-working Robert Maxey.

Flanked by relatively dingy casinos in the middle of an area of Las Vegas mired in urban decay, the Golden Nugget would always suffer from its downtown location. Its $44-million Spa Tower's foyer, opened in 1984, would resemble the Garden Room of the Frick Museum, and the suites—designed by Parry Thomas's son, Roger Thomas—would offer everything but a view, since they looked out on pawnshops and the rooftops of fifty-year-old buildings.

The splurge on renovations of an old casino drew mixed and cautious commentary from Wynn's peers.

"I don't think it's necessarily a good business decision for the Nugget to spend this much money, but it has helped the Nugget and downtown," casino boss Michael Gaughan said. "I don't know if it's going to pay off or not. I would not have done it, but Steve is brighter than me."

Hilton executive vice president Henri Lewin admired Wynn's chutzpa: "He's a gambler; he puts all his chips on the table and goes for the whole thing. He goes downtown and builds a white castle. This might come out as the best ever, or it might teach him a lesson. I hope the first thing happens. You don't go to St. Vincent's dining room in a mink coat. But he has the nerve, the money, and the team to make it."

———

It was not long after the Golden Nugget takeover that stories of Wynn's legendary temper tantrums and public dressing down of employees began to be heard. So did the tales of sexual harassment.

One Golden Nugget executive who quickly fell out of favor with Wynn was nearly knocked cold when the boss punctuated his displeasure by throwing a glass ashtray. The ashtray whizzed past the executive's ear, thus signaling the end of a short-lived corporate honeymoon. There was no need to terminate the executive; he took the hint and immediately looked elsewhere for work.

From the president's office to the engineering crew, no employee was too great or too small to feel Wynn's wrath. His outbursts of impromptu primal-scream-therapy sessions reduced common kitchen personnel to tears and goaded construction workers to the brink of violence.

Wynn's sexual appetite was established years before he assumed a leadership position at the Golden Nugget, but by the late 1970s, the stories became legion. His never-ending fascination with the casino's female blackjack dealers was nothing short of notorious even in a gaming industry known for its sexpot culture.

In her 1980 book, *Dummy Up and Deal*, a study of the subculture of blackjack dealers, University of Nevada–Las Vegas sociologist Lee Solkey recounted an incident involving a "Big Boss" at a downtown casino. Solkey, who herself used a pen name in publishing the book, revealed to friends that the anonymous executive in question was Steve Wynn. Solkey recounted one of her interviews:

"One day this girl tripped up to the casino manager who was a helluva playboy himself. 'That one's got the job already,' Ron (the floorman) said to me.

"Well, the casino manager looked her up and down and you could just see his eyes asking the question, 'Should I take her on myself or save her for the Big Boss?' Well, the Big Boss just happened to be standing nearby with a twinkle in his eye. The casino manager noticed this and said something to the girl. He pointed out the boss, the girl went over to him, and the conversation started. In a few minutes, the boss took the girl by the elbow and steered her toward the executive offices.

"A couple of hours later, the girl came down. She was wearing her own short skirt but now she had on one of our casino shirts.

"...Well, the Big Boss took her over to the floorman who does the scheduling, told him to give her a table, and left. The floorman put her on a [blackjack] table and went back to his podium. She shuffled, nervously, seemed very unsure of herself and just before pitching the cards, she turned to the floorman and asked, 'How many cards does each player get?'"

Those who know Wynn well are skeptical. They say he was particular about whom he put to work.

———

During these heady days, as he was well on his way to becoming known as a visionary with big plans for himself and Las Vegas, Wynn suffered an unexpected body-blow: he was diagnosed with retinitis pigmentosa, an inherited and incurable degenerative retinal eye disease. Through the years, some of Wynn's closest friends, including his mother Zelma, would assert that it was the effects of his eye disease that caused his mood swings and apparent tyrannical behavior. There was a bitter irony attached to Wynn's persona as a sightless visionary.

"The rages are more since he can't see," Zelma Wynn said years later. "There's an expression in business, 'I want to sit down and talk to him eyeball-to-eyeball.' Well, he can no longer do that; he has to rely on other people to do it...He's so frustrated. This is how he gets rid of his frustration."

Steve Wynn disagreed.

"Think of guys from Vietnam with no legs that get into these races with wheelchairs," he said. "Are they laughing? You bet they're laughing. They're having fun? Yeah. Then I'll show you some good-looking son-of-a-bitch with a thirty-two-inch waist and money and everything going for him that's contemplating suicide and goes to see a shrink every week. So the relationship of your physical condition and your mental health and happiness in this world is not direct. It's obvious the answer's somewhere else.

"You say eyes, and it's the most horrible thing to all of us. There's a lot of pity. The most horrible thing about this and the reason I hate to discuss it is someone will say, 'Oh, I heard about your eyes ...' I'm about as sympathetic as Attila the Hun."

Despite picking up occasional black eyes and contusions from slamming into walls and doors, Steve Wynn would not allow retinitis pigmentosa to slow him down. In the years following his takeover, the Golden Nugget expanded to 1907 rooms and would rate as the only Four-Star, Four-Diamond resort in downtown Las Vegas. By 1977, the six-month hold (the money dropped by players that exceeded what they won) climbed to $12.78 million with a net income of $579,000. A year later, thanks to the traffic generated by the additional rooms, the hold jumped to $17.34 million with a $2.25 million net income for the same period.

By then, Wynn had his sights set not only on the fledgling Atlantic City casino market, but also on the potential windfall to be had if Florida were to legalize gambling. He spent $300,000 for an option on the Castaways Resort in Miami Beach, a one-time hot spot not far from the Fontainebleau where he had first danced with Elaine Pascal. But his future hinged on the continued success of the Golden Nugget downtown.

"I used to come here all the time. We were in the liquor and wine business, and I used to come downtown and call on the Golden Nugget, try to hustle vodka and gin and stuff like that, and beer. And couldn't get the business," Wynn said. "But it seemed like this place had something special all of its own, even with its old red-flocked wallpaper and its red carpet and the dark wood. It was charming. It was sort of a unique kind of spot. It had its own personality, and I liked it a lot. And I was younger. And if you looked at the Del Webb Corporation, it was too big for a young kid to buy or get his arms around. But the Golden Nugget, you could almost have an audacious idea that you might get away with it. And in fact we did get away with it, for a relatively little bit of money."

If only Horatio Alger were alive to chronicle the magical event. With Parry Thomas as his mentor and father figure, there was no telling how far Steve Wynn might go—as long as he chose his friends wisely.

CHAPTER 5

LITTLE LOUIE AND THE GOLDEN BOY

Steve Wynn has always been shadowed by notorious men and events, but few characters in his charmed life offer a more checkered portfolio than his friend Louis Patrick Cappiello.

Born in 1940 in Trenton, New Jersey, Cappiello has at various times in his Las Vegas residency been accused of murder, cocaine trafficking, narcotics sales, and living off the earnings of a prostitute. Arrested on felony charges no fewer than three times, he has been indicted twice by the federal government over the past two decades on drug charges.

In 1973 Cappiello and two associates were indicted by a federal grand jury on charges of selling two pounds of cocaine to undercover Drug Enforcement Administration agents.

Jennifer Lynn Josephs, youngest of the Cappiello trio and a college graduate, accepted full responsibility for trying to sell cocaine, pleaded no contest to a single felony count, and received a five-year suspended sentence. Codefendant Andrew Ira Alkin, whose name would resurface later in another cocaine investigation of Cappiello, was slapped with a fifteen-month sentence and three years' probation. Charges against Cappiello were dismissed.

In November 1977, Cappiello, with no casino work experience, was handed a coveted shift boss position at the Golden Nugget and awarded stock options. Cappiello and his partner, Camilo "Neil" Azzinaro, Wynn's hairdresser and also an accused cocaine trafficker, were allowed to buy 5,000 shares each of company stock at a heavily discounted $10 a share only weeks before Golden Nugget announced its move to Atlantic City.

Wynn attempted to explain away Cappiello and Azzinaro by calling them colorful characters. Not choirboys, perhaps, but hardly dangerous.

"I knew that Louis and Neil were both considered to be half wiseguys. Now that's a Las Vegas term, it has to do with gambling, living high, not being particularly sure of what they do," Wynn told New Jersey Division of Gaming Enforcement investigators in 1980. "I had enough of an inkling about the fact that these kids had been living in the fast lane that I went and asked the sheriff, Ralph Lamb, about these guys and would he have any objection if they went to work. He said, 'We've always thought that these kids might get in trouble, that they might have a problem. We have never caught them doing anything, and I'd rather have them working and knowing that they're on the right track than not....'"

After being hired by Wynn at the Golden Nugget, Cappiello assumed his duties as casino coordinator and shift manager. Azzinaro, who as owner of Neil's East styling salon had cut the Wynn family's hair, rose to the rank of casino coordinator, second in line to the floor manager. He eventually hired his roommate, Michael Jones. (Jones was later fired by the casino's executive vice-president, Bob Maxey, after being suspected of stealing from the baccarat pit.) In 1980 Michael Jones would be convicted on trafficking-related charges and sentenced to four years in prison.

Neither job normally led to nonqualified stock options, yet Azzinaro and Cappiello, over the objections of Bob Maxey, each received them. The nonqualified stock option was later amended to allow its exercise after twelve months instead of the twenty-four months specified in the original statement. The adjustment was "confirmed and accomplished by telephone without a formal meeting or minutes of the Non-Qualified Stock Option Committee," according to a 1982 Gaming Control Board report.

On Jan. 18, 1978, Golden Nugget's board of directors approved a three-for-one stock split, turning 5 million shares of the corporation into 15 million. Suddenly, Cappiello and Azzinaro had not 5,000 but 15,000 shares apiece. By November 19 of that year, the market price of the stock climbed to $19 a share.

————

The Cappiello-Azzinaro duo brought intense scrutiny of Wynn and the Golden Nugget during the initial 1980 licensing investigation of the corporation's Atlantic City casino. The New Jersey Division of Gaming Enforcement recorded statements given under oath from three women who claimed they saw Wynn using cocaine. They made it clear Cappiello and, to a lesser extent, Azzinaro, were Wynn's cocaine suppliers.

The first statement came from an admitted prostitute, Shirley Ann Fair, who swore she saw Wynn use cocaine at a party in August 1977 and four months later at a New Year's Eve bash. Authorities also reported Fair said she saw Wynn in possession of drugs on the floor of the Las Vegas Golden Nugget.

On July 21, 1980, Fair was interviewed by Drug Enforcement Administration agents at their San Francisco office. Among those present were Senior Agent Thomas Dell'Ergo from the Reno office and Jack Adams, a New Jersey deputy attorney general working on behalf of that state's Casino Gaming Bureau.

"There was a get-together at Mike Jones's house with Lou Cappiello, Neil Azzinaro, Mike, myself, Steve Wynn, and like four or five other ladies," Fair told investigators. "It was a dinner party, cocktails afterwards and abundances of cocaine.

"... After dinner, we all went in the living room. Steve was very uptight, kind of wondering, this is not, you know, a normal party, and he and Louis were sitting like, at opposite ends of the couch, in the middle was Mike and myself and Frankie [De Angelo, a convicted drug trafficker] was in the kitchen fixing some wine or something, and Steve handed Mike like you know how bills are wrapped up with a wrapper around it, like that. He handed that to Mike, and Mike handed that to Louie, and Louie just put it on the coffee table. He opened one up and just dumped it in the ashtray and handed one to Steve, and Steve was just packing his nose, making a pig of himself. There was a spoon on the coffee table, and Steve was the first one to grab the ashtray."

Fair swore she saw Wynn snort cocaine at a New Year's party at Michael Jones's house.

"Steve, everybody notices when Steve does it, because you either do cocaine in a line and do it through a straw, or do it with a spoon and most spoons are tiny. His spoon is huge. It's called a shovel. As a matter of fact, he doesn't spoon it, he shovels it."

Question: How much do you think he did?

"That night, probably three or four grams," Fair said. "He was gone. He was, he doesn't get exactly schizophrenic but close. He gets mad real easy, real easy."

Question: And who supplied the coke that time?

"Cappiello had some, and Mike Jones was handing it out," she said.

Fair swore she held no animosity toward Wynn and was not promised anything from the government in exchange for her cooperation. She later refused to testify at the New Jersey hearings.

Wynn called her a liar.

"That's one outrageous allegation I have not yet heard," Wynn said at the Atlantic City Golden Nugget's 1981 licensing hearing. "I've never set eyes on her."

A second woman, Kathy Thomas, alleged Wynn used cocaine at Azzinaro's home in Las Vegas and on his corporate jet. In a separate statement, Thomas changed her mind and recanted her accusation. Wynn accused Thomas of filing the document with New Jersey investigators in exchange for help with drug charges in Nevada.

The third woman, former Golden Nugget blackjack dealer Anita Cosby, alleged drugs were sold inside the casino and that she once witnessed Azzinaro giving Wynn a quantity of cocaine placed inside a matchbook. But Cosby had been fired after being arrested on drug charges.

Wynn has always denied ever using cocaine and never was required to submit to drug testing to settle the matter. Years earlier, DEA investigators had compiled a thick confidential report that assigned Wynn a Narcotics and Dangerous Drug Identification System number, 894134, and outlined information of his suspected involvement in narcotics investigations dating back to the early 1960s, when he managed his father's bingo parlor at Wayson's Corner. Whatever the government's suspicions, Steve Wynn was never indicted. Nor has it ever been proved that he used cocaine.

In October 1981, New Jersey gaming authorities issued a one-year license for the Atlantic City Golden Nugget. The 504-room, $160 million resort had opened eleven months earlier and generated $17.7 million in earnings the first six months of 1981—more than the seven other Atlantic City casinos combined.

With such profits, the golden boy easily was able to rise above the drug and questionable stock option allegations.

———

In an established Las Vegas neighborhood with mature cypress and Russian olive trees sits a three-bedroom, two-bathroom house at 3413 S. Eastern Avenue, on the east side of the Sahara Country Club.

It is the house in which Louis Cappiello lived and where in 1980 he shot Joseph Conlan to death and badly wounded Philip Taft.

At approximately 2:30, on the morning of January 8, 1980, a maroon-colored 1978 Cadillac Coupe d'Ville pulled into the driveway outside Cappiello's residence. Two men got out of the car. A blonde woman, later identified as Conlan's stepsister, Jeanne Wilson, remained behind.

The two men knocked at Cappiello's door, Taft carrying a hidden blackjack wrapped in tape as well as a hot box—an electric heater used to melt and test the quality of cocaine. He said he had come to test Cappiello's cocaine.

Shortly before midnight, Cappiello's associate, Vincent Petitto, had come to Taft's Koval Lane apartment to have him test a gram of cocaine. The gram was a sample from a much larger amount of drugs Cappiello wanted Taft, who admitted he did most of Cappiello's testing, to test for purity.

Not long after Petitto left the apartment, Taft began receiving calls from Louis and Kathy Cappiello to come over and conduct the tests on the larger batch. Finally, shortly after 2 a.m., Taft gave in, taking along Conlan for protection.

A smiling Cappiello ushered them inside the house, Taft entering first, followed by Conlan.

As Taft reached the kitchen, gunshots roared behind him, hitting him in the left side. He fell onto the kitchen floor.

"I have two more for you!" Cappiello screamed.

Taft rolled to one side, regained his footing, staggered into the living room, and knocked the sliding-glass door off its runner.

Bleeding from the side, he stumbled into the backyard, crawled over a six-foot chain-link fence and onto the quiet golf course. He reemerged on Eastern Avenue, two houses away from the Cappiello house.

Conlan lay dead in the entryway of Cappiello's home, blood seeping from wounds to his chest, shoulder, and head.

Waiting in the Cadillac, Jeanne Wilson heard the gunshots and the screams of Kathy Cappiello. When Louis Cappiello emerged from the house with a pistol, Wilson, sure something had gone wrong, started the car and hurriedly backed out of the driveway.

Two doors down the street, she encountered the bleeding, wounded Taft.

"Philip, where is Joe?" she asked.

"Joe's been shot two or three times," Taft gasped. "Get me to the hospital. I've been shot."

Heavily sedated in Sunrise Hospital, with a .22 slug lodged near the base of his spine, Taft was coherent long enough to answer a question from Det. Jan Lesniak.

"When asked why Mr. Cappiello would shoot him, he said it was that he was set up, and it was because he owed Mr. Cappiello some money."

Taft said he owed Cappiello a little more than $4,000 in cash and cocaine.

An autopsy performed by county pathologist Dr. Sheldon Green later revealed the twenty-four-year-old Conlan suffered seven .22-caliber hollow-point bullet wounds at close range.

One bullet wound in the chest passed through vital organs, Dr. Green reported. Another hollow-point round entered the back of Conlan's head, five inches behind his left ear, downward at a 45-degree angle. The bullets were fired from a High Standard Sentinel model .22 magnum revolver. Powder-burn tattoos on Conlan's left arm, wrist, and hand gave convincing proof that he had been within arm's reach of Cappiello when shot.

———

On the afternoon of January 8, police executed a search warrant at Cappiello's residence and recovered a .38-caliber Luger revolver in the den. In a floor safe, the police found a small bag containing what they believed to be cocaine.

Cappiello maintained his innocence.

He claimed not to have recognized the strangers who knocked at his door in the middle of the night. He said he thought they had come to rob him, that his wife had been robbed a year earlier, and that is the reason he had answered the door clutching a .22 pistol. He also said one of his alleged assailants, the one he killed, shot first. Fearing for his life and the life of his wife, he returned fire.

It was a story police found laughable.

Philip Taft had worked for Cappiello for two years at the Golden Nugget; Joseph Conlan had met Cappiello and had enjoyed complimentary meals on Cappiello's written approval at the Golden Nugget's Lily Langtry Restaurant.

Yet Cappiello maintained that he hadn't recognized either man.

With neither time nor opportunity to arrange a common story, Taft, Jeanne Wilson, and Vincent Petitto all agreed the late-night meeting had been arranged at Cappiello's request for the purpose of testing cocaine.

Petitto: "I took a gram of coke to Philip Taft's apartment for Louie, and I just dropped it off."

Wilson: "I was with my brother Joseph Conlan and Philip Taft, and Philip was supposed to go over there to see Louis. I went over there because Louis had called. I can't remember who called, Louis or Kathy....When Kathy called, somebody called anyways, before 1:30, and we went on our way over there. He knew we were on our way over. Philip went over and took the box with him. The box is to test cocaine with. He was supposed to do it for Louis."

But why would Taft bring along the young, muscular Conlan?

Wilson: "...I knew they suspected something pretty funky. They hadn't been getting along so well. Louis was even cross with me because I was very mad at him. He threatened my brother's life, and I told Louis this. I went over to Louis's house another time and said, 'If anything happens to my brother you will have to deal with me.'"

During his statement after the shooting, Cappiello continued to maintain that he did not recognize the intruders even though he admitted Taft was a frequent visitor to the house on Eastern Avenue.

Yet in another series of police interviews, Cappiello said: "Phil came in first"—this, after previously stating he didn't know the man who had forced his way into the house bent on robbing him.

The second intruder, whom he had comped at the Golden Nugget but swore he had never seen before, fired bullets no one could find from a gun that no one had seen. Although police later recovered a slug that may have come from a .38 caliber weapon, trace metal tests indicated Conlan had not held a pistol in his hand.

Charged with murder and possession of a controlled substance, Cappiello was released after posting a $20,000 bond. Shortly before Valentine's Day, he entered a plea of innocent in district court. A trial date was set for March 17 before Judge Howard Babcock.

But in late March, all charges against Cappiello were dismissed after he passed a lie-detector test. Taft, recovering from his wounds, refused to take the test and left town.

Only hours after Cappiello had killed her brother, Jeanne Wilson swore nothing would come of the case because Louis had too much power and money behind him.

"He has the cops in his pocket," she said.

When news of the fatal shooting hit the papers, State Gaming Control Board members Jack Stratton and Glen Maulden called for an inquiry into Wynn's hiring of Louis Cappiello and Neil Azzinaro. Although both had submitted applications for key employee licenses, they left their jobs before a state investigation could begin.

"We feel there may be some problems in certain areas," Maulden said. "We don't understand why the Golden Nugget would place two people with such relatively little experience in such responsible positions."

Added Stratton, "I have a lot of questions about their background. They have no gaming experience, and yet they are coming in as shift bosses. I would like some answers."

Stratton would have to settle for silence.

———

All this trouble didn't stop Cappiello from going on to secure gainful employment in the highly regulated casino industry.

In 1986, he went to work across the street from the Golden Nugget as a blackjack floor supervisor at Binion's Horseshoe Club.

It wasn't until 1990 that Cappiello's presence at the Horseshoe was evaluated by the Gaming Control Board. The board voted to recommend him for key employee licensing scrutiny, a process that involves an in-depth background investigation.

Twice Cappiello appealed on the grounds that he was not really a key casino employee. He was just one of many workers on the floor, he said. It was an obvious attempt to avoid the kind of scrutiny that was certain to embarrass him and his friend, Wynn. Moreover, Cappiello must have known that his chances of qualifying as a trusted key employee were slim to none.

In May, 1990, he produced a letter from Horseshoe owner Jack Binion that stated Cappiello watched over only four blackjack tables and was supervised by either a pit boss or a casino shift boss. It also said Cappiello had no authority to issue complimentaries to Horseshoe guests.

Binion, who had hired Cappiello as a favor to his downtown neighbor, Steve Wynn, then appeared at a June control board hearing to further vouch for Cappiello's character but had to admit that Cappiello could indeed grant minimal gratuities and also had supervisory authority over Horseshoe casino assets.

The three-member control board voted to call forward Cappiello for suitability in the industry. The Nevada Gaming Commission confirmed the board's findings by a narrow 3-2 vote. The year was 1990.

Louis Cappiello, who had been caught up in the cocaine trade in Southern Nevada for nearly two decades, didn't undergo control board scrutiny.

Instead, he quit his job and faded into the Las Vegas scene.

———

And that's where it might have ended had Cappiello and Wynn had merely a passing acquaintance. Instead, the casino mogul and the shady character continued to associate.

In March 1991, former Golden Nugget President Dennis Gomes was deposed as part of a heated civil litigation between Wynn and his New Jersey nemesis, Donald Trump, for the rights to Gomes's services.

Gomes had left the downtown Golden Nugget under what he described as duress for an executive casino position with Trump, sparking a fight with an embarrassed Wynn.

The early legal sparring was highlighted by ferocious representation by attorneys Donald Campbell, on behalf of Trump and Gomes, and Morton Galane, on behalf of Wynn. Gomes responded with testimony confirming Wynn's continuing relationship with Cappiello despite more than a decade of trouble.

Gomes told about the time Wynn sent Cappiello to help secure a second executive position at the Golden Nugget. Gomes's contacts at gaming control surely would come in handy in clearing Cappiello for a top spot. At least, so Wynn thought.

After meeting with Cappiello, who admitted to having overcome a personal struggle with cocaine, Gomes wisely had a former Gaming Control Board investigator and associate, Joe Dorsey, learn more of Wynn's pal's background. What was discovered startled Gomes and convinced him Cappiello was not the right person for the Golden Nugget.

"... I was kind of shocked that Steve Wynn wanted this guy in our company," Gomes said. "...I decided I didn't want anything to do with this guy and certainly wasn't going to put my reputation at stake by pushing him with the Gaming Control Board. So, I decided not to help him. And he kept coming and visiting me at the Nugget all the time and bugging me about helping him. And then one day, either in person or by telephone, I can't recall, Steve Wynn—I believe the first one was by telephone—called me and he said, how are you coming with Cappiello? And I said—and he indicated something to the effect that—I think I may have asked him what kind of position he was thinking of for the guy, and he indicated something to the effect that—he said, I was thinking of casino manager at the [company's Laughlin resort on the Colorado] River or a high-level marketing...job at the Golden Nugget. And I said, well, I don't think it would be advisable for me to approach the Gaming Control Board on behalf of Cappiello, and I don't think it would be good for the Golden Nugget or for you for me to do that, because I don't think this is a good person for us to have around. And he asked me why. And I explained all the different things I found in his background. And he said, 'I'm familiar with all that stuff, I've researched it and I know there is nothing to it, I'm perfectly satisfied with it, and I want you to go forward with this.' So, I said, I think the gaming board won't take kindly to it and I think...they may just call him forward for licensing, and it's going to be a problem for him."

Wynn called Gomes again to lobby on behalf of Cappiello but eventually dropped the issue.

During the deposition, Gomes repeated a story told to him by Golden Nugget Food and Beverage Director Bob Sado about Wynn's interest in buying a specific brand of sausage called Botto.

"He said, 'When I first got here, I found that the sausage we were buying...was terrible quality and it was way, way overpriced,' and he said, 'so I just cut it out. I went to some other company's sausage that dealt with local vendors, and shortly after I did that,' he said, 'Steve Wynn called me, screaming, and he said, "What are you doing?" He says..."I don't like the sausage you're using, it's shit sausage, go back to what we were using before, this stuff tastes like garbage, or something"—I don't recall his exact words, but, it's horrible.' And Bob Sado told me at the time he'd never seen Steve Wynn take a bite of sausage in his life."

Following his boss's orders, Sado resumed purchasing the other sausage. Then, for a time, Sado had Golden Nugget's butchers make their own sausage. This triggered another angry phone call from Wynn. Finally, a blind tasting was set up.

"They cooked it all up and it was sitting there, and Steve Wynn was supposed to come in for this tasting. So, Steve Wynn comes walking in for this blind tasting, and he's got his arm around the representative from Botto Sausage.

"And the representative just happened to be Louis Cappiello. [At the time, Cappiello was employed by the Las Vegas-based Best Sausage Company.] And he walks in with his arm around this guy....'See that sausage? That's what we're going to have and don't fuck with it.' And well, he [Sado] said—he didn't taste it, he didn't do anything, he just walked in, gave those instructions. And Bob Sado told me at that time, he said, that's why I've never tried to change it after that and we're stuck with it.

"Later, when the thing with Cappiello came up, I didn't put the two guys together right away. Then I realized, after looking at his background, that it was the same Cappiello that he had told me about."

The same Cappiello who had managed to land in the middle of multiple cocaine-trafficking investigations; who hung out with street hoods and call girls; who had killed Joey Conlan and nearly sent Philip Taft to the morgue.

The same Louis Patrick Cappiello who for years remained a sidekick of Steve Wynn's even though it is against Nevada Gaming Control Board regulations for a casino licensee—under a penalty ranging from a fine to gaming license revocation—to associate with persons of ill repute.

Steve Wynn was fast becoming Nevada's Teflon kid.

PART
II

CHAPTER 6

INTO ATLANTIC CITY

In 1977, Atlantic City discovered legalized gambling. It was the greatest tourist attraction since the diving horse and the boxing kangaroo. The Boardwalk had been a magnet for freak shows and carnival pitchmen for more than a century by the time a collective of businessmen, including a wide assortment of organized crime figures, began buying up its real estate and pushing for the political changes that would lead to the legalization of gaming halls.

At only 12.9 square miles and a 1980 population of approximately 40,000, Atlantic City in 1977 wasn't much to look at even on the sunniest summer day.

Riddled with poverty, drugs, and decay, the once-sparkling ocean resort town had become a regional embarrassment and an easy mark for pro-casino forces. Where midget bellhops and the Miss America Pageant had failed to retain the public's interest, city fathers hoped that casino gambling would generate the tax revenues needed to fund Atlantic City's massive urban renewal projects.

On June 2, 1977, New Jersey Governor Brendan Byrne ushered in a new era of promise for Atlantic City by welcoming the

Boardwalk's latest industry. Voters had approved casino gambling a year earlier. Resorts International, which had its roots in Meyer Lansky's Bahamian casino experiment, bought the Chalfonte-Haddon Hall, then Atlantic City's largest hotel, for $5.2 million. This was only weeks before voters approved a gambling referendum in November 1976, and Resorts International would be the first corporation to try its luck by the sea.

"I've said it before and I will repeat it again to organized crime: Keep your filthy hands out of Atlantic City. Keep the hell out of our state," Byrne said with much conviction before television cameras that June day.

His line must have elicited laughter in some of the darker segments of the community. After all, the mob was not exactly intimidated by Byrne's tough rhetoric. In fact, representatives of organized crime had laid the groundwork for legalized casinos in Atlantic City years before Byrne got around to signing the paperwork.

"Organized crime has been here for decades," Atlantic City Police Chief William tenBrink said in 1978.

He was right.

———

The Gambino and Genovese families had invaded from New York. The Decavalcante family of New Jersey was exploring its own backyard, and the Bruno *brugad* [family] from Philadelphia also made the trip to what in reality was a drug- and crime-infested slum. It must have looked to them like a slice of paradise.

Without legalized casinos, they would have had to rummage for scraps like common alley rodents. But the approach of Las Vegas-style casinos meant a flowing river of cash that could be slyly skimmed or outright stolen. Gambling also meant the urgent need for construction materials and union manpower—trades dominated by the mob.

Mob contractors would help construct five of the first nine Atlantic City hotels and control the services—everything from taxis to exotic dancers—the expected flood of customers would demand. Hotels did not get built without pouring Anthony Salerno and Paul Castellano's cement and being gouged mercilessly for using it. Developers who balked at the system found themselves mired in union problems, perhaps dealing with Tony Provenzano's Teamsters Local 560 or Little Nicky Scarfo's Local 54 of the Hotel Workers and Restaurant Workers International Union.

In short, if you planned to operate in Atlantic City, organized crime investigators believed, you had to expect to see the region's crime families on your list of partners.

Nevertheless, the success of Resorts International and the casinos that followed it attracted nationwide attention to the slum by the shore.

———

Wynn, who was well acquainted with Resorts President Jack Davis, visited Atlantic City's first hotel-casino in June 1978 to see what all the excitement was about. The place was all right as far as casinos went, but the players were something else again. They stood three deep at craps tables like alcoholics at the only bar in town.

"It made Caesars Palace on New Year's Eve look like it was closed for lunch," Wynn recalled years later.

But it wasn't so much that Resorts was breaking new ground in the industry. It was the magic of the moment. Atlantic City was hot. Wynn decided to seize the magic, and another legend was born.

Davis induced Wynn to meet Boardwalk innkeeper and real estate investor Manny Soloman, who owned the Strand Motel at the lower end of the Boardwalk.

Wynn walked into the Strand wearing sandals, shorts, and a Willie Nelson T-shirt. He was the quintessential casino industry

iconoclast and would provide a welcome relief from the pretentious faux-royalty of Donald and Ivana Trump who were to come
along later.

In keeping with the casual negotiation theme, he offered Soloman $8.5 million for his motel and the adjacent property. Solo-
man accepted the offer. After cutting a check for a $1 million as
a down payment, Wynn walked out twenty-five minutes later the
owner of one of the most valuable pieces of real estate on the
Boardwalk. He also obtained an option on property at the other
end of the Boardwalk and, in short order, owned enough sand to
build a casino the likes of which Atlantic City had never seen.

The Strand was razed and in its place rose the opulent, $160
million Golden Nugget Atlantic City, a monument to Wynn's ability to seize the moment. With 506 plush rooms upstairs, the
Atlantic City Nugget boasted enough brass, marble, and glass to
remind everyone who entered that they were in a magical place.

The lobby featured a four-story gilded birdcage with five talking mechanical parrots singing in the voices of Louis Armstrong,
Bette Midler, Maurice Chevalier, Mae West, and Don Adams. An
automated, light-hearted Buddha named Tung Yin Cheek would
impart wisdom to visitors on the second floor.

The high-rollers' suites on the twenty-third floor would feature everything from saunas to "opium dens" and bars outfitted
to serve monied guests and their hundred closest friends. The Con-
stellation Suites, designed by Norwood Oliver, would be lavishly
appointed with the finest materials: Italian marble, raw silk, even
lacquered goatskin.

Wynn would cater to high rollers and use stars such as Frank
Sinatra and Diana Ross to draw them from competing resorts. The
Golden Nugget Atlantic City would beat its competitors at their
own game.

"We perceived back in 1978 that the East Coast experience is
basically a gray one," Wynn said. "And if Atlantic City was ever

gonna be excitin' and successful it was because it offered the people in this part of the world a chance to break their ordinary course of disciplined daily life and get a big dose of color and excitement and distraction. So we said everything in our building is going to be bright and twinkling, maybe too much so. The Golden Nugget's gonna be the last place in the world you would fall asleep. People come into this building, and they get what they're looking for, a shot in the arm, a zap. It's like bein' on speed. The spectacle of the casinos—the sound of the stickmen, the Big Six wheel, the roulette wheel, all the noises, that incessant roar, that low-level hum of the slot machine arms. People love that. And when they've had enough of it, they turn around and walk out."

———

If the Golden Nugget's success had made Wynn a celebrity in Las Vegas, then making a splash in the nation's newest casino metropolis—Atlantic City—promised to make him a media star to rival New York City tabloid poster-boy Donald Trump in the gaming industry.

Although Trump was the ultimate political and social icon in Atlantic City, Wynn possessed two things The Donald did not. A genuinely successful casino, for one: Trump's burgeoning one-man Monopoly game was impressive on paper, but his highly leveraged financial arrangements made him fall into bankruptcy court before the end of the decade.

More importantly, Wynn found not only a brilliant financier but a close friend in up-and-coming junk bond genius Michael Milken.

Wynn was introduced to Milken through Stanley Zaks, chairman of Zenith Insurance and Milken's cousin. Wynn and Zaks had met and befriended each other in college. If Wynn was going to score the kind of financing necessary to erect the Golden Nugget Atlantic City, then Milken—a summa cum laude graduate of the

University of California at Berkeley and the wunderkind of Drexel Burnham Lambert Corporate Finance Department—was the man to make it possible.

———

Using the charismatic Wynn's gift for self-promotion, Milken quickly assembled backers for the $160 million in high-interest financing. Basing much of his philosophy on the strategies of billionaire high-risk maven Meshulam Riklis, Milken believed in the power of junk bonds in the hands of intelligent, energetic entrepreneurs.

Wynn, who already was acquainted with Riklis, fit the mold in classic style. His charismatic road show impressed industry analysts and potential investors alike.

"He was mesmerizing," gushed one casino executive who witnessed the rhetorical whirlwind. "Steve Wynn had some of the brightest people on Wall Street eating out of his hand. He presented them with a vision, and he managed to get around answering some tough questions. He knocked them off their feet."

Milken was equally pleased.

"In time [Milken] would do much larger financings for Wynn, but he always retained his affection for that first deal—not because it was his debut as an investment banker, but because of its size," Jesse Kornbluth writes in the Milken-friendly biography, *Highly Confident*. "Nothing pleased him more in those days than to provide a boost to smart and struggling outsiders; that was service, that was functional idealism, that was what his father would have done."

Establishing himself as a presence in Atlantic City with less than $15 million in cash, Wynn was rapidly emerging as the new face of legalized gaming. Once he had the financial wherewithal, the Golden Nugget's foundation was all but poured.

That he was not yet licensed by the hard-nosed New Jersey Casino Control Commission did not seem to matter.

In December 1980, Wynn's Atlantic City Golden Nugget, the Boardwalk's sixth casino, opened and set the East Coast ablaze with its opulence and success.

In its first six months of operation, it rewrote Atlantic City's meager casino record books, piling up $17.7 million in profits. Wynn's attention to in-house detail, and his superior high-roller marketing and entertainment policy attracted players of all levels to the palace. Golden Nugget players ranged from high rollers to low rollers to wiseguys and grandmothers.

"That's why I'm never gonna be without money again," Wynn said a few years later. "The biggest opportunity of a lifetime and I didn't have the dough for it. It was so clear, so easy. It took until the next summer to finish the financing. It was venture capital; it really wasn't financing. They should have taken a piece of the hotel—the people who lent me the money, the bond buyers, the institutions we got so close to. They bought the notes and made a lot of money. Once you keep the promise and do good like that, then you're wired.

"You don't have to be flamboyant to be successful, although there's room for that in this business. Be in the right place, take advantage of friendships, capitalize on opportunity, and have courage to initiate action. You don't exactly have to be fearless, but you can't be afraid of making a mistake. There comes a moment when you've measured the situation to the best of your ability, sought the advice of your people, and come up with a balanced position. Then, you make up your mind and go. It never comes down to a lock."

But New Jersey Division of Gaming Enforcement investigators were proving harder to impress than the high rollers who inhabited the top floors of the Golden Nugget and the action-starved low rollers who bused in from hundreds of miles away to gawk at the mechanical birds in the gilded cage. Wynn still wasn't licensed to operate the resort he dreamed up and dared to finance.

In mid-November 1980, he had resigned from the board of directors of Golden Nugget Atlantic City in an effort to keep from delaying the Thanksgiving weekend opening of the resort. In part, investigators were awaiting the outcome of a federal grand jury probing allegations of corporate insider trading and cocaine trafficking at the Las Vegas Golden Nugget.

Wynn's granting of generous nonqualified stock options to his friends and family had raised the regulators' suspicion, and allegations of drug use and his embrace of reputed cocaine traffickers at the downtown Las Vegas casino had also sent investigators sniffing for scandal among the company and its key players.

Golden Nugget Atlantic City (GNAC) had been incorporated May 1977, but neither Wynn nor his corporate officers had chosen to publicly disclose their interest in operating along the Boardwalk. His reason for the early incorporation, Wynn stated, had been to protect his company's logo. New Jersey regulators found that explanation plausible.

Of course, secret incorporation for any other reason might lead some cynics to believe Wynn was protecting his interests at the expense of common stockholders—a violation of federal securities laws. By designing an extensive nonqualified stock option plan, which was implemented a few months later, Wynn's actions prior to the official announcement to stockholders of the Atlantic City foray reeked of insider trading.

There were other problems, to be sure. A year before Wynn's purchase of the Strand, he and his mentor, E. Parry Thomas, had taken trips to Atlantic City on the company jet in the summer of 1977 to scout future investment territory. They were accompanied by a female companion, who confirmed the purpose of their flights.

"We are aware that our incorporation of a New Jersey subsidiary in May 1977 was one of the central issues involved in the insider trading allegations," Golden Nugget Vice-president and General Counsel Bruce Levin wrote the curious Gaming Control Board in September 1982. "The issue of whether such incorporation was the first step of a secret plan to prepare for gaming in New Jersey or was accomplished solely to protect our name and trademark as a matter of general corporate interest was directly dealt with in all of the investigations described above."

The controversial nonqualified stock options were issued months before the purchase, as was a three-for-one stock split which effectively tripled the stocks' value. The official registration statement for issuing the nonqualified options makes no mention of the Atlantic City project. Previous proxy statements also had neglected to mention the forthcoming $160 million deal that was sure to send Golden Nugget stock into the stratosphere.

Wynn faced some internal dissension, as well. Not everyone was pleased with his autocratic operating style. His biggest critic was Edward Doumani, then the second-largest stockholder in the company.

Doumani, whose name years later would surface in federal casino-skimming, money-laundering, and tax-evasion cases related to the Tropicana Hotel in Las Vegas, believed Wynn's lavish lifestyle was harming the company. Doumani also suspected that Wynn wanted to force him out through a cagey political maneuver—having New Jersey Division of Gaming Enforcement agents severely scrutinize Doumani's background as Golden Nugget made its move to Atlantic City.

As with many veteran casino operators in Las Vegas, there was plenty to find. Doumani was a friend of mob front Joseph Agosto, who was the Kansas City Outfit's inside man at the Tropicana during the years its casino was skimmed into bankruptcy. Doumani also was close with transplanted New York wiseguy Joseph

Cusumano, a former Golden Nugget casino employee who later would be convicted of conspiring to corrupt the Las Vegas Culinary Union insurance fund. Cusumano eventually was placed in the Nevada Black Book of persons excluded from casinos.

Doumani, an attorney by profession, also maintained contact with Frank "Lefty" Rosenthal, the Chicago Outfit's in-house skimming operative at the Stardust Hotel. Doumani failed in a bid to buy Allen Glick's Argent Corporation hotels and by the early 1990s had distanced himself from the casino industry.

In early 1980, Doumani knew he was on his way out of the Golden Nugget corporation. Doumani said Wynn called him repeatedly in an attempt to persuade him to resign from the Golden Nugget's board of directors. Wynn used the argument that the corporation's fund-raising attempts would be hampered by someone who could not provide satisfactory explanations for his relationships with known gangsters.

Convinced the move to New Jersey would be jeopardized if he kept his hand on the company's reins, Doumani acceded to Wynn's request. Doumani eventually sold his block of Golden Nugget stock for fifteen million dollars.

Weeks later, Doumani regretted his decision. It was too late. By selling when he did, Doumani lost future interest in the Golden Nugget Atlantic City and the triple stock split. Angry over feeling he had been tricked into stepping down—and humiliated by being made to pay for his food at the hotel—Doumani lashed out at Wynn in a widely circulated letter dated January 19, 1980.

Nothing was held back. Wynn was criticized for everything from his monopolizing of the corporate jet to his friendships with suspected drug traffickers Neil Azzinaro and Louis Cappiello.

"Never in the annals of a public company has anyone taken more advantage than yourself," Doumani wrote. "The G2 is truly your private aircraft, not really a corporate one. You personally maintain its scheduling to cater to your whims. Rumor has it you once sent the plane merely to pick up (and fly) Chinese food from the Nugget to Sun Valley. And no one can deny that the food on the plane is catered for your personal appetite.

"Anyone can conjure up a business purpose for most things, but I am sure if the truth be known we would find Mr. Wynn to be taking full advantage. This would hold true with the million-dollar mansion in New Jersey, its staffing, and the food served there as well. It would also apply to the Mercedes, the Rolls-Royce limousine, the Cadillac limousine, and the limousines which await you wherever you travel. I need not inquire why that same public company policy concern does not inhibit you from using Golden Nugget employees extensively to remodel your personal residence and that of your mother's.

"And I do not have to comment regarding the calibre of people trafficking in drugs whom you protected over the years as casino executives, with large stock options, one of whom recently was the assailant in a murder case.

"Steve, you have single-handedly alienated every associate who started with you in this endeavor. I am relieved not to be on your spineless Board of Directors who are manipulated by you as a puppeteer does with his marionettes, at least those who are not your relatives and therefore not subject to your dominance.

"But Steve, the one test you have not passed even with all your magic is a disgruntled large minority stockholder."

The Doumani letter would surface repeatedly over the next decade and haunt Wynn as he unsuccessfully attempted to expand his casino operations from Las Vegas and Atlantic City to England, Canada and South America.

Doumani's record was far from spotless, but he was an insider who had watched Wynn rise like a white shark to consume a corporation one voracious bite at a time.

Doumani was not alone in his alarm at Wynn's creative corporate style.

Seemingly special treatment for Wynn's friends also aroused the suspicions of investigators from the State Gaming Control

Board, New Jersey Division of Gaming Enforcement, Securities and Exchange Commission, and the federal strike force, who were drawn to three examples of questionable stock option deals: the choice plans served up to Michael Pascal, Wynn's brother-in- law; to Peter Thomas, son of E. Parry Thomas; and to suspected drug traffickers Louis Cappiello and Neil Azzinaro.

Michael Pascal had been a certified public accountant in Miami before joining the Golden Nugget in May 1978 as corporate treasurer and being put in charge of the corporation's stock option files.

His annual salary was $75,000, but Pascal also received options on 50,000 shares of Golden Nugget stock at a $13-per-share market price. A few weeks into his new job he realized his 50,000-share promise had not been recorded, so he did the paperwork himself and presented the document to Chairman George Mason and former Nevada Supreme Court Chief Justice David Zenoff of the stock option committee. It was approved, and by June 14, 1978 Pascal was able to exercise 10,000 of those 50,000 shares in the first twelve months.

Investigators thought the timing most fortuitous, considering the company's purchase of the Strand property was made public June 22, eight days later. That quick action gave Pascal a large advantage over other investors, and, as anticipated, Golden Nugget stock began making a steady climb. (In 1978, the stock price fluctuated from 5 ⅝ to as high as 44 ⅝ as Golden Nugget stock trading moved from the Pacific Stock Exchange to the American Stock Exchange.)

Pascal accepted a demotion to assistant treasurer the following spring but not before another stock agreement was drawn up, reducing his options to 33,342 shares at the same $13 market price. In November 1979, Pascal assumed the casino coordinator duties of Neil Azzinaro, who by then had plenty of problems of his own. Pascal resigned from the Golden Nugget in May 1980 but received the remainder of his options after writing a letter of hardship to corporate counsel Bruce Levin.

The brother-in-law's stock option package had been unortho-
dox from the start, but he is hardly the only member of Wynn's
Golden Nugget crew to be enriched by the relationship.

The second example that drew the attention of investigators
was the deal given to Peter Thomas, son of the Las Vegas legend.

The younger Thomas had been elected to the board of directors of Golden Nugget in November 1976 at the same time Valley Bank led a group of institutions backing Wynn's expansion
downtown and, later, into Atlantic City.

Peter Thomas received 10,000 shares at $17.25 on Dec. 16,
1977. When Golden Nugget's stock split three-for-one the following February, Thomas's nonqualified options tripled to 30,000 shares
at a purchase price of $5.75 per share with a five-year vesting period.

In June 1978, Peter Thomas sold 2,000 shares of Golden
Nugget at $32 per share. In July, he exercised his option to pur-
chase 2,000 shares at $5.75 per share without waiting at least six
months between stock transactions as the law requires. By accel-
erating Thomas's vesting period, the nonqualified stock option
committee enabled him to enjoy a potential profit not otherwise
available to investors, an act that appeared to be a clear violation
of Section 16 (b) of the Securities Exchange Act of 1934.

The apparent SEC violation was mitigated when Thomas, who
resigned from the board of directors of the Golden Nugget in July,
1978, agreed to repay the company $30,000.

The third example—the deals given to Neil Azzinaro and Louis
Cappiello—was even more notorious.

In December 1977, Azzinaro and Cappiello each were
handed 5,000 shares of stock at $10 a share and watched it triple
two months later. Steve Wynn's loyal "half wiseguys" worked at
the Golden Nugget in key casino jobs until rumors of cocaine

trafficking and their own behavior drove them back into the shadows.

Their vesting date on their nonqualified stock gift was changed from twenty-four months to twelve months, apparently without even notifying the company's committee. Strangely, no one seemed to remember who altered the original documents. And no one argued or disagreed when Wynn ordered the change.

No one dared.

Added to these oddities was the case of the Houssels, a pioneer gaming family in Las Vegas.

At one time, J.K. Houssels, Sr., had owned all or part of nearly every downtown Las Vegas casino and a sizable percentage of the properties on the rapidly expanding Strip. After his death, his widow, Alice Houssels, still held much of his stock, including 90,000 shares of Golden Nugget.

But in late May 1978, Alice Houssels was ninety-one years old. Her son, Union Plaza Executive Vice-president J.K. Houssels, Jr., handled the stock sale to the Wynn group of 90,000 shares at $9.50 per share, with 19,600 shares being transferred directly into Wynn's personal portfolio. It seemed like a solid deal at the time, but Houssels, Jr., later recalled no mention was made of the Atlantic City operation. A month later, when the announcement was made, Golden Nugget stock climbed to unprecedented highs.

Nevada Deputy Attorney General Samuel P. McMullen wrote in a confidential memorandum to the Gaming Control Board, "...it seems to indicate that the parties to and facilitators of this purchase and transfer were aware of this date well in advance of the actual closing. No mention of this transfer of additional stock to some of the officers and directors of [Golden Nugget] was made in the April 1978 Proxy Statement forwarded to the stockholders."

Indeed, at Golden Nugget's annual stockholders meeting on May 26, 1978, Wynn neglected to voluntarily mention the company's plans to expand its eastern horizons. When the subject was broached by a curious stockholder, "the Golden Nugget's attitude was 'wait and see,'" McMullen wrote.

McMullen determined that Golden Nugget had established "four major patterns" which would give the Gaming Control Board cause to recommend sanctions.

Company officers gave "series of misleading statements and omitted material in disclosure documents and at shareholder meetings relating to the New Jersey corporate opportunities; (b) the use of corporate assets, i.e., the stock options at less than market value, as a means of reimbursing Cappiello and Azzinaro; (c) the profiting by insider directors and officers by non-qualified stock options floated out before the public announcement of the New Jersey expansion; and (d) the insider trader purchase by and through Chairman Wynn of the Houssels' stock without disclosure of the pending New Jersey announcement."

One former New Jersey investigator, who worked Wynn's file for years and often pored over his burgeoning portfolio, came away suspicious of several transactions. But suspicion and proof were two different things. He also was fascinated by Wynn's seemingly limitless propensity for psychological games.

On an investigative trip to the Las Vegas Golden Nugget, the New Jersey agent entered Wynn's posh office for an interview. As he took his seat in a chair across an expansive desk from the boss, all the doors in the sprawling office slammed shut and locked. Wynn watched the agent's expression for a sign. The agent refrained from jumping out of his shoes, but barely.

"He was trying to see how I'd react," the investigator recalled, laughing. "When I didn't respond, he apologized for accidentally hitting the lock button. I think he controlled it with his feet. That's the kind of guy he is."

Wynn's inner office at the Golden Nugget was outfitted with remote-control locks and a metal detector built into the doorway. One wonders whether Walt Disney took such precautions.

———

These problems aside, the control board investigation would hinge, in large measure, on the outcome of the federal grand jury evaluating evidence regarding allegations of narcotics trafficking and insider trading.

Las Vegas Strike Force Special Attorney C. Stanley Hunterton and his assistant, Geoffrey Anderson, headed the insider-trading investigation. The Securities and Exchange Commission, through its well-respected attorney Hille Cohn, also scrutinized the insider-trading rumors.

By the summer of 1982, the Gaming Control Board's investigation was complete, but the federal cases were headed nowhere.

Hunterton, who ruled no harm, no foul, would later become a member of the President's Commission on Organized Crime before trading his promising position with the Las Vegas Strike Force office for private practice. His biggest client: Steve Wynn and the Golden Nugget.

The SEC investigation sank with the resignation of the attorney Cohn, who became associated with a Los Angeles law firm that had supervised the authorization of millions in subordinated debenture offers by the Golden Nugget.

The federal narcotics investigation resulted in the conviction of former Golden Nugget employee Michael Jones, who received a four-year sentence largely on the testimony of Shirley Ann Fair, the same woman whose affidavit implicating Wynn in cocaine use had been discounted by the casino commission.

Cappiello was found not guilty at trial, and charges were dropped against Azzinaro.

The New Jersey commission decided Wynn had "answered forthrightly and with candid demeanor denied Fair's accusations." Wynn had provided the commission affidavits from witnesses placing him in Sun Valley, Idaho, during the time Fair said she had seen him hungrily shovel cocaine up his nose.

On Nov. 13, 1981, the New Jersey Casino Control Commission voted 4-0 to license Wynn.

———

By the fall of 1982, Stephen Wynn was the toast of the gaming industry from Las Vegas to Atlantic City. He had affixed a bright, energetic face to an age-old racket. The golden boy was in his glory. Nothing, it appeared, could slow his rise as America's most prominent casino operator.

"If it hadn't been for our reputation of catering to the best people in Atlantic City, I don't believe our rather radical departure in downtown Las Vegas would have been easy to do," Wynn reflected in a 1984 interview. "To compete successfully with Caesars Palace from Fremont Street would have been laughable. Even though it did evoke a few chuckles when we started last year, the laughter was a little shallow because we were taken very seriously on the East Coast.

"We had competed [for high rollers] with Caesars in Atlantic City, and they didn't think of us as a downtown casino operator on Fremont Street anymore. Our drop per table exceeds anything in the state of Nevada, including Caesars."

Said Lee Isgur of Paine Webber in 1984: "Right now he's the best there is."

Others fawned shamelessly. "He's the true American dream," Daniel Lee of Drexel Burnham Lambert said. "Wynn is almost every ambitious man's idol. He combines the showmanship of P.T. Barnum and the wisdom of Solomon."

Lee is now a Mirage Resorts executive where he can conveniently worship Wynn at close range.

CHAPTER 7

UNCLE CHARLIE

"If you're ever in New York," Charlie Meyerson told Steve Wynn, "I'll take you to lunch or dinner. Give a call.'"

Wynn called, and thus began a relationship that would eventually lead to Meyerson coming to work at the Golden Nugget in Atlantic City.

Steve Wynn has often said he loves colorful people, and Meyerson easily fits that description.

The son of a cap cutter in New York's garment district who never made more than $50 a week, Charlie Meyerson dropped out in the ninth grade. After serving in the U.S. Marines during World War II, he took a job at the Meyers Brothers Parking Lot and spent his spare time bookmaking.

His paid advocates would argue vehemently otherwise, but Meyerson was not merely a small-time bookmaker with a few no-name clients. He was known as a major force in bookmaking in

New York City, although some claimed he was not that important, and, in fact, served a small ethnic clientele. His partners were directly associated with the Genovese crime family and its eventual boss, Anthony "Fat Tony" Salerno. So, for that matter, was Meyers Parking.

The union that held the parking contracts, the International Brotherhood of Teamsters Local 272, was controlled by Salerno's brother, Cirino "Speed" Salerno.

Payoffs from parking company operators to the Genovese and Lucchese crime families were a tradition in New York. Although some investigators considered the millions that changed hands a form of extortion, others considered the payoffs part of a long-standing partnership.

It wasn't until the early 1980s that the FBI, which had managed to plant a listening device in the ceiling of Anthony Salerno's headquarters at the Palma Boy Social Club in East Harlem, learned the names of the key players involved in New York's parking lot industry.

Vincent "The Fish" Cafaro, who spent decades in the service of Salerno as a Genovese lieutenant before cooperating with the government against his boss, later explained the setup.

"Speed [Salerno] is a union official in the garage and parking lot Teamsters union which is located in Manhattan....This union represents garage employees and parking lot attendants....the union is ours; it belongs to our brugad," Cafaro told investigators.

"Speed Salerno has the New York City garage and parking lot industry locked up through sweetheart contracts with the owners of these businesses....Speed collects money from garage and parking lot owners and delivers this money to East Harlem. Speed used to deliver this money to his brother Fat Tony or to me in East Harlem. The cash ranged from two thousand dollars to five thousand dollars per score [garage]....Speed has never had problems negotiating or collecting payoffs from the owners of garages and parking lots in New York City. This used to be because everyone knew that Fat Tony was the 'power' behind Speed and 'our union.'"

Cafaro would later remember Meyerson, who became a millionaire several times over, as a "big earner" for Fat Tony Salerno.

———

If Parry Thomas has been a father figure to Wynn, and Michael Milken like a brother, then Charlie Meyerson, whom Steve Wynn fondly recalls acting as Mike Wynn's bookmaker as far back as the mid-1950s, has been a favorite uncle.

When Wynn opened the Atlantic City Golden Nugget in February 1980, Meyerson became the casino's chief junket representative in New York City. He was hired to procure customers, not to grant them credit. As the story goes, Meyerson, the longtime bookmaker and taxi-company owner, was concerned about succeeding in the marketplace.

During his bookmaker days, he would have his wife tell people he sold carpets. Then, when her back was turned, he announced that he was a bookie.

Meyerson divorced his wife thirty years ago, leaving her to care for their four children. Shortly thereafter he married again and started a second family.

"You know, I've been out of business so long, my customers are all dead," Meyerson has said. "It's been fifteen, twenty years since I had my list and I knew anybody in the city."

Not all Meyerson's friends were deceased or incarcerated for that matter. In fact, Charlie had enough customers to fill a penitentiary and soon became an integral part of Wynn's New York City marketing strategy, ranking up there with the purchase of a $3.5 million S76 Sikorsky helicopter, which was used for the forty-minute shuttle of high rollers from New York to Atlantic City.

Wynn would provide the fancy transportation; Meyerson would make sure the helicopter was filled. Meyerson's phone book of underworld gamblers helped make the Golden Nugget on the Boardwalk an immediate success.

Come 1983, old Charlie was busy toiling for the Atlantic City Golden Nugget as the head of its New York City marketing office when the casino's preferred customer credit list began to be scrutinized by Division of Gaming Enforcement (DGE) investigators.

As they pored over the credit files, they kept seeing the funniest thing: Select files were marked with "CM" or "friend of CM." Charlie Meyerson, the Golden Nugget later admitted, was granting credit for his customers.

And he was granting it to plenty of them—to the tune of more than 600, in clear violation of New Jersey gaming regulations. Meyerson was allowed only to lure customers, not to grant credit.

"Indeed, it appears that certain of Nugget's patrons received a credit line precisely because, and on account of, Meyerson's participation in the credit decision," DGE Director Thomas O'Brien wrote in August 1984. "Furthermore, it also appears that Meyerson participated in credit decisions during the period of time from and after March 1981 when he resigned from the Nugget and before his re-employment in May 1982."

Focusing their attention on Meyerson's customers, investigators also noticed something peculiar about his preferred guests: dozens of them were mobsters.

Included among them, for example, was John Novick, a New York pretzel manufacturer described by gaming investigators as an associate of organized crime, who gambled up to $50,000 each time he visited the Golden Nugget as Meyerson's guest.

There was Genovese crime family member "Joe Pepe" Sabato —another friend of Uncle Charlie with a $50,000-per-visit line of credit—who gambled and received the largest of the resort.

There was mob soldier Tony Grieco, whose line was $100,000. Tommy Cestaro and Abe Margolies, pals of Matty Ianniello, the

Genovese capo and longtime New York racketeer, also gambled large sums of cash as Meyerson's guests at the Golden Nugget.

Frank Manzo, a Lucchese mob soldier who in 1985 was implicated in a $900,000 fraud case at Kennedy Airport, was another good customer.

Not all of Meyerson's customers were such unsavory characters, to be sure, for the New York City gambling market is second only to California in size.

But his list of customer contacts was littered with gangsters: big fish and little fish, frontmen and hit men.

In August 1986, during Golden Nugget's relicensing hearing, Meyerson was called to testify before the Casino Control Commission about his customer list. Investigators were seeking an answer to a compelling question: Was Charlie Meyerson a conduit to the mob at the Golden Nugget?

If Division of Gaming Enforcement and Casino Control Commission officials ever were to find answers to such questions, they would have to do so without Meyerson's assistance. He talked, but he didn't say much.

An example of Meyerson's old-school reluctance to provide details was cited during the stormy relicensing hearing, when the state asked how the aging ex-bookmaker came to know so many notorious fellows. Meyerson said that New York businessman and mob associate, John Novick, had introduced him to the array of mob guys.

From there, Meyerson's memory became fuzzy.

DGE: And he introduced you to Benny Eggs?

Meyerson: Yes.

DGE: And you are pretty sure he introduced you to Johnny Barbato, too?

Meyerson: I have to check that, I don't know. I am sure I met Benny Eggs through John Novick.

DGE: What is Benny Eggs' reputation?

Meyerson: His reputation is only hearsay, that he is somebody important.

DGE: What does that mean?

Meyerson: I don't know what he does.

DGE: What is his reputation? You said that he is somebody important. What does that mean?

Meyerson: Somebody that people respect.

DGE: What people?

Meyerson: Everybody respects him.

DGE: What does it mean that he is important?

Meyerson: I never pursued it to the point that he was important.

DGE: You have told me he is somebody important.

Meyerson: That is right.

DGE: What does that mean?

Meyerson: It means that he is a man you have to respect.

DGE: Why do you have to respect him?

Meyerson: Because he's a big man.

DGE: In what?

Meyerson: I don't know.

Deputy Attorney General Mitch Schwefel asked Meyerson how Benny Eggs got his nickname.

"Maybe he liked a lot of eggs, I don't know," Meyerson replied.

The old bookmaker's reponses often sounded like a wiseguy version of Abbott and Costello's "Who's on First?" routine.

———

Still, Meyerson was right. "Benny Eggs" Mangano was a big man.

Mangano was a respected member of the Genovese crime family, a big man with an impeccable reputation. He was capable of setting up meetings with Genovese bosses Anthony Salerno and Funzi Tieri, according to *The Last Mafioso*, the biography of mob-killer-turned-informant Aladena "Jimmy the Weasel" Fratianno written by Ovid Demaris.

"Benny Eggs" Mangano was later nominated for the New Jersey casino exclusion list, but the bid was rejected when it was ruled investigators had failed to compile sufficient evidence that he was a threat to the industry.

"Whether he did or didn't or should or shouldn't have known is a central issue in his own pending case," Commissioner Carl Zeitz said. "But Mr. Meyerson, as indicated by the excerpt from his sworn testimony cited above, which was typical of his testimony in those interviews and before this commission, was not a cooperative witness. He was evasive. He was not forthcoming."

Added New Jersey Division of Gaming Enforcement Director Thomas O'Brien in an August 27, 1984, letter to Chairman Walter Read: "Moreover, and of far graver concern, pertains to the identities of numerous of the Nugget's patrons involved above. That is, Meyerson has facilitated the extension of credit by the Nugget to individuals either who possess criminal records or who are reputed to be or associate with organized crime members."

O'Brien offered Genovese mob associate Cestaro as one of several examples of Meyerson's peculiar clientele. Meyerson assisted in establishing a $35,000 credit line for Cestaro in August 1982. The Nugget's own surveillance department identified Cestaro as a pal of Matty Ianniello, the Genovese capo, a longtime New York racketeer and frequent Las Vegas visitor who once was a silent partner in the Dunes Hotel.

Despite the fact many of his notorious customers were the subject of constant media scrutiny, Meyerson claimed to know them only as good players and not reputed members of organized crime. They came, they played big, they were "comped." It was as simple as that to the grandfatherly fellow with the Florida tan.

Yet Meyerson was hardly the only Golden Nugget marketing specialist to be linked by investigators to organized crime, especially the Genovese family. "Fat Tony" Salerno and "Matty the Horse" Ianniello had other friends on the Boardwalk.

Among Ianniello's other acquaintances at the Atlantic City Golden Nugget was Julius "Big Julie" Weintraub, an affable six-foot, six-inch casino host and junket representative who had run with the Mafia bulls since his New York youth and was rumored to have once had his legs broken after a misunderstanding with some of his old gangland friends.

Wynn had known Weintraub nineteen years, but apparently gaming's golden boy was unaware of Weintraub's odd associations.

At least, so Wynn indicated to the New Jersey casino regulators. He claimed not to know that Nevada's gaming commission had twice denied Weintraub permission to acquire a percentage of the Dunes because of his unsavory friendships.

Weintraub's woes had, in fact, made the newspapers, but Wynn claimed to know nothing of his problematic past when he lavished $900,000 on Big Julie to acquire the junket rep's list of high-flying, high-rolling customers. New Jersey investigators believed the deal smacked of a payoff to Anthony Salerno through his acquaintance, Julie Weintraub.

Wynn neglected to fully disclose the terms of the company's agreement with Weintraub and settled their contract differences through litigation for $585,000 after the big man was ousted by the regulators. The fact Weintraub sued and won more than a half-million dollars did not preclude him from later enjoying a $2,000 comp at the resort.

"Inexplicably, Golden Nugget failed to include in its agreements with Weintraub a condition precedent requiring his licensure," Chairman Read said in his 1986 report.

Wynn, the rising star in gaming's corporate era and a man prone to hiring a small army of high-priced attorneys when threatened, seemed too naive to be true in his association with Weintraub.

The presence of Big Julie so close to the Golden Nugget team, however, created nowhere near the controversy as the sight on the casino floor of mob conduit Irving "Ash" Resnick.

Tales of Resnick's exploits up and down the Strip continue to be told years after his death. He was known as the Caligula of Caesars Palace at a time when the Genovese and other crime families held a controlling interest in the Teamsters-funded resort.

In January 1983, Wynn hired Resnick—at $200,000 a year plus 10,000 stock appreciation rights worth an additional $237,000—to develop the Atlantic City casino's Hawaiian market.

Golden Nugget Security Chief James Powers, who conducted a background check, wrote a memo informing Wynn of some trouble spots with his new employee.

Resnick, who had been twice convicted of illegal bookmaking, had cashed casino markers and kept the money, later writing off the debts as uncollectible.

He had refused to testify before the Securities and Exchange Commission in a case involving Caesars Palace.

He had been convicted of income tax evasion but acquitted on appeal.

He had survived two murder attempts.

He had been recommended for denial of a gaming license in 1978 after the Gaming Control Board discovered that he held a hidden interest in the Tropicana Hotel.

He had associated with mob types, especially members of the Genovese and Patriarca crime families, for decades.

In his memo on the subject, Powers questioned Resnick's honesty and integrity and wrote in part, "[Resnick] has a reputation as a low-class type of guy. Associate of Meyer Lansky and was bagman for "Fat Tony" Salerno. Was a target on two occasions for bad gambling debts, one they tried to dynamite his automobile, the other, they tried to shoot him."

Despite Powers's findings, Wynn denied knowing anything about Resnick's obvious mob ties and longstanding practice of skimming. The New Jersey commission accepted the excuse that Powers, the former head of the Las Vegas office of the FBI, apparently did not report all his findings to the boss.

Once on board, Resnick didn't change his style at the Atlantic City resort. He bounced checks and mishandled markers. He was fired in November 1983 after Golden Nugget executives finally got through to Wynn.

"We are breaking our neck arguing with this guy and keeping track of him all the time," Wynn said, recalling his employees' frustration. It was almost as if someone else had done the hiring.

Commissioner Kenneth Burge put it cogently: "...Golden Nugget surely had adequate guideposts which should have convinced it to steer clear of Resnick. What happened, however, was that Mr. Wynn, through his forceful and persuasive personality, hired Resnick without the GNI board receiving a full and complete disclosure of Resnick's background information.

"To be sure, Mr. Wynn's dynamic personality is a major factor in the success of the Golden Nugget. However, providing Resnick with stock appreciation rights troubles me. In my view, SARs were a substantial inducement the Golden Nugget used in order to keep key personnel. In bestowing those rights on Resnick, Mr. Wynn demonstrated a willingness to embrace, much too quickly, a man whose only apparent saving grace was his alleged ability to increase the bottom line. While hindsight is 20-20, Golden Nugget's own experience with Resnick demonstrates that this supposed virtue of his cannot be separated from his all too apparent vices."

New Jersey Division of Gaming Enforcement Director Anthony Parrillo was more blunt.

Resnick represented "a most arrogant choice of business concerns over regulatory interests," Parrillo said.

But it was Uncle Charlie who was something else.

No one ever accused Charlie Meyerson of stealing. He was popular with other employees, and even the casino commission's most cynical investigators would have to admit his mug book of customers often gambled away small fortunes at the Golden Nugget. From the beginning, Charlie Meyerson remained an earner with few peers.

What investigators appeared to be implying, however, was that his customers' very presence on the casino floor was enough to warrant concern. After all, how could the casino control commissioners say with confidence the mob was out of the casino business when so many of its junior executives were standing shoulder to shoulder at the Golden Nugget's craps tables?

Fact is, they couldn't. Not without acknowledging the fact that casinos act as magnets for such people. Nor, for that matter, was the Golden Nugget the only casino frequented by wiseguys.

Indeed, in the end, the omnipresence of hoods in every other casino is the fact that mitigated the issue in Meyerson's favor.

"In so much as that is an issue, it appears not to be confined to the Golden Nugget but is probably prevalent in most or all of the casino hotels," Casino Commissioner Carl Zeitz said.

It wasn't that anyone believed Meyerson's story that he never had met a gangster—only Wynn and his busload of attorneys clung to that uproarious notion. The issue was more basic: To punish Meyerson without vilifying his counterparts in other casinos would be unfair.

"I do not think it had been demonstrated that Golden Nugget is a significantly greater offender than the other casinos in this regard or that this is a matter reflecting negatively on its suitability for relicensure," CCC Chairman Walter Read said in 1986.

But to assume Meyerson genuinely didn't recognize a wiseguy when he saw one would seem naive at best.

Going by Wynn's description of Meyerson, one begins to wonder how the sweet old fellow ever survived in the big city. Far from a simple fellow who wouldn't know Benny Eggs from scrambled eggs, Meyerson was a thirty-year survivor of New York's treacherous taxi, bus, and limousine industry.

In the cab racket, it also pays to have friends such as the one Meyerson found in City Taxi and Limousine Commission Director Jay L. Turoff. Their relationship was the point of controversy in 1984 when state investigators uncovered information indicating Turoff was a secret investor in a Yonkers cab company. The deal, investigators believed, was arranged by Meyerson.

By the early 1980s, when Meyerson had begun concentrating on luring customers to the Atlantic City Golden Nugget at the hefty annual salary of $365,000—more than the president of the hotel received—one of his customers was the same Jay Turoff, who received free trips and complimentaries while heading the taxi and limousine commission.

Meyerson became a center of controversy after escorting Harvard-educated attorney and heroin-trafficking money launderer Anthony Castelbuono at the Atlantic City Golden Nugget in late 1982. Castelbuono laundered $1.187 million in cash, a sum filling several suitcases.

Although targeted for prosecution by a federal grand jury, Meyerson was not indicted in the Castelbuono case and denied knowledge of any money laundering.

Golden Nugget was approved for relicensing with strict conditions in 1986, but Meyerson's hearing was severed from the proceedings. More information was needed, and Uncle Charlie wasn't exactly a bubbling fountain of facts.

In the aftermath of the super-heated relicensing hearings, Wynn quickly moved to sell his Atlantic City resort for a staggering $440 million to Bally. At the time, the Casino Control Commission had not finished its inquiry into Meyerson. The investigation would remain incomplete.

After a brief stint with Bally on the Boardwalk, Meyerson followed Wynn west to Las Vegas, where the well-liked casino uncle of so many wiseguys continued to attract high-rolling and often highly notorious players. Thanks to Wynn's politically influential attorney, Frank Schreck, Meyerson did not, however, attract scrutiny from Nevada's Gaming Control Board.

Just the opposite, in fact.

Schreck submitted a literate but sanitized version of events to the Nevada Gaming Control Board, which did Wynn and Meyerson a huge favor by simply dropping it in a file drawer. Meyerson went to work for the Golden Nugget and later for the Mirage, where his starting salary was more than $400,000 a year to welcome his distinctive customers to Las Vegas.

Uncle Charlie had found a new home three thousand miles away from his New Jersey critics.

CHAPTER 8

BOARDWALK BLUES

In the early 1980s, Atlantic City gained a reputation as a Mafia laundromat of illicit cash. Dozens of members and associates of La Cosa Nostra were spotted inside casinos playing with large sums of cash and on credit. The thought that these mobsters might be laundering their ill-gotten gains through the casinos was not lost on the cops.

Lieutenant Colonel Justin Dintino, executive director of the New Jersey State Police, was adamant in his evaluation of the use of casinos for money laundering and warehousing street cash. In two months of 1983 alone $64 million in cash deposits took place at Atlantic City casinos.

"Members of organized crime, drug traffickers, and some legitimate businessmen made these deposits," Dintino said. "We found some hit men with over $1 million deposited."

Part of modern-day law enforcement's problem is the size of the multibillion-dollar drug cartels dominated by an international combination of highly organized criminals. The sophisticated drug lords are by no means limited to Sicily, but are literally citizens of the world, hailing from Bulgaria and Venezuela to China and the former Soviet Union.

But no matter how successful they become, they still must launder their ill-gotten wealth.

One example that stands out conspicuously is the case involving Anthony C. Castelbuono and Steve Wynn's Atlantic City Golden Nugget.

━━━━━━

At Thanksgiving in 1982, Anthony C. Castelbuono appeared to have plenty for which to be thankful.

But Castelbuono also had his share of troubles. For one, his cocaine and gambling habits were exacting a nasty toll on his health and personal life.

Then there was his immediate business dilemma.

His Sicilian organized crime associates were anxious to have the millions in proceeds from their heroin-trafficking venture turned from five, ten and twenty dollar bills into less cumbersome cash.

The crew that Castelbuono served included his Sicilian connections Gaetano Giuffrida and Italian national Antonio Turano, whose name, address, and phone number would find its way into Golden Nugget casino host Charlie Meyerson's client book.

Another key figure in the heroin-smuggling ring was Victoriano Molina-Chacon, a shoe manufacturer from Alicante, Spain.

The Molina-Chacon group was capable of moving eighty kilograms of heroin to the United States every two weeks. The narcotics were hidden in a shipment of shoes sent by Molina-Chacon to a Manhattan shoe store.

In 1982, Italian authorities intercepted a shipment in Florence, and the international ring began to unravel.

Drug Enforcement Administration agents in New York had seized fifteen kilos of heroin from a Thai national, made the connection to Turano, and began to piece together the worldwide puzzle.

Weeks later, the bullet-pocked corpse of Antonio Turano was plucked from the marshlands of Queens.

Castelbuono's associates were impatient men, and it was his job to convert the cash and see that it found its way across the ocean and into a safe, anonymous account in Switzerland's Credit Suisse Bank. But his was not an easy job involving piddling sums of money. In 1982, for example, eighty kilos of heroin had a street value of $130 million. Thus did Castelbuono find himself in Atlantic City with enough cash to open a small savings and loan.

Indeed, when he hit the Gold Nugget, he toted along suitcases filled with $1.187 million in small bills.

The junkie money—consisting mostly of fives, tens, and twenties siphoned from the arms of New York City heroin addicts—would find a home-away-from home at Steve Wynn's Golden Nugget.

———

The sequence of events that led to the infamous affair and one of Wynn's most embarrassing moments on the Boardwalk began innocently enough on Nov. 26, 1982, when casino host Charles Meyerson received a phone call from his Tropicana counterpart Gus Lauro, who advised the Golden Nugget's top procurer of gamblers that a "substantial cash player" was headed his way.

After midnight, Anthony C. Castelbuono appeared at the Golden Nugget with his bodyguard and personal valet, Ben Valenza. He was immediately escorted to a penthouse suite.

Outfitted with saunas, remote-control curtains, commercial-size bars, "opium dens," and green marble toilets, the hotel's top accommodations were known as some of the most opulent in Atlantic City.

Castelbuono had no complaints.

With Meyerson serving as his personal escort, Castelbuono met in the casino manager's office with D. Boone Wayson, then the Golden Nugget's marketing vice-president, and was introduced as

"Tony Cakes," an obvious misnomer he later said was intended to reduce the risk of kidnapping.

Castelbuono carried with him a mountain of money. Valenza began opening suitcases jammed with $1,187,450 and piling up the cash. It took five hours to count.

The staggering cache of money, Castelbuono claimed, was proceeds from successful restaurants he owned.

"It didn't enter my mind to believe him or not believe him," Meyerson told the New Jersey commission four years later in 1986.

Wayson officially expressed his discomfort with the amount of small bills present, and so the money was temporarily segregated from the river of cash in the casino cage.

Later that day—several hours after Castelbuono had begun gambling—Wayson contacted Golden Nugget Director of Surveillance Sabino Carone to investigate the mysterious restaurateur with the abnormal distrust of banks.

However, Wayson was not so uncomfortable with Castelbuono as to keep the high roller from the baccarat pit. At 3:38 a.m., approximately $300,000 was deposited in the cage, and Castelbuono went to the tables.

He played like a man on stimulants.

Betting from $10,000 to $50,000 per hand, Castelbuono played cards for one hour, forty-five minutes. He lost $295,000. By the time he finished pushing the last of his chips across the table, back in the casino manager's office another $600,000 had been counted. It was deposited in the cashier cage. Castelbuono made a pair of withdrawals totaling $10,050, then retired at 5:30 a.m. to his penthouse. It was named the President's Suite.

———

Carone, who had twenty years experience as an investigator, checked in with Wayson before noon.

He reported that Tony Cakes was really Anthony Castelbuono, a Fordham University graduate and a 1969 graduate of Harvard

Law School. He was an attorney with a successful limousine business in New York. He was also a commodities trader. No trace of any restaurant ownership.

Castelbuono's luck at the baccarat table didn't improve that night. At 9:41 p.m., he withdrew $850,000 and bet up to $50,000 a hand. Forty-five minutes later, he left the baccarat pit, a $14,000 loser.

Castelbuono handed his chips to bodyguard Valenza and instructed him to return them to the cage. But cage personnel prevented him from making the deposit. Instead, Valenza opened an account under his own name and, in effect, took possession of $800,000. The segregated money no longer existed.

"At 11 a.m. on November 29, 1982, Castelbuono and his party left the Golden Nugget, after withdrawing the $800,000 in Valenza's account in large bills," New Jersey Casino Control Commission Chairman Walter Read said.

"...Subsequent indictments and convictions in federal court have established that the money originated from the importation into this country and the sale of heroin, and that, as part of a criminal conspiracy, Castelbuono was assigned to convert the small bills to large bills at Atlantic City casinos."

———

Case closed?

Hardly.

On June 24, 1985, Wynn appeared before the President's Commission on Organized Crime in New York City in the company of a cadre of Golden Nugget executives, including company vice-president Alfred Luciani, a former deputy attorney general; in-house counsel Marilou Marshall, a former staff attorney for a previous presidential commission on gambling. Also present was Vice-president of Community Affairs Shannon Bybee, a former member of the Nevada Gaming Control Board.

Wynn was a master of rhetoric and the technique of interviewing the interviewer, but his explanation of the Castelbuono affair met cynical opposition from President's Commission on Organized Crime counsel James Harmon.

In his statement to the president's commission, Wynn remarked, "Anthony Castelbuono appeared at the Golden Nugget one evening in November 1982. He deposited over one million in cash, and by the time he departed three days later, he had lost more than $300,000. Because he was unknown to casino executives, our surveillance department was requested to conduct an investigation."

During the hearing, Harmon proved Wynn's toughest sell.

"Mr. Wynn, perhaps I could draw your attention more particularly to this," Harmon said. "Cakes gave you an address of 436 East Eighty-sixth Street, which your investigator could not verify, is that correct?"

"Correct, he could not verify," Wynn said.

"And the date of birth that Cakes gave was not the correct date of birth. Your investigator found that out, correct?"

"We have two different birth dates, the one that he claims and the one that we thought we found in the *Fordham Law* [magazine]," Wynn said. "Sab says in the report December 26, 1943, which is different from the November 26, 1944, believed to be his correct birth."

"I ask you to refer to page 3 of the report which reads as follows:

"'In addition to the above, information was developed that he [Castelbuono] deals in gold and silver but there is no information as to why he had such a large sum in small bills in his possession.'

"Correct?"

"Correct," Wynn admitted.

"So that as of December 2, the date of this report, the Golden Nugget knew that he had originally come in with street money, that he had used a false name of Tony Cakes, that he had given a false date of birth, a false address, that he was allegedly a gold and silver trader, and that he had no apparent source for the small bills that he had brought in," Harmon said. "Correct, Mr. Wynn?"

"No sir. He gave his correct name as Castelbuono, number one," Wynn said. "He gave his birth date, and in our preliminary report we came up with a conflicting date. I still don't know what the correct one is. The man gave us his correct name, though. When you say that the man had no apparent source for the money--"

"I don't say that, Mr. Wynn," Harmon interrupted. "The report says that."

"Yes, that is right," Wynn said. "There is nothing wrong with that. The fact that we can't verify a source for the money is not in itself morally compelling. We don't know where your money comes from or anybody else's. The issue is, Cakes was the subject of this report because they were suspicious of it, and this report was prepared after the fact. This was after the man came and lost $300,000, Mr. Harmon.

"The money was counted, and Mr. Castelbuono was told that the money would be isolated until it was clear that he had come to gamble and not to make change," Wynn said. "We don't do that. 'That's fine,' said Mr. Castelbuono. 'I came to gamble.'"

But Castelbuono had not merely come to gamble; he had come to launder suitcases packed with small bills, and no amount of rhetoric could change that.

After gambling, he left the casino with $800,000 in hundreds neatly bundled in $10,000 packets in Golden Nugget wrappers.

———

Wynn and his spokesmen insist that "The casino acted within the law. It should not be examined...by selective moral judgments that do not attach to specific legal violations because there were none.

"Casinos are not churches or towers of theological construction. They are businesses.

"There was then and is now no crime called money laundering. There is now but was not then a federal casino cash transaction report regulation....Castelbuono's alleged intention was to violate the law in a conspiracy to hide and send out of the country the proceeds of illegal narcotics trade. The Golden Nugget's intention was to win his money and it did."

The fact is that on July 14, 1983, the Golden Nugget paid $40,000 to Castelbuono for an antique Rolls Royce.

The fact is too that after the much-investigated Castelbuono affair, Wynn visited Castelbuono in New York and was persuaded to invest $50,000 in an account at Kidder Peabody to trade commodities, relying on Castelbuono's advice.

Wynn lost his $50,000.

Wynn told the President's Commission on Organized Crime, "I did not trust Mr. Castelbuono. That's why I was there [on hand at the casino]."

This didn't stop Wynn from subsequently going on a ski trip with Castelbuono.

Even after Castelbuono was indicted, Wynn vehemently argued with New Jersey gaming officials and Senate organized crime investigators that Tony Cakes returned to the Golden Nugget with the $800,000 in casino wrappers and gambled it away.

Castelbuono did return to the Boardwalk resort, making a $500,000 cash deposit on December 2 and an $815,000 deposit on December 11, 1982. Untrained observers easily could be confused by Wynn's expert rhetoric, but the Golden Nugget's own video camera did not lie.

Thomas Sheehan, an investigator with the President's Commission on Organized Crime, explained the exchange to the panel, which had spent the morning listening to Wynn attempt to explain away Castelbuono's disturbing presence. As the videotape played, the commission learned the truth.

"This is the early morning hours," Sheehan said. "You see Mr. Castelbuono on the left, Mr. Wynn, and Mr. Meyerson leaving the pits about 1:45 a.m. on the twelfth of December, 1982.

"Could you cut to the other tape please?

"This picks up at approximately 6:14 a.m. in the morning of the twelfth. It is the cashier's cage. Mr. Castelbuono is cashing out. You see the top individual putting $100 bills, stacks, on the counter, and putting them in a bag. This cashing-out event, as Mr. Wynn would say, took seventeen minutes. We have edited it down to about four."

The tape showed Castelbuono picking up $983,000 from the Golden Nugget cage. (New Jersey gaming regulators used $800,000 as their laundering figure.)

"You see the cash being placed in bags by casino employees. This is the first bag being given across the cashier's counter to Mr. Castelbuono," Sheehan said. "There is a shot of Mr. Castelbuono on the other side of the cashier's cage. He is accompanied by two women, and there is a casino security guard standing behind him. They are getting ready to leave the cashier's cage. The money is being carried by two security guards. It's in three bags....As he is exiting, an individual will appear from the top left, identified as Mr. Meyerson, casino employee. He greets Mr. Castelbuono and escorts him out of the casino. There you see the casino doors opening, Mr. Castelbuono is leaving with, as I said, $983,000 on December 12, 1982. The indictment charges that on December 16, 1982, $1 million in cash was placed in a Swiss bank account."

Commission member Philip R. Manuel noticed the discrepancy between Wynn's intriguing tale under oath and Sheehan's report and video presentation.

"I have one question," Manuel said. "When Mr. Wynn testified earlier today, he stated, I believe, that all the money in question was actually lost in the casino on subsequent occasions. Do you have any knowledge of that?"

"I have no knowledge of that," Sheehan said.

In fact, only Wynn appeared to possess such knowledge.

Why did the golden boy of Nevada gaming admit traveling to New York and seeing Castelbuono's operation, called Castelbuono and Price Associates, at New York's Turtle Bay Towers?

"I said I went there because I wanted to see if he really had a business," Wynn said.

"And you saw his business, and it was the business of placing trades in precious metals?" Counsel James Harmon asked.

"Silver," Wynn said.

"By way of computer?"

"Right."

"Saw no cash?" Harmon asked.

"Saw no cash."

"No large amount of bills in small denominations?"

"No."

"Did that cause you to wonder"

"No," Wynn said.

"Is it consistent with your experience that Harvard-trained attorneys accepted cash fees in amounts of small bills, Mr. Wynn?"

"No....I did trust him after I went there," Wynn told the commission. "That's the point. Mr. Castelbuono, you know, in terms of what we learned subsequently, is a very deceptive man. I did trust him. I saw that he was in fact doing what he said he was doing. He did have the firm that he said he had. He was a real person."

A real person who had claimed he owned restaurants, then admitted he was a government- securities and commodities trader.

By an intriguing coincidence, the federal accounting experts who analyzed the Castelbuono case were able to track all but approximately $50,000 of his laundered cash. Only Wynn and Castelbuono know whether Wynn's $50,000 investment was a way of balancing the laundering transaction.

Wynn also neglected to mention that in December 1980— more than two years before he laundered cash at the Atlantic City casino—according to a New Jersey investigative report Castelbuono had begun to negotiate a contract to place his Two For the Road Car Corporation limousine service at the Golden Nugget.

———

On the same day Wynn testified before the President's Commission on Organized Crime that Castelbuono must have been a mere bettor because Tony Cakes lost more than $300,000 from a $1 million bankroll, attorney Harmon explained the concept of exchanging small bills for large.

"The commission has heard within the context of this hearing that a Cuban organized crime group known as 'The Corporation' has so much cash that it is willing to pay 100 percent to launder its profits," Harmon said. "In other words, to get the use of $1 million, it was willing to pay $1 million."

For example, the so-called Pizza Connection heroin traffickers who laundered $13.45 million through E.F. Hutton in New York had paid dearly. The Sicilian Mafia's money eventually found its way to Switzerland but not before the traffickers spent $10.5 million in precious metals trades through Hutton.

"Put another way, the Sicilian Mafia was apparently willing to gamble $13.45 million to legitimize less than $3 million in the process of paying a laundering fee of over 75 percent," Harmon told commission members.

Internal Revenue Service Agent Martin Molod—balding, bespectacled, and presenting a strong contrast to the dapper, forceful Wynn—was the next to testify before the commission.

But Molod's looks were deceiving. He had helped detect a $100 million drug-money-laundering scheme at the Deak-Perera Group, a multibillion-dollar international currency exchange firm.

Exercising his expertise in the physical properties of cash, Molod, who had seen it all before, offered perhaps the day's most compelling testimony.

All concerned agreed Castelbuono had brought $1.187 million to the Atlantic City Golden Nugget Casino. Molod showed just how cumbersome that sum must have been that night near Thanksgiving in 1982.

He divided the bills into three categories, $5, $10, and $20, and divided the $1.187 million into equal thirds: $395,817 each. It added up to 79,163 $5-bills, 39,581 $10-bills and 19,790 $20-bills. In all, 138,534 bills.

Using the Department of Treasury's standard 490 bills to the pound, Molod was able determine the approximate weight of the deposit: 160 pounds worth of $5-bills, 80 pounds of $10-bills, and 40 pounds of $20-bills.

Total weight: 280 pounds, about the average heft of an NFL defensive tackle.

Total mass: 5.81 cubic feet, a stack nearly six-feet high, six-feet wide and six feet deep.

After Castelbuono finished his initial trip to the Golden Nugget, removing the better part of $1 million, the difference was startling.

"My analysis of the withdrawal, using the same formula, would consist of 8,000 $100-bills weighing 16 pounds and consisting of one-third cubic foot," Molod said.

Even a child could understand Molod's explanations in Money Laundering 101.

———

Between his mountain of small bills and rabid baccarat technique, Anthony Castelbuono made for one pathetic money launderer. He gambled frantically, and lost much of the more than $3 million he hauled to Atlantic City over the course of a few weeks. There was no indication that he was holding hands with Golden Nugget officials. Beyond their open-door policy to a fellow packing hundreds of pounds of small bills, that is.

In his opening remarks at trial, Assistant U.S. Attorney George Daniels elaborated on Castelbuono's plan and why it went awry:

"Anthony Castelbuono and Sheila Silvetti and Dirk Velton and all their friends were given complimentary rooms and shows and limousine rides for their friends, and even helicopter rides to carry them to Atlantic City.

"They are there and you will see video tapes of Sheila Silvetti and Anthony Castelbuono at the baccarat table with stacks and stacks of chips. They were doing their job putting the small bills in the casino to take them out ultimately in $100 bills so the money could be more easily transported.

"During this period, they gambled hundreds of thousands of dollars. They stayed [in Atlantic City] for several days.

"During this period of time, Anthony Castelbuono is gambling a lot of money. Unfortunately what happens at this time, he ends up losing a lot of money that doesn't belong to him. A lot of money entrusted to him to sneak to the Swiss bank account so that the heroin dealers can get their money.

"At that time, Anthony Castelbuono decides he—he is going to have to make arrangements to have the money transported, the money he hasn't lost on this trip.

"In December he goes down, he is gambling at Bally's and ends up going to the Golden Nugget that gives him complimentary room service and transportation and shows. He and all his friends."

For Castelbuono, the trouble began in earnest when—like so many high rollers—he lost more money than he'd planned.

Daniels: "After Francis DiTomasso deposits the money, there is still problems because the fact is this money is not all the money that was given to Anthony Castelbuono. Anthony Castelbuono...lost over a million dollars at the baccarat table.

"Now he has a problem. He's got to make up this money. He begins to run around to try to make it up. Before Mr. DiTomasso comes back from Switzerland, you will hear during that period of time, Mr. DiTomasso is talking to Dirk Velton reporting every leg of the trip about where he is, whether the money has been deposited."

In December 1987, Castelbuono was sentenced to fifteen years in prison and fined $50,000 for his role in helping launder millions in illicit profits in a federal case linked to a Sicilian-based heroin-smuggling operation.

In all, nine persons were charged in that narcotics case. Andrew J. Maloney, then the U.S. attorney for the Eastern District of New York, told the *New York Times* Castelbuono led a money-laundering operation that moved millions from drug sales in New York City to a secret Swiss bank account via Bermuda and Canada.

Molina-Chacon, the footwear manufacturer who owned Mintor Shoes in New York City, was sentenced to twenty-five years in prison and fined $750,000. Francis DiTomasso was sentenced to ten years for his conviction on currency and drug charges.

New Yorkers Rudolpho Risatti and Sheila Silvetti also played key roles. Risatti and Silvetti, convicted of conspiracy to import heroin and conspiracy to violate American currency laws, counted approximately $2 million in small bills and passed the cash to Castelbuono at Thanksgiving. That December, DiTomasso transported $1 million through London and Bermuda to Switzerland and a law enforcement-proof bank account.

Had Tony Cakes been more prudent, his run of luck might have lasted a while longer. But hard living and cocaine took its toll.

"I was successful at everything except as a criminal where I was a complete failure," Castelbuono said at his sentencing. "I spent the first thirty-six years of my life sane. The last six years ..."

Cocaine had taken control.

"The dope was at the end of it," Drug Enforcement Administration case agent Joel Gutensohn said. "It caused him to spend lots more than he had. He eventually became indebted to the people. He became indebted to them for a large amount of money and began moving the money out of the United States for them."

As a result of his cocaine blues, Castelbuono alias Tony Cakes operated as a rather crude money changer.

After the heated 1986 hearing, Golden Nugget Atlantic City was relicensed, but Wynn quickly moved to sell the resort. He found a willing buyer in Bally, which paid the then preposterous price of $440 million for the Golden Nugget—about twice what the experts believed the property was worth.

Although the Castelbuono affair did not prevent Golden Nugget Atlantic City's relicensing, New Jersey Casino Control Commission Chairman Walter Read acknowledged the resort's attempt to identify Castelbuono's actual identity and keep his strange fortune separate from its casino cage but was frank in his opinion of the operation's business practices.

"One might question whether Golden Nugget acted too quickly to accept Castelbuono's money, with no idea of its origin other than for his obviously false claim that it came from restaurants," Read said. "One might also question whether Golden Nugget was too willing to return $800,000 in large bills to Castelbuono and was too quick to deposit some of his money in the bank, particularly since Wayson's explanation for doing so necessarily assumes that Castelbuono either was not going to gamble any more or was going to continue to lose.

"Golden Nugget has complained that this affair has exacted a great toll on its resources and on its reputation. If the company had displayed slightly less concern for the bottom line, and a bit more concern for the policies on which the Casino Control Act is founded, it might have saved itself, and the commission and the division, much time and turmoil."

In 1986, the law requiring the use of Currency Transaction Reports was still fairly new. The Currency Transaction Report (CTR) required a report to be filled out when any cash transaction involved sums of $10,000 or more. Prudent businesses and banks often request their customers to fill out reports for half as much. The casino's CTR includes a patron's name, address, employer, social security number, passport number, and amount of currency involved.

The crime commission reviewed 128 of these reports filed by the Golden Nugget. Most showed no irregularities, but fourteen were peculiar for the lack of information provided on the form.

Harmon directed Wynn's attention to two examples, gamblers named Anthony Lombardo and Joe Pepe. Lombardo gave his name and no other information; Pepe listed his address as Manhattan. Wynn claimed he was unfamiliar with either. And, no matter, a failure to provide information did not in his estimation constitute criminal activity.

"Were all fourteen of these people Italian?" Wynn asked. "You picked two examples. I wonder why you picked those two."

"Because they refused to furnish the information," Harmon said. "I don't know who Anthony Lombardo is, frankly, and if he gave his address and social security number maybe we would know."

Harmon may not have possessed background on Lombardo, but he did know Joe Pepe.

"Joe Pepe" Sabato, whom Castelbuono's gracious host Charles Meyerson once described as a "very good player," is a Genovese crime family associate.

For his part, Wynn's view of the government's meddling through the use of the Currency Transaction Report was clear.

"In providing tools for law enforcement to deal with serious problems, we should be careful not to give them a broad ax where a scalpel would suffice."

More than a decade after Castelbuono stepped into the Atlantic City Golden Nugget, Wynn continues to stick by his version of events.

"Anthony C. Castelbuono did not launder money at the Golden Nugget. I don't know how many times I have to tell you that," Wynn said to a skeptic in 1993.

At the Nevada Gaming Control Board headquarters, the Castelbuono affair did not even raise a public pulse. No hearings were conducted; not one of the state's casino watchdogs stepped forward to challenge the propriety of the transaction or the logic involved in Wynn's explanations.

Meanwhile, Anthony C. Castelbuono a.k.a. Tony Cakes was scheduled for release from Pennsylvania's McKean Federal Correctional Facility in 1995.

CHAPTER 9

THE TROUBLE
WITH MEL HARRIS

The trouble with Mel Harris began after Wynn invited his old acquaintance to the Golden Nugget for what later was described as a job interview.

They had known each other since the 1960s, Harris having attended high school in Miami with Wynn's wife, Elaine Pascal. Wynn called on his friend to discuss a rather remarkable career opportunity: a vice-president's position at the wildly successful Golden Nugget Atlantic City.

The offer was remarkable considering that Mel Harris, a successful Florida condominium developer who sometimes played at the Golden Nugget in Atlantic City, had no casino experience. In most cases, such a shortcoming would be enough to get a fellow laughed out of a personnel office, but Wynn said he noticed something special about Harris—so special, in fact, that Wynn was able to overlook the fact that Harris's recently deceased father, Allie Harris, had been a notorious Miami-based mob bookmaker.

Wynn also was aware that Harris was the former son-in-law of Canadian sleight-of-hand specialist Louis "Uncle Lou" Chesler, "the big fat money machine" who had worked closely with Meyer Lansky to establish a casino on Paradise Island in the Bahamas. Harris had, in fact, met Lansky many times and, as Wynn would later acknowledge, young Mel had over the years also been acquainted with notorious Allie's gangster friends.

Despite those glitches in the Harris portfolio—the sort of flaws sure to set off bells with New Jersey gaming officials—Harris was named in August 1984 to the board of directors of Golden Nugget Las Vegas and vice-president of marketing at the Atlantic City resort.

On August 16, Golden Nugget attorneys submitted an employment suitability document, officially known as a Personal History Disclosure Form, on behalf of Harris. The Casino Control Commission granted him temporary approval, from September 21 to December 20, 1984, pending a standard background investigation.

The terms of Harris's employment contract made him easily one of the highest paid executives not only at the Golden Nugget but in all of legalized gaming.

His five-year deal paid an annual salary of $400,000 and gave him an option to purchase 250,000 shares of convertible preferred stock, which in 1984 sold at a year-ending price of 9 ⅜. That's potentially another $4.6 million. Harris also was handed a stock option agreement that would enable him to purchase up to 500,000 shares at a 25-percent discount.

But there was a hitch, one quickly pointed out by the New Jersey Casino Control Commission during the Golden Nugget's relicensing hearing in 1986.

Harris had a circle of dubious friends.

In August 1984, the time of his employment at the Atlantic City Golden Nugget, Harris was well-connected to Genovese crime family boss Anthony "Fat Tony" Salerno.

Steve and Elaine Wynn are joined by daughters Kevin (left) and Gillian for a gathering of Nevada's unofficial first family.

"I wasn't sure what he was going to do," the former Elaine Pascal said, recalling cocky young Steve Wynn, "but on the first date I knew that we were going to do it together." Despite obstacles ranging from Steve Wynn's reputation as a ladies man to their divorce and remarriage, the couple has managed to remain together for more than 30 years.

Wynn took up high stakes poker for several years, but he proved better suited at playing host to major events than winning them. (Jim Laurie/ *Las Vegas Review-Journal*)

"Give a gambler a good excuse, they'll thank you for doing that," cowboy gambler Benny Binion once told Steve Wynn, who spoke at the Horseshoe Club patriarch's funeral service. (Jim Laurie/ *Las Vegas Review-Journal*)

Steve Wynn is a formidable spokesman for the casino industry. Here he finds himself in a rare position of agreement with rival Donald Trump on the subject of 24-hour gambling in Atlantic City. (Associated Press)

Culinary International official John Wilhelm has been one of Wynn's biggest supporters. The hotel and restaurant service workers union has a long history of mob influence. It represents approximately 35,000 workers in Las Vegas.

Steve and Elaine dazzle former Nevada Senator Howard Cannon at a black-tie affair for Las Vegas mob attorney Oscar Goodman. (Wayne C. Kodey/*Las Vegas Review-Journal*)

The Kid and the Chairman of the Board. Until his temper got the best of him, Frank Sinatra proved one of Wynn's greatest casino high roller marketing tools.

Kenny Rogers and Steve Wynn have been friends since the late 1960s when the young singer and his band, the First Edition, headlined in the Golden Nugget lounge. (Jim Laurie/*Las Vegas Review-Journal*)

Before a child abuse scandal drove Michael Jackson into hiding, he was a regular guest at the Mirage's exclusive Villa suites. Plans to create a Jackson attraction at the Mirage are now on hold. (Jeff Scheid/*Las Vegas Review-Journal*)

Kevin Wynn began traveling with an escort shortly after she was kidnapped and released. Steve Wynn paid a $1.45 million ransom. "I thought they were driving me out into the desert somewhere," she testified at the trial of her abductors. Her father said afterward, "We will resume our lives, but we will do so with deep personal understanding and compassion for victims of violent crimes." (Jim Laurie/*Las Vegas Review-Journal*)

A former circus performer, Ray Marion Cuddy was the so-called mastermind of the Kevin Wynn kidnapping. "They left a paper trail...that would choke a goat," one federal prosecutor said upon Cuddy's conviction. (Jim Laurie/*Las Vegas Review-Journal*)

Cathy Lee Crosby is one of the many entertainers who have shared the spotlight in commercials with Steve Wynn. Wynn's best known television spots remain the series of commercials he did with Frank Sinatra. (Jim Laurie/ *Las Vegas Review-Journal*)

Other men whose names have become associated with Steve Wynn and the Mirage: (clockwise from lower left) Genovese crime family soldier Carmine Russo; Anthony Salerno associate Willie Cohen; former Golden Nugget casino boss Neil Azzinaro; and longtime Wynn friend Louis Patrick Cappiello.

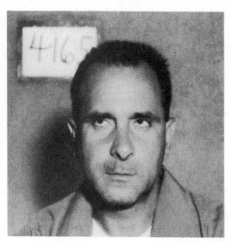

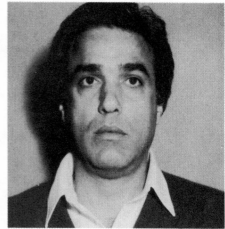

Old acquaintances Willie Cohen (background, left) and Mirage casino host Charlie Meyerson take their morning stroll before their relationship became a point of controversy. "He walks a little earlier in the morning than I do," Meyerson later testified before the Gaming Control Board. "I bicycle ride now."

Wynn was at his articulate best during his campaign to place a dolphin exhibit on the grounds of the Mirage. Although the U.S. Marine Fisheries Service objected, Wynn eventually prevailed with the assistance of several of Nevada's most important political players.

Flanked by corporate counsel Bruce Levin (left) and brother Kenny, Steve Wynn looks tense in a hearing during his lawsuit against Donald Trump and former Golden Nugget president Dennis Gomes. He need not have been. Wynn eventually forced Trump to settle their dispute over the services of Gomes. (Jim Laurie/*Las Vegas Review-Journal*)

The consummate Las Vegas casino pirate announces arrival of Treasure Island, the Adventure Resort, on the grounds of the Mirage. (Jim Laurie/*Las Vegas Review-Journal*)

Salerno was then recognized as the most powerful gangster in America with an estimated net worth of $200 million. Salerno had managed by 1984 to advance through the ranks of the most ruthless American corporation without collecting a vast scrapbook of *New York Post* headlines such as would eventually come to haunt the more flamboyant family boss, John Gotti. Quietly holding court at the Palma Boy Social Club in East Harlem, Salerno preferred that club members avoid publicity in the tabloids.

With his untaxed wealth, his family's hands in scams around the world, and a life spent mostly outside of jail, it is easy to see how Salerno would feel confident saying, "I'm the fucking boss, that's who I am. Connecticut is mine; New Jersey is mine." And there was truth in his observation, "Without me, there wouldn't be no mob."

Salerno believed the Palma Boy was a safe haven for the Genovese family to conduct its business.

The FBI proved him wrong.

Not only would the FBI's surveillance halt Fat Tony's sixty-year career; the agency's so-called Salerno Tapes would help end Harris's casino career almost before it started.

On March 6, 1984—only a few weeks after the death of his father—FBI surveillance recorded Mel Harris entering the Palma Boy escorted by Genovese associate and frequent Las Vegas visitor Sammy Spiegel.

At the Palma Boy, Salerno and Harris talked for twenty-four minutes. In his deposition before New Jersey gaming investigators, Harris recalled only exchanging "pleasantries concerning his late father" with the man experts considered the *capo di tutti capi* of America's La Cosa Nostra.

Two weeks later, this time in the company of convicted racketeer Milton Parness, Harris again met with Salerno at the Palma Boy. Parness and Salerno had served time together in prison.

This second Salerno-Harris sit-down lasted forty-nine minutes, but Harris recalled that meeting only after being confronted with the fact of the federal law enforcement surveillance. Harris grudgingly admitted making the visit but swore he did not remember what was discussed with the cigar-chomping head of organized crime.

Harris explained to investigators how, after the death of his father, he had been contacted in Miami by longtime family friend John Tronolone of Cleveland who said that one of Allie's old pals wanted to speak to Mel in person. Out of respect, Mel Harris flew to New York City and strolled into the Palma Boy for a sit-down chat with the Godfather.

Tronolone, nicknamed "Peanuts" Tronolone, was a ranking and respected member of Cleveland's La Cosa Nostra family. In addition to operating a travel agency in Miami, Tronolone was also a trusted mob messenger who supervised the mob's business in South Florida.

Well-liked by small-time associates and caporegima, the aging but effective Tronolone was able to communicate with mob bosses from all over the nation when they arrived in Florida on business or pleasure. He also was a key communications link to Fat Tony Salerno, one of the heads of the American Mafia's five-family ruling commission.

When the New Jersey Division of Gaming Enforcement scrutinized the Harris-Golden Nugget relationship in 1986, officials presented the testimony of New York State Organized Crime Task Force investigator Joseph Coffey, who mocked the idea that the Harris visit possibly could have been anything other than for business purposes. Coffey, now an author, said that Harris's acquaintance through the late Allie Harris would hardly have enabled him to enter the "citadel" of the Genovese crime family.

The Palma Boy was not a place for casual chats with the sons of old business partners. It was as much a business office as anything constructed eighty floors above Wall Street, and in his office Fat Tony Salerno was all business.

A conversation at the Palma Boy between Salerno and Tronolone, overheard by FBI eavesdroppers on November 27, 1984, confirmed Coffey's perspective.

———

The conversation was sparked by a dispute that had developed over the mob-dominated Teamsters pension fund.

Before being forced out of the lending business by federal mandate, the Teamsters' Central States Southeast and Southwest Areas Pension Fund had provided more than $200 million in loans for operators of Las Vegas casinos.

From shopping centers to ice rinks, Strip casinos to golf courses, Central States loans had played a pivotal role in the growth of Las Vegas.

The fund lent $1 million to finance construction of Sunrise Hospital. It lent money to enlarge the Stardust Hotel and Casino, then the largest hotel in Las Vegas with 1,060 rooms. Another $1.2 million was doled out to develop the 241-acre Stardust Golf Course and Country Club.

Jimmy Hoffa's own attorney, Morris Shenker, joined a group of fascinating fellows at the Dunes in grabbing a $4 million loan—later gradually increased to $9.5 million—to construct the casino's twenty-story tower that Steve Wynn more than three decades later would dramatically implode.

In 1963, portly big-idea man and mob front Jay Sarno used $9.7 million in Teamsters loans to construct Caesars Palace. Through a series of frontmen and carefully placed casino plants, Caesars maintained a close association with some of the biggest names in American organized crime history. By 1968, the Teamsters had upped their investment in Caesars to $19.4 million.

San Diego real-estate maven and mob front Allen Glick surfaced in 1974 in time to score the largest Teamsters loan in Nevada history—$62.75 million to take over the Stardust and Fremont casinos and the Echo Bay resort at Lake Mead. Another $25 million was heaped on Glick's Argent Corporation in the name of renovation.

Years later, federal investigators would strip off the mob facade from Glick's Teamsters-backed operation of the Stardust and Fremont casinos. A classic straw man who turned informant against his dangerous benefactors, Glick was the pension fund's largest borrower: $100 million in three separate transactions with $87.75 million devoted to the Stardust and Fremont.

After his connection to organized crime was exposed, Glick sold his holdings in late 1979 to Allan D. Sachs's Trans-Sterling Corporation, which was put under the trusteeship of Victor Palmieri and Co. Federal investigators quickly surmised Trans-Sterling was little more than a mob-connected holding company for Glick's sponsors.

In 1984, Sachs, in turn, agreed to sell out as part of a settlement with the Nevada Gaming Commission; the settlement came after federal indictments outlined a mob-skimming operation at the Stardust.

The $73.9 million Trans-Sterling promissory notes, Teamsters-generated mortgages on the Stardust and Fremont hotels, would be the mob's last pension fund score.

———

Palmieri's initial attempts to find a buyer for the Trans-Sterling notes failed. On October 15, 1985, Palmieri contacted Irwin Molasky—a man intimately familiar with the Teamsters pension fund—who, in turn, reached out for Steve Wynn.

Wynn wanted at least a 20 percent profit, and over the next two weeks, Golden Nugget Corporate Vice-president Clyde Turner negotiated with Palmieri. By Halloween, a final draft of the deal had been cut.

Backed by three separate $20 million loans, Golden Nugget plucked the Trans-Sterling notes. At $58.6 million, with the notes set to reach full term in 1991, it was a steal in more ways than one.

On February 28, 1985, the Boyd Group, then owner of Sam's Town and the California Club, prepaid the Trans-Sterling notes at the $73.9 million face value. In a mere four months, Wynn had made $14.4 million profit on his investment.

Palmieri quickly filed an eleven-count lawsuit in April 1985 on behalf of the Teamsters pension fund against Golden Nugget Corporate Vice-president Clyde Turner, seeking to rescind the transaction, recover $18.4 million it believed Golden Nugget gained from the purchase, and receive another $20 million in punitive damages.

The allegations included civil racketeering, fraud, breach of contract, and breach of good faith. The racketeering-related charges were later dismissed, and Golden Nugget vehemently denied the allegations.

A federal judge in Los Angeles eventually ruled that Golden Nugget had acted improperly and forced it to divide the $14.4 million with the Teamsters.

The case was resolved and went all but unnoticed in Las Vegas, where Wynn's record of business victories rivaled the success of the Harlem Globetrotters.

It was later revealed that Golden Nugget's board of directors had not even been officially informed that its chairman had floated $60 million in loans to purchase the notes of two scandal-plagued casinos. Only after the deal had been signed was the board brought into the picture.

Wynn's explanation of his high-handed action sounded distinctly like double-talk: "You can argue for many months about when does...an acquisition of an asset become a material event and when does the purchase or sale of an asset become the normal conduct of a management managing large cash reserves. It is a murky and gray consideration. A lot of it has to do with intent and a host of other factors. When in doubt, have the board rectify it....So, in order to avoid any possible conflict in the future, it's very easy to say we would like to have board ratification for this in case someone would interpret such was necessary."

In other words, Wynn told New Jersey Division of Gaming Enforcement investigators, next time he would do it correctly.

———

At New York's Palma Boy Social Club, the business office of Anthony Salerno and the site of an FBI surveillance microphone, the following post-Thanksgiving conversation about the pending sale of the notes to the Boyd Group was recorded between the Genovese boss and his trusted messenger John "Peanuts" Tronolone.

Tronolone: Jack Zero [Cerone] told me, he said you got to do this. No fucking telephones. Nothing. You gotta go and see this thing move right away. You gotta tell Salerno to tell Vince [Vincent Vinci] to get somebody to get Steve Wynn to stop. He's blocking the sale. He's blocking the sale.

Salerno: What can I do with Steve?

Tronolone: Humm?

Salerno: Who am I going to get?

Tronolone: Mel Harris. He's our guy. Mel Harris.

Salerno: Where is he, over there.

Tronolone: He's from the office. He's right under him. He's the secretary.

Salerno: Yeah?

Tronolone: Yeah. Vice-secretary, first vice-president in command. Mel Harris is. Remember I told you all of this. The only guy who can talk to Mel Harris is you.

Salerno: He's blocking the sale?

Tronolone: He's blocking the sale. Now, if the sale is made, there's plenty of money in there for everybody. He told me to tell you.

Salerno: Is that the Stardust?

Tronolone: Huh?

Salerno: Stardust?

Tronolone: Yeah. Stardust. He's blocking that sale. He wants somebody to tell these people not to block it. Let the sale go through. If the sale goes through, he said, 'Tell Tony that there's money for all of us.' He says, 'It's paramount to tell him that.' How much, I think Mel and he can sit down after. 'If he lets that fucking sale go through, there's plenty of money for all of us.'"

Salerno: How much time we got?

Tronolone: Right away you have to start on it.

Salerno: Yeah, but, ah, you sure Mel could tell him?

Tronolone: Huh?

Salerno: Mel could talk to him?

Tronolone: Mel, Mel's a shrewd man. Mel's his right-hand man. Mel, Mel could find a way to tell him.

Salerno: In other words, Steve Wynn is looking to buy this, right?

Tronolone: Right. He's looking. You see. But he's blocking it. That shit, that's not for sale. But he's blocking the sale, see? The combination from Chicago. Their people are buying...now trying to...they put, put a fifty-two million dollar bid in for it.

Salerno: How can he [Wynn] go in it when I'm in it?

Tronolone: You can't call him no more. You gotta send word to him.

——

Although aging and the victim of a 1981 stroke, Salerno had spent a lifetime practicing the mob's tradition of veiled conversation. Salerno knew that by late November 1984, Mel Harris no longer was in Atlantic City. New Jersey gaming authorities already had busted him out. Harris was in Las Vegas at the downtown Golden Nugget.

——

Salerno: Tell him [Jackie Cerone] I'm gonna do it, but I don't know if I can do it.

Tronolone: Yeah, yeah, that's what I'm gonna tell him. He's gonna do it, but he don't know what's gonna happen.

Salerno: I'm gonna tell him myself. Now let's get this money and insurance out of it. Everybody wants me to.

Tronolone: But this is a big job. Napoleon said, 'Tell Tony there's enough for all of us there.' And the money, ah, minga, money. 'If he lets that fucking sale, if he don't block that sale and the sale goes through, tell Tony we'll all be in good shape.' They've even got control of the other end.

Salerno: (Unintelligible)....in Vegas right now. But Stephen Wynn sent him to Vegas.

Tronolone: Who's that?

Salerno: Mel.

Tronolone: Yeah, he's there now!...He's there, right now.

Salerno: That's what I say...I don't know how I'm gonna get a hold of him.

Tronolone: How will we know you got word to him?

———

Salerno and Tronolone agreed that the best way to safely communicate with Harris was to go through convicted racketeer Milton Parness, Salerno's messenger and investment adviser.

With government wiretaps listening at nearly every phone and federal agents keeping mob members under constant surveillance, business meetings and decisions involving millions of dollars were accomplished through a series of trusted messengers.

Tronolone was one. Parness was another.

But what did it all mean?

———

The Salerno-Tronolone conversation aside, the Trans-Sterling transaction appeared to be an example of Wynn's sharklike aggression in corporate matters.

But did the move connect Wynn to Fat Tony Salerno and the Genovese crime family?

Unquestionably, the answer was "yes" in the opinions of the attorneys who prosecuted Salerno and fifteen other mobsters and their associates on forty federal charges ranging from murder to union corruption.

The indictment alone was 116 pages. Salerno and company were accused of fixing the elections that brought Jackie Presser and Roy Williams to power as presidents of the Teamsters, rigging construction bids, and corrupting New York's food and construction industries.

As never before, the trial illustrated the mob's generations-old stranglehold on New York.

Salerno and his associates had a piece of everything from hot-dog stands to hospitals and controlled the city's largest numbers and bookmaking operations.

The Cosa Nostra collective rigged the cement contracts for construction projects as large as Trump Plaza. Through Edward "Biff" Halloran, Salerno and Gambino boss Paul Castellano had acquired control of Manhattan's three concrete supply companies. Halloran operated the Transit-Mix Concrete Corporation. Through Nicholas Auletta, the mob locked up the S and A Concrete Company. In partnership with Richard Costa, Salerno controlled Marathon Enterprises, a food distributorship.

———

In the end, Salerno was acquitted of the union-election fix but was convicted of other corruption and racketeering charges. Those charges netted Dunes hidden-owner Matthew Ianniello as well as

Edward Halloran, former owner of the Halloran House Hotel. Among a host of other mob men convicted was Giuseppe "Joe Pepe" Sabato, at one time a favorite customer at the Atlantic City Golden Nugget.

Salerno's old Cleveland friends Milton "Maishe" Rockman and John "Peanuts" Tronolone were the only defendants acquitted of all charges.

Federal prosecutors Alan Cohen and Mark Hellerer overwhelmed some of the best defense attorneys in the country, including Byron Fox, Michael S. Washor, and John Jacobs, with more than 100 witnesses, 1,000 pieces of evidence, and 400 audio and video surveillance tapes. U.S. District Judge Mary Johnson Lowe successfully waded through the year-long trial that often resulted in emotional outbursts by each side.

Although Salerno was ill and already serving a 100-year sentence in the commission racketeering case, surveillance tapes showed he had been a national force in organized crime just a few years earlier.

From his chair at the Palma Boy Social Club, Salerno was capable of manipulating the skimming at Las Vegas casinos and fixing cement contracts in New York City. He was the mob's squatty, maniacal $200 million man.

Fat Tony Salerno would eventually receive a seventy-year sentence.

———

But did he have the ear of Steve Wynn?

When it came to the acquisition and sale of the Trans-Sterling notes, some lawyers believe there was no question about it.

Outside the presence of the jury, with Judge Lowe, both sides staged a heated debate.

"They were unhappy with [Wynn] at that point because they thought the offer was high enough," federal prosecutor Alan Cohen told the judge, "but Wynn was holding out for full face value and enough was enough. Let's go through with the deal. Stop holding out for the full amount."

Judge Johnson Lowe was not easily satisfied.

"More basic, what evidence is there of the reason that Salerno would be acting against his apparent best interests by dumping on Wynn because Wynn was holding up the sale, which is what this refers to?" she asked.

Cohen: "The answer to that is on the tape, and that is that while Salerno was going to get a piece out of Wynn's end, the people in Chicago and in Kansas City were going to get a piece out of the other end, and you'll see in the transcript it says, the message that Tronolone carries is, 'We can all make money from both ends.' And what Salerno had to do was to get Wynn to go ahead and sell so that the people in Chicago and Kansas City could get out of their end the Stardust and Fremont owners and Salerno could get out of his end what he could get out of Wynn. Each of the respective organized crime families had, as they say in the tapes, 'We have it on each end. We have it in Las Vegas and you have it here.'"

Defense attorney Mark Washor attempted to obfuscate the argument. He questioned the evidence. He questioned the prosecution's sense of logic. He argued the pertinence of including the Wynn remarks, which amounted to three pages out of thousands of pages of evidence.

Jacobs also saw what was coming and chose a slightly different course of rhetoric.

"We are opening up a Pandora's box to other criminal conduct not charged in the indictment which we did not have notice of," Jacobs said. "The problem is, how far do we go? Do we start trying this case and have a [Vincent] Cafaro take the stand and get into this criminal activity in detail?

"That's the problem, Judge. By allowing, as Mr. Washor is pointing out, by allowing these three pages to come in, you're now allowing the government to try their major criminal fraud here, and I think that's the problem Mr. Washor is upset about....You are in effect—we got no notice, we made our opening statements on what the criminal conduct charged here is. I have not been given notice that they were going to put a $25-million fraud on a company that every juror knows about.

"They see Steve Wynn on TV every night, our jurors here, Judge, our jurors see him on TV with Frank Sinatra every night. This isn't some minor criminal activity that we can gloss over in a transcript, Judge."

The defense argument, which in effect was an attempt to block the Wynn-Salerno connection from the jury, was crumbling. Finally, Washor grasped for a compromise.

"There is no objection to the tape and the language," Washor said. "We are asking the court to define for this jury that that has nothing to do with this indictment. You can play whatever you want for this jury, as far as I am concerned, but that doesn't pertain to the indictment."

But it did, of course. It showed Salerno's influence over the Teamsters pension fund. Presser and Williams—not Salerno and the mob—were supposed to be in control. As if the previous admissions of Presser, a longtime FBI informant, were not evidence enough, the tapes made Salerno's strength self-evident.

That made Salerno's comments regarding the Trans-Sterling sale more than pertinent.

"This tape is absolutely crystal clear enterprise proof...of what Tronolone does on behalf of this enterprise," Cohen said. "He is acting here clearly as a conduit between the organized crime people and Chicago, Jackie Cerone, and Salerno, and carrying a message to Salerno asking Salerno to get Wynn who is demonstrably —and Mel Harris, demonstrably under Salerno's control, to do something which would financially advantage the people in Chicago and the people in New York."

The defense cried uncle.

"Judge, can I just say something, might save a lot of time?" Washor asked, scrambling for legal footing. "Now, you want to hear the offer of compromise, that's the offer of compromise. I am not disputing the admissibility or relevancy for enterprise purposes, I can't do that in all conscience. What I asked you at the beginning to do I am asking you now, a limiting instruction that this does not apply to the underlying RICO [Racketeer Influenced and Corrupt Organizations] specific acts. That's all I wanted from you."

"If the government wants to use the transcript, Judge, in summation, show relationships and enterprise, that's one thing," Jacobs added quickly. "What we want to avoid is thousands of documents, Judge, and trying a major fraud with the Golden Nugget, and I think that's the difference."

Judge Johnson Lowe allowed the tape to be played as it showed the activity of the three groups involved in the transaction. "That's what's on the tape, so the jury has to have something to anchor it," the judge said. "Defense lawyers—did you hear what I said?…Once more, New York group, Las Vegas group and Chicago group and how they make money."

———

Confronted with the facts about his connection with his shady friends, Mel Harris acknowledged his relationships but said he had remained independent of his father's notorious friends.

Golden Nugget security officials insisted that, to their knowledge, all of Harris's business activity was legitimate.

Expert witness New York State Organized Crime Task Force investigator Joseph Coffey might disagree, but by the time the New Jersey Casino Control Commission got around to publicly scrutinizing Harris, Wynn already had conveniently terminated his business relationship with his old acquaintance.

In their confidential report to the commission, New Jersey Division of Gaming Enforcement investigators Ernest Tiberino and Michael Iannacone outlined a series of concerns about Wynn, his organization, and the depth of previous investigations.

They wrote, "Major Issue: Alleged associations with Anthony 'Fat Tony' Salerno, Boss of the Genovese organized crime family, and with other members of the Genovese crime family as well as the members of other organized crime cartels."

In his 1986 summary of the Golden Nugget Atlantic City's relicensing hearing, Chairman Walter Read of the New Jersey Casino Control Commission summed up the matter.

"The qualifications of Mel Harris for licensure are not at issue in this case," Read said. "It is nonetheless appropriate to comment that, in my view, his testimony at the deposition and at this hearing clearly lacks credibility. I do not think it is necessary to detail all of the reasons for this conclusion, and indeed some of those reasons must be obvious from what I have already said. It should also be unnecessary to describe the seriousness with which I, and I am sure my fellow commissioners, view this matter. However, at the risk of belaboring the obvious, I must note that the prospect of a person having uncontested access to Anthony Salerno sitting as an officer and director of a casino enterprise is, to say the least, frightening. Such a situation carries with it the potential to undo all of the past efforts of the commission, the division, and the industry to foster and protect public trust and confidence in the casino industry....It is equally perplexing that [Security Chief James] Powers and [Golden Nuggest Officer Al] Luciani, both of whom knew that Harris was acquainted with Salerno, apparently never imparted this knowledge to the GNI board or its chairman, Steve Wynn."

In his final remarks during Golden Nugget's 1986 Atlantic City relicensing hearings, Commissioner Carl Zeitz consistently sided with Wynn and Golden Nugget.

"Mel Edward Harris brings to mind a Churchillian expression uttered in the context of far more momentous events. I do not mean to demean that remark, but Harris is 'a riddle wrapped in a mystery inside an enigma.' In this hearing that is the best Harris is.

"Why, knowing all there is to know about his background but less than he told anyone at any give time, probably including this commission on the occasion of his testimony here, did Mel Harris accept Steve Wynn's invitation to join his company? Surely Harris, who is clearly a man of experience and had been warned he would be closely examined, knew at some keen level that the regulatory oversight of legal casinos is a boiling cauldron. Yet he chose to do more than test the heat, he chose to immerse himself in it."

The commissioner apparently forgot the multimillion-dollar employment package Harris was offered by Wynn.

Forgotten, too, was that Wynn admitted that his acquaintance with Harris extended back to the 1960s, and that the two men had maintained contact in the 1970s, and that Harris was a family friend of Elaine Wynn.

Even Wynn, rarely one to admit a mistake, has described the botched Harris hire as "the most embarrassing of my career."

He has been reminded of the fact more than once, but never so visibly as during an April 1988 edition of the CBS News *West 57th* TV magazine.

Wynn was interviewed by veteran reporter Meredith Vieira, who began her segment by mentioning Benjamin "Bugsy" Siegel, Meyer Lansky, and the mob. She described Wynn as a new breed of operator. Pretty standard stuff, at least for starters.

"Gambling has changed over the years, especially with the entrance of Wall Street into the game, but still [is] a money-making machine worth $7 billion," Vieira said. "But the industry says it's gone legit, and no one says it louder than Steve Wynn. Wynn is the new symbol of success in Vegas. He turned a $10,000 grubstake into a multimillion-dollar empire. As chairman of the Golden Nugget, he's a forty-six-year-old businessman looking for respect amid the glitz."

All well and good.

Then came the mention of Mel Harris.

Wynn: What Drexel Burnham was sure of is that the Golden Nugget couldn't have any involvement with nefarious people unless I was in on it. It couldn't happen around me, it couldn't happen in spite of me, it would have to happen with my consent or my approval or my allowing it to happen.

Vieira: You mean, if it was happening at the Golden Nugget, you would know it.

Wynn: I'd have to know.

Vieira: But you didn't know about Mel Harris. You said you didn't know about Mel Harris.

Wynn: Mel Harris never got involved with the Golden Nugget longer than twenty seconds after it was brought to our attention.

Vieira: (voice-over) Mel Harris was a vice-president of the Nugget. In 1984, federal agents secretly videotaped him entering the New York headquarters of "Fat Tony" Salerno, head of the Genovese crime family. In wiretapped conversations, the mob referred to Harris as "our guy at the Golden Nugget."

Wynn: All of a sudden, Mel Harris—we find out that Mel's talking to the wrong kind of people, and we throw him out on the street, you know. Goodbye, Mel.

A new voice comes in. It is that of Frank Pulley, one of the New Scotland Yard detectives who investigated Wynn during Golden Nugget's failed attempt to open a London casino.

Pulley: It's that sort of association, direct links to the Genovese family, which give grave cause for concern to investigators in both America and Britain when it comes to consideration of licenses.

Vieira: That's sort of guilt by association, right?

Pulley: Well, that's the way the mob operates.

Then it was Wynn's turn.

Vieira: How can you trust anyone around you? You trusted Mel Harris.

Wynn: The question is, how can you be sure, how can you be positive, how can anybody—well, you can't in this world. What you can be sure of is that in the end honest people will do the right thing. That's why we all survived Mel Harris and we kept our gambling licenses, and the state of New Jersey renewed our license after they investigated this. And if I don't see that sentence in this edited version of this tape, I will kill both of you after this question and answer.

Even in 1988 Wynn was obviously still sensitive about the trouble with Mel Harris.

CHAPTER 10

A BATTLE WITH THE BRITISH

At Steve Wynn's Treasure Island Hotel and Casino, the adventure begins a few feet off the Strip with a fantasy battle waged hourly in Buccaneer Bay. Like a larger-than-life scene from Disney's Pirates of the Caribbean, a crew of acrobatic buccaneers from the Hispaniola engages naval forces from the Royal Brittania in a mock display of high-seas swashbuckling.

To the few who recall the story of Steve Wynn's failed attempt at opening a casino in Her Majesty's backyard, the irony obtrudes like a peg leg on a show girl: When the last cannon has been fired and the final scalawag has thrust his sword, the pirates come from behind to defeat the British and capture Her Majesty's ship.

If only expanding the empire were as simple for Steve Wynn as that staged pirate battle in the man-made lagoon. But crossing swords with the British in reality has been much less kind. After an impressive string of business successes, Wynn ran aground in Great Britain when he attempted to open a casino in London.

In 1981, Steve Wynn seemed to be on a roll.

His hotel expansion had turned the Golden Nugget into the class of downtown. After successfully maneuvering through a New Jersey Division of Gaming Enforcement licensing investigation, Wynn's Golden Nugget Atlantic City was the talk of the Boardwalk. His next move, a three-million-pound ($5.8 million) investment in property zoned for a casino in London, appeared a natural.

London in the 1980s was a popular place with high-rolling Arab princes and monied gamblers from across Europe. Wynn meant to seize a sizable piece of that action at the old Park Lane Casino on Hertford Street.

He also planned to gain acceptance by taking control of the Mecca Sportsman gaming and recreation network in partnership with controversial British gambling figures Max Kingsley and Phil Isaacs.

He never got the chance.

Wynn butted heads with British licensing authorities over the directorship of Golden Nugget's London subsidiary and became a veritable punching bag for New Scotland Yard inspectors, who in 1983 presented a blistering—if not entirely accurate—report to their supervisors.

It was their belief that Wynn operated in partnership with the Genovese crime family.

Wynn insists it was a mistaken belief.

The lengthy report from the Criminal Investigation Department, researched at a time Wynn's Golden Nugget was being scrutinized by United States law enforcement, rounded up scads of historical information as it chronicled his rise from running a single Maryland bingo parlor to climbing to the top of the casino industry.

Inspectors wasted little time in highlighting what they considered problematic about Wynn's portfolio. Borrowing from law-enforcement informant files, the inspectors believed they shattered

Wynn's image as the cleanest face in the gambling trade and produced the most damaging investigative report of his career.

"Dealing with the latest developments first, it can be shown that there are numerous strong connections between GNI, some of its officers and so called 'key employees,' and the Genovese Cosa Nostra family based in New York and New Jersey.

"The strong inference which can be drawn from the new intelligence is that Stephen Wynn, the president of GNI, has been operating under the aegis of the Genovese family since he first went to Las Vegas in the 1960s to become a stockholder in the New Frontier Casino.

"It must be said that some of the data supporting this view, taken on its own, is not conclusive. However, the connections are so numerous and significant that it would be impossible to accept coincidence as a reasonable explanation."

Using confidential sources and raw intelligence data, the inspectors attempted to draw a link between Wynn's father, Mike, and Anthony "Fat Tony" Salerno.

All the names from Wynn's past were presented in chronological order: New York City bookmaker Herbie Liebert, who had introduced Wynn to organized crime associate Maurice Friedman, who had let Wynn in on the Frontier deal, which had soured when several of the owners were discovered to be acting as mob frontmen.

Wynn's association with casino-junket specialist Julie Weintraub and Las Vegas wiseguy Ash Resnick—both of whom were negotiating for employment at the New Jersey Golden Nugget—was presented as damning evidence of a connection to the underworld.

So, too, was the $10 million contract to which Wynn signed Frank Sinatra.

The Doumani brothers, Ed and Fred, also were evaluated: Their reported organized crime ties were presented as further evidence not only of Wynn's character flaws but of theirs as well.

Then came the bad news.

"Wynn's personal association with the Genovese family has been established beyond doubt by a series of meetings which took place last autumn. In September 1982, according to a confidential and reliable source, Wynn and Anthony Salerno met in New York City at one of Salerno's social clubs. The exact reason for the meeting is not yet known."

There was one problem with that specific item in the report. The FBI would not confirm whether its agents on surveillance had actually seen Wynn entering Anthony Salerno's Palma Boy Social Club. Wynn later asserted that Mel Harris had been mistaken for him.

The fact is that despite the long life of that charge, no one has ever testified to such a meeting and the probability is that it never took place.

The report continued: "The following month a meeting in New Jersey was observed by federal agents. Among those attending the meeting Stephen Wynn, Anthony Salerno, Charles Meyerson, and Abraham and Robert Margolies were identified positively. The meeting was held to discuss casino ownership and junket business.

"In November 1982, a meeting was attended by Abraham Margolies, Charles Meyerson, Julius Weintraub, and Milton Wekar. This meeting was also held to discuss casino ownership and the finance and organization of junkets into Atlantic City."

Abe and Robert Margolies were businessmen and associates of the Genovese family, the inspectors concluded. Wekar and Meyerson were a couple of aging bookmakers who stood on either side of the law.

The second meeting, Wynn's attorneys said, never happened. Neither reported Wynn-Salerno sighting surfaced during Wynn's Atlantic City licensing hearings.

Moreover, Wynn had never been turned down for a license by U.S. authorities who had access to the same information the Scotland Yard inspectors cited.

Sensing imminent rejection, Golden Nugget's attorneys in early 1982 asked the Gaming Board of Great Britain to withdraw the company's licensing application rather than have it refused outright. The reasons given were reasonable: They did not want to be forced to inform the New York Stock Exchange of the rejection, and a withdrawal would enable Golden Nugget to try for future licensing. Detective Superintendent C.P. Coxall of the Special Intelligence Section ended that hope with a scorching report on March 30, 1982:

"This sudden change of plan by Golden Nugget may be considered to represent a successful thwarting of the attempt by U.S. syndicate criminals to obtain control of a major holding in London's casinos, inasmuch as the overt approach has been blocked, but it cannot be considered to be an outright victory.

"...It now seems likely that Golden Nugget will have realized that the authorities in this country have divined their strategy and that they will now resort to more devious tactics to achieve their end.

"It is still suspected that, hidden behind the complex interrelationships between the various groups and individuals involved in the current round of takeovers and licensing applications, there are various and powerful interests who are seeking to establish a casino cartel in London."

———

Wynn has vehemently denied knowledge of the suspicions of the Gaming Board of Great Britain. Nevertheless, on January 26, 1982, the Golden Nugget made a move to improve its overseas image by asking for, and getting, the resignation of David Zenoff from the Golden Nugget board of directors. British investigators had become concerned about the Golden Nugget when they learned that Zenoff, a former Nevada Supreme Court justice, had provided legal representation for the controversial La Costa Country Club.

If Wynn and the Golden Nugget were leaving Great Britain under the cloud of alleged organized crime association, the stockholders never knew it. The company's Form 10-K, on file with the Securities and Exchange Commission, only spoke of the promise of expansion and failed to note the humiliating rejection.

The 10-K for fiscal year 1982: "In December 1981, the Registrant purchased certain leasehold interests in premises in London, England which were previously the site of a small casino which has not been in operation since December 1979. The purchase price was 3 million pounds (approximately $5.8 million at the then-current exchange rates). In order to conduct gaming operations on these premises, it is necessary for the registrant to obtain approvals from various governmental authorities in Great Britain and from the Nevada Gaming Commission. The initial approval required is a Certificate of Consent from the Gaming Board for Great Britain. On February 26, 1982, the registrant was advised that it would not be granted a Certificate of Consent at that time. The Gaming Board for Great Britain did not make any findings or articulate any reasons in support of its decision, which is not subject to appeal. However, the Registrant believes that a significant issue was the degree of control over the proposed London casino it was willing to vest in British residents. The Registrant has recently submitted another application for a Certificate of Consent from the Gaming Board for Great Britain and anticipates a hearing thereon within four months."

The paragraph was repeated in the 1983 10-K. The only change was the tentatively scheduled date for the supposed license hearing.

———

By the time the 1984 Form 10-K was submitted to the SEC, Wynn's grand London plans—and the status of that supposed second application before the Gaming Board of Great Britain—had disappeared. Neither the status of the project nor the results of that second application were noted.

Although Wall Street, Golden Nugget stockholders, and federal securities officials might have forgotten about the London casino that never was, Scotland Yard inspectors are known for their acute memories. When CBS News *West 57th* aired its story on Wynn, it was obvious he had failed to charm interviewer Meredith Vieira and was damaged by the comments of Scotland Yard Inspector Frank Pulley.

Vieira: (voice-over) Wynn's own reputation in Vegas has always been first-rate, but when he ventures beyond the desert, people tend to ask questions. In 1981, he tried to expand his gambling empire to England. Wynn bought a London hotel but he failed to receive a gaming license.

Vieira: The British turned you down?

Wynn: Well, they don't exactly turn you down. What they do is they don't hear you calling. You apply for a certificate of consent, and it does not issue.

Vieira: So you pulled out.

Wynn: There was nothing left to do. You can't argue with them. They don't want American control.

Frank Pulley: If you get into bed with the American gambling industry, you're getting into bed with the mob. Whether you know it or not, that's what's going to occur.

Pulley: The man has made an untold fortune in an industry which historically has been proved to be replete with organized crime. It was invented by the mob, it was modernized by the mob, the mob have put money into it, and they've taken vast amounts of money out of it.

Vieira: Do you think the British made up their minds about you before you even walked in there?

Wynn: Oh, I don't know why I would think a thing like that. I mean, the fact that the Scotland Yard guy came to investigate us in my office, he did everything but ask me to put my hands against the side of the wall and frisk me.

━━━━━

In Wynn's defense, it should be noted that Golden Nugget could not have been entering the lucrative London market at a worse time politically.

Not only were British authorities highly suspicious of attempts by American companies to enter the legalized gambling market, some of their suspicions had been realized by the comportment of two London casinos operated by Hugh Hefner's Playboy.

Victor Lownes, a member of the Playboy family for more than a quarter century, was dumped by Hefner at 4 a.m. after British authorities uncovered a series of relatively minor credit-policy violations. Replacing Lownes with a retired British naval officer didn't help. Told Playboy's licenses would be revoked, Hefner decided to abandon the country, selling not only his three London casinos and two others outside the city but also interests in two other casinos and the company's eighty bookmaking parlors. The move lent credibility to Wynn's claim that the British were looking for any excuse to minimize American influence.

"They did not want American control," former Golden Nugget President Bob Maxey recalled.

Maxey unsuccessfully attempted to carve out an agreement with British authorities. "It was my impression that they would do anything to keep the Americans out. It was a star chamber proceeding. They did brutalize Steve."

━━━━━

The Scotland Yard investigation sunk Wynn's chances of opening so much as a pinball parlor in Great Britain in the early 1980s. The damaging report, riddled with so many allegations, not all of them accurate, returned to haunt him in the 1990s as he worked to add casinos outside Nevada.

Like that tall ship in the mock bay of the Treasure Island, Wynn's attempts to expand outside Nevada get sunk time and again. But unlike the play-acting pirates, who spring back from battle, Wynn suffered deep wounds to his image and finances.

The rejection in Great Britain was the first of an extended string of increasingly expensive defeats on the road taken by the golden boy of Las Vegas gaming. Wynn, who racked up a string of firsts and wowed the casino establishment with his bravado and big ideas, was beginning to show signs of aging in the industry.

Until he prevailed over the British, Wynn's fight to expand his empire would be fated to fail.

PART

III

CHAPTER 11

THE ULTIMATE INSIDER

At the Gourmet Cafe in downtown Las Vegas, the local legal community's denizens ducked in out of the wicked afternoon wind to drink coffee, eat a late lunch, and lament the state of the American justice system.

The Gourmet occupies the bottom floor of a building that houses the Las Vegas office of the Federal Parole and Probation Department. Ex-cons from the federal system wishing to spend a weekend in the city must register there before checking in at a Strip resort.

That knowledge didn't prevent a few of the cafe's patrons from nearly spitting out their coffee at the sight of Steve Wynn pressing his celebrated face up against the restaurant's window before escorting Michael Milken, the convicted felon of Drexel Burnham junk-bond fame, sans toupee, to the federal parole office.

And why not?

Not only are the two close friends, but Milken is largely credited with fueling Wynn's climb in the industry he now dominates.

Milken's system of high-interest, high-yield financing, commonly known as junk bonds, financed $2.25 billion in new resort construction and massive remodeling efforts in the new Las Vegas, accounting for, by Milken's reckoning, 100,000 Southern Nevada jobs.

The casino companies to benefit from Milken's junk bonds make up a Las Vegas Who's Who: Bally's, Caesars Palace, Circus Circus, Harrah's, Holiday Inn, Sahara Resorts, Sands, Showboat, Riviera, and Tropicana. And even those not funded by junk bonds were forced to refurbish their properties or face extinction in an increasingly competitive marketplace.

If Jimmy Hoffa's pension fund bankrolled the old Las Vegas, Michael Milken's black magic constructed the new one.

And there Milken stood, on the sidewalk, about to take the elevator to the parole and probation department and sign in just like any other wiseguy or white-collar con.

In Nevada, a casino executive caught consorting with felons and persons of ill repute can lose his privileged state gaming license. But Steve Wynn isn't just any pit boss.

Despite Milken's six felony convictions and reputation in federal circles as the biggest Wall Street criminal in the history of the United States—he paid $1 billion in fines and spent twenty-two months in a yuppie prison—no member or agent of the Gaming Control Board dared broach the subject of Milken to the king of Las Vegas.

In a brief interview on the sidewalk outside the cafe, Wynn playfully called his friend "Milken, Schmilken." He referred to Milken's time in the Federal Correctional Facility at Pleasanton, California, as being "away at camp." He said Milken was in Las Vegas not for some wild weekend but to celebrate his grandfather's ninety-fifth birthday.

Wynn did most of Milken's talking. But when Milken spoke, the slight, piqued fellow was pleasant and quietly talked of creating a public-private partnership to redevelop the poor and minority neighborhoods not far from where he stood on the wind-swept sidewalk. Community service was a condition of his probation, and Las Vegas was a community he was familiar with serving.

However, the details would have to wait.

Before Milken could finish, a gold Mercedes pulled up to the curb and the two men disappeared into it.

In 1978, Wynn was a brash young casino operator riding the success of the Golden Nugget.

Then came his summertime visit to Atlantic City and his peek into the future of gaming at Resorts International where he was impressed by wide-eyed gamblers standing three-deep at the slot machines and "21" tables. Legalized gambling was new on the Boardwalk, but construction in mob-dominated New Jersey wasn't cheap. Wynn needed to find a traditional financial institution willing to lend a casino man $120 million.

Wynn, while sometimes without capital, has never been short of contacts. And the second most important business contact of his life, next to his friendship with Nevada banking legend E. Parry Thomas, was about to be made through his college pal, Zenith Insurance chairman and investment specialist Stanley Zaks.

Wynn and Zaks had discussed the vast possibilities of Atlantic City; both agreed the potential profits were astronomical for the best operators. Not long after their discussion, Wynn received a phone call from an excited Zaks.

"He said, 'Get your ass on a plane and meet me at 1901 Avenue of the Stars, the thirteenth floor, and I will introduce you to the only guy who can do this—my cousin,'" Wynn said in Connie Bruck's 1988 book, *The Predators' Ball.*

"I got there and Stan introduced me to this young kid, thirty-two, wearing jeans, a plaid sports shirt, and black loafers. Stan told him he'd known me for ten years and that I was good at my business.

"I told Mike about Atlantic City. He asked me brief, terse questions. He asked for the annual reports of Golden Nugget. Asked where I'd gone to school (I'd gone to Wharton).

"'I'll tell you what I'm going to do. You think you need a hundred million. I think you need a hundred twenty-five million. I don't like people to be underfinanced. I'm going to do your deal.'"

───────────

Patterning much of his business philosophy after high-risk financial shark and Riviera Hotel owner Meshulam Riklis, Milken knew more about the financial inner workings of the gaming industry than most casino bosses. He saw a Las Vegas others did not. Peeking beyond the facade, he recognized a sound business based on mathematical laws. It was gambling for the player, good business for the owner.

"In the late seventies I'd take money managers and pension fund people into the casinos and show them that it wasn't a gambling business, it was a business that was built on the laws of probability and statistics," Milken revealed to his literary ally Fenton Bailey in *Fall from Grace*.

"We'd go up in the catwalks looking down on the gaming tables and really see the inner workings of the industry. Once these people had all these stereotypes stripped away and they saw that it was basically a business, their attitudes changed."

In two years, Wynn received $160 million from Milken's junk bonds. This was $35 million more than he'd asked for.

Prompted by Milken to make up-close contact with bond buyers, Wynn became a smashing success, something of a P.T. Barnum in his selling of the casino industry to conservative financial backers. Time and again Milken used Wynn's charisma to generate confidence in his pyramid-shaped system of corporate financing.

"'The gaming industry needs a White Knight,'" Wynn recalled Milken saying. "'They need somebody they can believe in who's not just capable but stands for integrity.... If someone emerges like that the marketplace will give him everything he wants. You can be that guy, Steve. You've got an unblemished career. But I'm gonna tell you, there's no home runs. You hit singles, and hit singles, and some day you can do anything you want. That's the way it works. The most important thing is to keep your promises [and] if you do good, the day will come when you'll be able to raise a billion dollars.'

"When he said that I thought the man was certifiably insane. I was willing to sell my soul that day for $65 million. But look what's happened. Counting all the deals, I've done $1.6 billion so far, and we're just getting started."

———

The $620 million Mirage is a 3,049-room, thirty-story testament to the power of junk bonds.

The property's signature fire-spewing volcano and five-acre lagoon would be grand. Its white tiger exhibit would stop traffic, and illusionists Siegfried and Roy would pack the showroom year-round. The tropical rain forest and 20,000-gallon aquarium featuring small sharks would intrigue even the most cynical casino customer. (The tropical theme, warm and understated by gaudy local standards, was not original; the Tropicana, which for years had called itself the "Island of Las Vegas," lost a lawsuit to prevent Golden Nugget from borrowing its motif.)

Other resorts' accommodations were unsophisticated grist for newspaper feature stories, but the Mirage's cabanas were spotlighted in *Architectural Digest*.

With oriental rugs and inlaid marble floors, antique furniture, four-poster beds, separate master bathrooms and dressing facilities, a private pool, and a miniature putting green, the Mirage Villas are tailored to the most expensive tastes. Each luxury apartment cost nearly $3 million to construct and decorate. "If Queen Elizabeth and Prince Philip came here, the queen would say, 'My dear, we are at home,'" Wynn boasted.

For the high-rolling gambler seeking the equal of the Villas at the gaming tables, the Mirage would offer the Salon Privé. Minimum credit line: one million dollars. It comes complete with a private gourmet kitchen.

"Steve is a lot more detail-oriented than he would like people to believe," former MGM Grand President Bob Maxey said. "He likes to portray himself as a fellow who paints with a broad brush, but he's involved in every aspect of the process."

To wit: Although Joel Bergman is rightfully recognized as the architectural force behind the design of the Mirage and Treasure Island, his office was equipped with two drafting tables: one for him, and one for Wynn.

The Villas became an immediate success with high rollers and celebrities. Before revelations of his alleged abuse of young boys became public, Michael Jackson set up house in one of the palatial super suites. Jackson, who eventually paid a reported ten million dollars to silence one twelve-year-old critic, entertained his young friend, Joey Randall, and Randall's mother, Molly, at the Villas. The trio flew into Las Vegas and moved into a $3,000-a-night suite. They watched Siegfried and Roy and Cirque du Soleil as Steve Wynn's special guests, and they swam with the dolphins in the Mirage's so-called educational dolphin pool, and according to Christopher Anderson's *Michael Jackson, Unauthorized*, dined at the resort's Moon Gate Chinese restaurant.

Before his child-abuse scandal made international headlines, Jackson was often at Wynn's side for interviews and photo opportunities. Wynn often talked of wanting to create a family-themed attraction with Jackson at the Mirage.

After it became apparent the damaging tales of pedophilia weren't going to subside, the Vegas King and the King of Pop no longer appeared together in public. Plans for a "Jackson Attraction" at the Mirage are on hold.

━━━━━━━━

But what about those junk bonds? Surely they would be Wynn's undoing. Not even the golden boy of gaming could guarantee record profits.

"We are concerned about the high leverage," industry analyst Marvin Roffman told the *New York Times*. The Mirage would have to clear $1 million-a day to cover its operating costs and bond-interest payments. Roffman was not alone in his grim assessment.

Thanks to Milken, the $540 million worth of Mirage bonds would contain a clause that enabled the company to escape paying full interest to bondholders if Mirage earnings equaled 150 percent of interest payments for nine straight months, a performance goal the hotel easily met.

Indeed, five weeks after the Mirage opened, Wynn announced the casino had set record profits for a single month: $40 million in winnings at the tables alone. Its food and beverage and even its rooms—loss leaders at every resort in the city—were turning a profit. The Mirage is credited with igniting the explosive Strip expansion that has become known in magazine feature stories as the New Las Vegas.

Yet even as the Mirage was becoming the symbol of the shining new city, the company was far from debt-free—even with Milken's friendly finance clause.

In early 1993, Mirage Resorts was hip deep in high-interest financing—$831.2 million in long-term debts with an average interest rate of 10.7 percent. A year earlier, the company had owed more than $1 billion with an average interest rate of a withering 12 percent. After refinancing and retiring some of the most usurious notes, the figure was reduced by approximately 30 percent.

Throughout 1993, Wynn devised methods of retiring the company's obese long-term debt. In March, Mirage issued $100 million in subordinated notes; in November, 13,750,000 shares of common stock were put on the market, generating $303.6 million "in order to build a strong base upon which to fund future growth." With the cash, Wynn paid off another $356.3 million in mortgage notes with interest rates ranging as high as 13 ¾ percent.

By year's end, Mirage's long-term debts nearly had been carved in half: $535 million with an average interest of 9.4 percent.

———

The dark heart of Drexel was captured, along with the supreme arrogance of the 1980s era, by a line written and posted by a corporate finance official in 1986: "Drexel is like a god in that end of the business, and a god can do anything it wants." That year, Drexel wrote $4 trillion in deals and scored $5 billion in revenues. Milken's cut has been estimated at as much as 25 percent.

As a financial facilitator for Drexel, Milken was peerless. He was the quintessential confidence man; his Herculean work ethic, ability to motivate sellers and buyers, and numerous successes created an atmosphere of supreme confidence among the nation's biggest traders and corporate raiders.

And in the junk bond carnival, Steve Wynn became one of his greatest barkers.

Nowhere was Wynn's influence more noticeable than in 1984 during Drexel's annual Institutional Research Conference, also known as the Predators' Ball. In the decade that made greed famous, the Beverly Hills conference was the supreme symbol of excess.

In spite of Milken and his lofty philosophy about big business making the world a better place, most of the attendees were typically present to massage their capitalistic libidos and score megadeals. Honored guests and potential clients included a long list of the nation's wealthiest men: Merv Adelson, Boone Pickens,

Marvin Davis, Rupert Murdoch, Carl Icahn, Ralph Ingersoll, Jay and Robert Pritzker, Peter Ueberroth, Kirk Kerkorian, Ted Turner, Henry Gluck, and Mel Simon.

Flashy starlets and models mingled in the crowd. High-priced call girls worked the conference, operating at times out of Bungalow Number 8 of Ivan Boesky's Beverly Hills Hotel.

Wynn not only addressed the conference, he also provided celebrities direct from the Golden Nugget. The golden boy's old friend Kenny Rogers made an appearance, as did Dolly Parton and Diana Ross. At the final conference, Sheena Easton performed.

But by far the biggest impression was made at the 1984 Predators' Ball by America's most famous chairman of the board, Frank Sinatra.

"You guys don't know how to do commercials," Milken said to Wynn during their Martin-and-Lewis shtick session before the packed audience.

"Oh yeah?" Wynn said. "Let's have an expert decide."

Sinatra strolled onstage, clutching a handful of greenbacks.

"Here you are, kid," Sinatra said, handing the money to Wynn. "Buy yourself a few bonds."

The crowd went wild.

———

Golden Nugget's Atlantic City foray was only the first deal for Milken and Wynn. The aborted 1984 takeover of entertainment conglomerate MCA, owner of Universal Studios, became their most notorious venture.

Early in 1984, Wynn secretly bought more than two million shares of MCA stock, at prices ranging from $38 to $43. He was on his way to accumulating just less than 5 percent of the company at an investment of approximately $100 million. After 5 percent, the law required that Wynn would have to make his intentions known to MCA and the SEC.

Takeover rumors began to appear in the daily press during the summer, and by late August the *Los Angeles Times* was all but predicting Golden Nugget might somehow manage to acquire a company many times its size.

MCA officials were not happy. Company President Sidney J. Sheinberg was blunt: MCA "didn't invite [Wynn] in" and "we don't see any commonality of interest with Golden Nugget." Despite Golden Nugget's inferior size, in the eighties even executives at America's largest and most successful corporations gained a healthy respect of the possibilities of junk-bond-fed corporate takeovers.

But by August it became evident that an attempt by Golden Nugget to swallow MCA would be suicidal. Wynn now had a problem: He owned more than 2 million shares of MCA stock. He would suffer a substantial loss if he tried to sell the stock on the open market. He needed help in a hurry, the kind only Michael Milken could provide.

For the tricky business of selling off Wynn's stock, Milken enlisted Ivan Boesky as a middleman. The arbitrageur was a willing participant in the textbook felony.

Milken laid out the deal to Boesky, guaranteeing the arbitrageur's investment against loss and promising to cut him in on future deals that would net him millions.

It was a favor for a friend.

Boesky jumped at the chance to have Milken in his debt. "Ivan was like an addict, and his drug was capital," one former Boesky employee told the *New York Times*. "Milken seemed to be playing the role of the pusher."

With his image as a fearless corporate raider and dealmaker, Boesky provided the ideal straw man. As the Wall Street remoras began swirling around the Great Whites, Boesky acquired more than half of Wynn's position. Moving quickly while the scent of blood remained in the water, Boesky managed to sell much of the stock, minimizing his risk.

Milken's guarantee returned to haunt him. The promise violated insider trading laws. Once the feds reeled in Boesky, it was a matter of time before Milken was also caught.

The MCA deal was one of six felonies Milken pleaded guilty to in April 1990.

———

Wynn has nothing but kind words for Milken—and nothing kind to say about Boesky, the snitch whose testimony helped put the Junk Bond King behind bars.

Without Ivan the Terrible, the government wouldn't have come within a block of Milken. With Boesky, the cases not only were simple to make but also were relatively uncomplicated to explain to a jury.

The federal investigation of his complex junk-bond network resulted in Milken and his brother, Lowell Milken, being hammered with ninety-eight felony charges related to insider trading and securities fraud. Investigators outlined a long list of insider trading allegations and illustrated instances in which Milken had used his influence over investors to reap hundreds of millions of dollars in commissions and bonuses. Steve Wynn's hero and financial wizard was depicted as the biggest confidence man since Ponzi.

"The three-year investigation has uncovered substantial fraud in a very significant segment of the American financial community," Acting United States Attorney Benito Romano said. "A serious criminal problem has infected Wall Street."

In an interview, Wynn lashed out at Milken's critics. "It's breaking our hearts," Wynn said. "They can indict him. They can attack him, but they will not destroy what Michael Milken is in the eyes of his friends because Michael Milken's credibility is a thousand, million times greater than anything in government."

Milken's advocates fought to preserve his freedom in the courtroom and to rehabilitate his image in the press with an impres-

202 J O H N   L.   S M I T H

sive assault in newspapers, magazines, books, and television programs.

Symbolizing the split, the *Wall Street Journal* published the government's massive case against Milken on its front page while extolling his business philosophy on its editorial page. Milken's allies published story after story recrafting what prosecutors called the biggest swindle in the history of American securities. By giving millions to charities through the Milken Family Foundation, Milken also reaped favorable publicity. Magazines that initially painted him as slightly short of Satan, later softened their editorial stances. "How Crooked Was Milken?" a 1990 *Newsweek* story asked. "Where's the truth about Milken?" *Forbes*, which championed his cause, wondered in 1992.

In Southern Nevada, where Wynn made sure locals understood Milken's importance in the gaming industry's growth, a seven-part series of articles extolling Milken's virtues appeared in the *Las Vegas Sun* newspaper, itself financed by his junk bonds. Written by freelancer Jack Sheehan, the series celebrated the billionaire's creative and charitable sides, depicting him as a family man who took pride in giving his sons a tour of the shimmering resorts he had financed on the Las Vegas Strip. Local leaders gave witness to Milken's stature in Southern Nevada.

"I have nothing but admiration for that young man," E. Parry Thomas said of Milken in a rare interview. "What he has accomplished is incredible. I think he's a fellow who tries to do the right thing. I hope he comes out of it all right."

"After almost two-and-a-half years of leaks and distortions, I am now eager to present all the facts in an open and unbiased forum," Milken said on the day he was indicted. But when the time came to support his case, Milken backed down.

Whether he was pressured into signing off on a plea agreement or finally was forced to come to grips with the strength of the government's mountainous case against him, in the end he buckled and avoided a trial. In April 1990, Milken cut his deal with the government: he'd plead guilty to six felonies.

His advocates accused the government of extorting a conviction out of Michael by using brother Lowell. One of the conditions of Milken's plea arrangement was that his brother not be prosecuted.

Federal Judge Kimba Wood sentenced Milken to ten years. The sentence was later reduced to three years, of which Milken served twenty-two months.

Milken's statement in court makes his transgression clear. He also made certain to protect his favorite client, Steve Wynn:

"As for count III and the second overt act of the conspiracy count, in the fall of 1984, a client of Drexel, Golden Nugget, wanted to sell a substantial amount of MCA stock. I wanted the shares to hit the market in such a way that would not identify our client as the seller and adversely affect the price that it might receive. So I turned to Boesky, whose business it was to buy and sell large amounts of stock and who I knew had an interest in entertainment company stocks, including MCA. I told a Drexel employee to ask him to buy the blocks of MCA shares as they became available from Drexel's client. I did not tell the client how I was disposing of the stock. Drexel crossed the blocks between its client and the Boesky Organization, which subsequently resold most of these shares into the market.

"When Boesky complained that he had lost money on his initial purchases of MCA, I promised that we would make up any losses the Boesky Organization suffered on its purchases and sales and thereafter it bought more stock from Drexel acting on behalf of our client. This promise was not recorded on Drexel's books nor made public, and it was wrong not to do so. It was my intent that the block sales would enable our client to receive a better price than it might have obtained if I had not agreed that Drexel would make up the Boesky Organization's losses on the MCA stock."

————

After paying $1.3 billion in fines and spending less than two years at Club Fed, Milken and his immediate family still possess a collective wealth estimated at $1.2 billion. Milken's personal assets are believed to total more than $600 million. The government may have halted the Wall Street sharks' feeding frenzy, but Milken and his closest associates, including his friend Steve Wynn, continue to feed on the schools of sucker fish.

Junk bonds victimized many people, Milken's champions to the contrary. His maneuvers led to the failure of fifty-five savings and loans, strapped taxpayers with more than $1 billion in direct costs, and soaked insurance companies with more than $100 billion in losses. Thousands of jobs may have been created in Las Vegas, but untold thousands were lost in other regions.

For the New Jersey Division of Gaming Enforcement, the collapse of Drexel and its junk bonds created something of a conundrum.

In January 1989, division officials attempted to grapple with the Milken question. The division asked the Casino Control Commission to ban Drexel from doing business with Atlantic City casinos. Up to that time, Drexel had facilitated $2.5 billion—about 70 percent of the long-term financing on the Boardwalk.

Nevada's Gaming Control Board also indicated that its agents were looking into the matter. Considering Drexel had fueled the growth of both resort cities with more than $5 billion in junk-bond loans, the issue was politically charged. Regulators knew too well how close high-profile operators at Golden Nugget, Caesars Palace, Sands, Holiday Inn, and Resorts International were to Milken.

Fortunately for Nevada regulators, Drexel eventually declared bankruptcy. The supernova that was the junk bond era had burned itself out. By the end of the 1980s, junk bonds no longer were the financial drug of choice for sharp-toothed entrepreneurs and corporate raiders.

Government regulators blamed Milken, his assistants and investor friends, and voracious greed for the demise of the high-yield industry.

Insiders clung to their belief that it was an overzealous government, prodded in large part by conventional industrialists who felt their world threatened, that had destroyed a money-raising system largely feared and little understood.

Cutting through the government's propaganda and the Great Milken Image Machine isn't easy.

Michael Milken was not merely a gifted, greedy devil in an ill-fitting toupee. He was a one-man white-collar crime wave. He also was not a brilliant saint given to elaborate visions of a kindhearted world economic order. If anything, he was addicted to a money game the likes of which the nation had never seen before. He was a charismatic, computerized pied piper capable of attracting dozens of followers who did not share his vision of a gentler and better-capitalized world.

He lived modestly; but he also accumulated more than $1 billion.

As Milken once said to his friend Steve Wynn, "It's not what you've got, it's what you stand for."

CHAPTER 12

WYNN-MORAN WAR

By July the weather in Las Vegas turns from merely uncomfortably warm to excruciatingly hot. Temperatures surpass 100 degrees daily, and 110-degree afternoons are common. The fastest growing city in America takes on all the climatic appeal of a pizza oven.

Even in the smokiest July heat, the Mirage pool area is crowded with baking tourists. Tall and short, anorexic and obese, they converge by the blue waters and sear their flesh in the name of fun and a healthy tan. Often as not, they come away looking like blood-rare New York steaks and spend the rest of their trip rubbing in ointments and walking gingerly.

The five men arriving from New York on July 15, 1991, didn't seem to mind the heat. They were living the life of Las Vegas high rollers, having a fine time hanging out at their pool-side cabana complete with cocktail and food service and a sweet view of the female talent cruising in the midday sun. But even as they watched the bikinis bake, the New Yorkers were, in turn, being watched and photographed by locals who had crashed the pool party: Metro and Gaming Control Board investigators.

Acting on a tip from New York law enforcement, Metro detectives had contacted Gaming Control Board investigators and picked up surveillance of the gamblers as they arrived at McCarran International Airport. The visitors gathered their baggage and traveled by a house limousine to the Mirage. There they were met by a casually dressed old gentleman with a Florida tan, gray hair, and glasses.

The guests registered under the name McKoy, a reference to Genovese associate and businessman Roy Frank McKoy, owner of Blackjack Fireworks near Pahrump, a rural community sixty miles from Las Vegas. They received complimentary rooms and meals; they gambled on credit.

Their names weren't McKoy, of course.

The crew consisted of Alphonse "Alie Shades" Malangone, a Genovese crime family capo; Carmine "Baby Carmine" Russo, a Genovese soldier; Elia Albanese and John Gagliardi, Genovese associates; and Carlo Lattinelli, a New York businessman.

Born in 1936, Malangone is reputedly hip deep in New York City's garbage-carting industry. He also managed Pastel's, an Eighty-eighth Street restaurant in New York that is a popular wiseguy hangout. New York investigators assert Malangone assumed responsibility for the rackets of aging Genovese capo Thomas Contaldo of Brooklyn. McKoy was Malangone's nephew and lifelong friend.

The Mirage surveillance was no small-time mob sighting. Malangone was a serious gangster.

The McKoy group, watched at the Mirage by undercover detectives, conducted themselves like most tourists: They hit the casino, dined in the resort's restaurants, and lounged in a cabana by the pool. Occasionally, they greeted the old fellow, who seemed to have the run of the 3,000-room carpet joint. During their stay, they received $9,400 in complimentaries and met with a couple of local businessmen and even a rookie cop.

On July 19, when the visitors from New York were chauffeured back to the airport at the end of their stay, Metro detectives, gaming control investigators, and investigative reporter George Knapp's television camera crew, tipped to the bust by intelligence bureau officers, were waiting.

Russo and Albanese, who had neglected to register as ex-felons when they entered the county, were arrested and taken downtown on the misdemeanor charge designed to legally harass mob guys.

It all ended up on the nightly news: Mob gamblers at the Mirage fail to register as ex-felons. In the fickle world of television news, it held the promise of a one-day story—until a column in the *Las Vegas Review-Journal* revealed that the host who had catered to the Cosa Nostra was Charlie Meyerson.

It was meant to be a one-day column, but Wynn reacted as if someone were trying to drive a stake through his heart.

The first shot in the Wynn-Moran War had been fired.

━━━━━

Going into their pit-bull mode with the media, Wynn's attorneys set up a summit meeting with Sheriff John Moran and his investigators. What began as a meeting of old friends—a major campaign contributor, Wynn always had enjoyed a good rapport with Clark County sheriffs—deteriorated into a shouting match with Wynn defending Charlie Meyerson and Moran taking up for his men.

As with many great battles, the early exchanges between Wynn and Moran were skirmishes meant to test the enemy's defenses.

After all, Wynn had employed the sheriff's sons. Metro narcotics detectives had used Mirage cash as "flash rolls" in undercover drug buys. Could these two powerhouses really be going to war?

Just after New Year's 1992, Wynn found out: Meyerson was notified that Metro had moved to revoke his sheriff's work card for his "continual association with persons of notorious reputation and the extending of complimentary hotel services to those people at the Mirage Hotel and Casino."

Without a work card, Meyerson could not be employed by any casino even as a dishwasher, much less a casino host pulling down $400,000 a year.

But the cops had a problem, too.

A complete background investigation into Meyerson's criminal and employment history had not been conducted when his work card originally was issued in 1987. Someone had expedited the process with the police and at the Gaming Control Board. Meyerson, despite his salary and status within the resort, had not been required to submit to a key employee license investigation.

Metro investigators privately pushed for the Gaming Control Board to act regarding Meyerson's status as a $400,000-a-year casino host. He qualified on many accounts as a key employee, and the cops pressed the issue directly and through the media.

In a tersely worded letter to Gaming Control Board Member Bill Bible, Moran chided the state for not moving with greater dispatch in the Meyerson case.

The letter—in all probability penned by Metro Intelligence Services Bureau Lt. Loren Stevens—sent Wynn into orbit.

━━━━━

On April 14, 1993, twenty-one months after the Malangone visit and nearly a year after the county work-card hearing, the control board finally opened a key employee licensing hearing of Charlie Meyerson—more than a decade after he had joined Wynn's inner circle.

The hearing revealed that Wynn's friend and adviser was a heartbeat from the Genovese family, that he had maintained friendships with mob bookmakers for as many as fifty years, that many of his friends and business partners were directly tied to Anthony Salerno.

Frank Schreck, Meyerson's attorney and himself a former member of the Nevada Gaming Commission, fought to dominate the hearing. In the end, there were some relationships even Schreck couldn't explain away.

There was, for example, Meyerson's half-century friendship with illegal bookmaker and mob associate Alfie Mart.

From New York to Miami, Mart dealt closely with Salerno as a bookmaker and moneylender. In a recorded conversation, Salerno recalled a $150,000 loan he made to Mart and, Nevada gaming officials argued, indirectly to Meyerson. The purpose of the loan was to fund a Miami Beach-based bookmaking collective operating out of a small sundries store on Collins Avenue. The loan was to be paid back at a rate of $15,000 a week, a percentage that even a sundries store the size of K-Mart would find difficult to repay.

Control board member Steve DuCharme argued that Meyerson, as well as Mart, was a recipient of the transaction. Meyerson's old friend and business partner, Herbie Liebert, helped bankroll Mart. His argument was bolstered by law enforcement interviews with Cafaro and former Lucchese crime boss Alphonse "Little Al" D'Arco. Both agreed Meyerson knew well the identity of his customers.

Cafaro went further still, claiming that the gray-haired casino host was a big earner for Fat Tony Salerno and the Genovese crime family. Although Cafaro's testimony had helped convict his friend and former boss, Salerno, in the end the word of a member of the Federal Witness Protection Program would not offset the passing years and the political strength of Steve Wynn's gaming machine.

Another example was presented.

Back in New York in the 1940s, Meyerson had hooked up with Nathan Teplis at the Meyers Parking Lot in Manhattan on Thirty-fourth Street. From 1965 to 1968, Teplis had operated a junket business affiliated with several Nevada casinos, including the MGM, Thunderbird, Caesars Palace, Frontier, Sands, and Golden Nugget.

His application for a race and sports book license had been rejected in 1960 at a time when the Nevada Gaming Commission was eagerly approving ex-bootleggers and bookmakers. Teplis, they determined, even by Nevada's forgiving standards, was unacceptable.

Then there was the problem of Meyerson's daily companion at the Las Vegas Country Club, one Willie Cohen who had been Anthony Salerno's best friend and a longtime pal of Genovese capo and mob casino overseer Vincent "Jimmy Blue Eyes" Alo.

When he wasn't spotted by investigators taking morning walks with Meyerson, Cohen was seen dining at Fratelli Restaurant in Las Vegas with Alo and, occasionally, Irving "Niggy" Devine, the former Lansky courier who had accompanied young Stephen Wynn on the yacht ride that ended in the mutilation death of Nancy Mottola.

In Las Vegas, Cohen once managed a massage parlor and had licensed the dime pitch concession at Circus Circus when the resort was under the influence of the mob. At the Aladdin, he had operated a travel agency with Jimmy Tamer's sister before selling out after gaming investigators moved to call him forward for licensing.

Cohen managed to remain close to the mob throughout his adult life without finding himself under police scrutiny even though his New York City drugstore and bar had been a notorious meeting place for bookies, loansharks, and members of the bent-nose fraternity. Cohen sold the bar in 1955, but his contact with the underworld did not end: In 1984 he was picked up repeatedly on the Salerno tapes discussing business and history with Fat Tony.

Did Willie Cohen complete the circuit that connected Meyerson, and in turn Steve Wynn, to the Genovese crime family?

That clearly was the contention of Metro investigators, who had waded into deep and treacherous waters when they decided to take on Wynn's formidable political machine. It was too tight a circle, and the meetings were too regular to be otherwise, they surmised. And the point of the control board's licensing hearing was merely to establish whether Meyerson had friendships and associations that could leave Nevada's legalized gambling industry open to ridicule.

Meyerson explained it another way: "Well, I came here in 1987, and I didn't run into him [Cohen]—one day I ran into him at the Golden Nugget, and I—we started to talk, and he told me he lived in [the Las Vegas] Country Club, and I told him I lived there, too. And about two-and-a-half, three years ago I used to run into him walking in the morning, I met him walking, and there's a lot of other people walking, and we all walk together. And they would branch off, and people go their own way. That's how I got reacquainted with Willie Cohen."

"But did it concern you that he had some former relationship or had been associated with Mr. Salerno?" Chairman Bill Bible asked.

"No, it never entered my mind," Meyerson said. "I didn't think much about it, because I never heard anything bad about Willie Cohen. But since that time, since this has happened, I do—he walks a little earlier in the morning than I do; I bicycle ride now."

Meyerson's problems were compounded by references on the Salerno tapes to a $150,000 loan.

On the Salerno Tapes, mob soldier Anthony Romieki is overheard cryptically saying, "He [Meyerson] had the orange juice joints of Florida...with Tommy Pappadio. Anthony Salerno... loaned him $150,000 that time."

"He [Romieki] knew that I don't know Tony Salerno," Meyerson told Nevada gaming regulators. "He never loaned me $150,000."

Schreck earned his substantial fee by ferociously arguing that in a 1992 prison interview by Metro detective Bob Conboy with a largely senile Salerno, the imprisoned godfather could not recall making the loan. But Schreck had to admit that Herbie Liebert, Charlie's bookmaking partner, also was Alfie Mart's partner in Miami.

"I mean, these guys are sitting around just talking all day long, and out of these two-and-a-half years of tapes, these are the only times Charles Meyerson's name is mentioned. And I can guarantee you they sat and BS'd about all kinds of other people. I mean, we're all a bit subject to that. I mean, I don't know how, you know, you can come in now and take some [guy] and say, well, why did this guy say this when you don't—if you don't even have no idea why they're even talking about you, except in the context, like Salerno was doing. He read something in the newspaper about the party for him, and he talks about what he heard Steve Wynn say."

Under gaming control regulations, appearances count—embarrassing the state's largest industry can get an operator fined and even lead to removal of a casino license—yet law enforcement still had a serious problem: Anthony Salerno, their devil, was by then dead.

———

Gaming Control Board hearings such as the one involving Uncle Charlie and Steve Wynn raised troubling questions. Wynn's reaction was swift.

His attorneys harangued members of the Las Vegas press who had had the audacity to write unfavorable stories on the subject. He accused Sheriff Moran, considered by many to be second only to the governor as the most powerful political boss in the state, of dispatching the intelligence bureau on a personal vendetta against the Mirage family.

Why? Well, there was the problem of Moran's sons.

Las Vegas juice attorney John Moran, Jr., had gained and lost business with Wynn's company, and casino floorman Richard Moran had failed to win a coveted promotion in the Mirage.

Could the sheriff have been retaliating for Wynn's failure to support his sons?

The scenario was possible. Las Vegas casinos have a long tradition of featherbedding their staffs with the relatives of prominent politicians.

A summit meant to resolve the issue ended in a warning from the aging but powerful Moran.

"He said, 'Don't you go to war with Metro, Steve, or you'll lose,'" Wynn recalled.

———

Wynn and his Mirage bulldogs initially argued that Meyerson had no knowledge of Malangone's organized crime ties. The argument lacked logic.

Gambling under the name Al Rizzo, Malangone had been Meyerson's guest in Atlantic City. They clung to this story until it no longer suited them, then abandoned it in favor of the "so what?" defense. That is, "So what if Meyerson knew they were gangsters?" As long as he was merely performing his duty as a gracious host, he was not violating gaming regulation or inappropriately associating with them.

Meyerson's defense was bolstered by the appearance of several friendly witnesses, including former New York police organized crime authority Ralph Salerno, twenty-seven-year FBI veteran James Mulroy, and former New Jersey gaming regulator Mickey Brown.

Of the three, Ralph Salerno's testimony proved to be just short of spellbinding. His memory for names, dates, and scenes was impeccable, and he assured the control board that in all his years spent working the streets, Charlie Meyerson's name had come up only once in connection to the January 1961 arrest of mob bookie Miltie Wekar.

After two days of hearings and almost a year of political infighting between Steve Wynn's Mirage, Metro police, and the control board, Meyerson received his key employee license on April 15, 1993. The vote to give it to him was unanimous.

Wynn still wasn't satisfied with the affirmation from the Gaming Control Board and Nevada Gaming Commission. It was time to make Metro pay for daring to challenge him.

A day after the Nevada Gaming Commission voted to affirm the control board's recommendation, Wynn sued Sheriff Moran, intelligence bureau lieutenant Loren Stevens, Det. Dave Kallas, and the department collectively for damages related to Metro's "plan of malicious, vindictive, and retaliatory harassment."

Former strike force prosecutor Stan Hunterton, who had investigated insider-trading allegations against Wynn before joining his stable of personal attorneys, claimed clear evidence of Moran Jr. overbilling existed. If it was discovered that the bad press cost Mirage casino deals outside the state, Hunterton said the company would ask for "tens of millions" of dollars in compensation from the department.

The war was on, and the police were pressing on many fronts.

The long-rumored drug use of Kenny Wynn, Wynn's younger brother, became an issue after a December 1992 Las Vegas police raid on the homes of attorney Michael Mushkin and convicted drug dealer Harvey Sackin.

Mushkin, Kenny Wynn's friend and one of a gang of attorneys employed by Mirage Resorts, was arrested and later convicted of possessing a small amount of marijuana. Sackin, who was arrested for narcotics possession, trafficking, and conspiracy to distribute cocaine and marijuana, gave police a list of his clients. Investigators also discovered an envelope containing $1,200 that was inscribed with the name and address of Atlandia Design, a Mirage Resorts subsidiary, of which the younger Wynn was president.

The Mushkin-Sackin case prompted Kenny Wynn to admit having used marijuana and cocaine. He underwent voluntary drug treatment, took a leave of absence from the parent company, and eventually paid a fine for violating Nevada's gaming statutes before being reinstated. He was never charged in the criminal complaint against Sackin and the Mushkin.

Mirage attorneys suspected the police investigation, which included interviews with Kenny Wynn's estranged wife and an attempt to enlist his gardener as an informant, was motivated by Steve Wynn's feud with John Moran.

———

Mirage Resorts embarked on its own investigation of the sheriff and his intelligence gatherers, circulating a letter to Mirage employees requesting assistance in uncovering attempts by the police "to recruit people as informants during the last year."

The lawsuit cost hundreds of thousands of dollars to defend before it was resolved with carefully drawn letters of conciliation from both parties. Both parties in the strange political wrestling match had plenty to lose.

Although his gaming license in Nevada was secure, Wynn was fighting to obtain casino licenses from Connecticut to Australia. Moran, on the other hand, was in the twilight of his lengthy and successful police career.

After standing up to Wynn, Moran coughed up an apology: "On Feb. 9, 1993, a letter was sent over my signature to members of the Gaming Control Board concerning the Meyerson matter. In retrospect, I realize that letter questioned the integrity of the board and the regulatory process. That was not my intent. In fact, this department holds the board and regulatory process in high esteem.

"The board and the [Nevada Gaming] Commission, after an extensive investigation in which Metro took part, each concluded unanimously that Mr. Meyerson should be licensed and that there were no unsuitable connections between Meyerson, or anyone else at the Mirage, and organized crime. Metro and I are completely satisfied with these conclusions.

"I also recognize the need for review of police investigations by independent bodies. In the gaming area, the Gaming Control Board and the Nevada Gaming Commission provide this oversight."

Neither Loren Stevens nor Dave Kallas agreed to add their signatures to Moran's surrender.

Wynn was gracious.

"We are very gratified with the statement issued today by Sheriff Moran. The reasons that caused the deterioration of the Mirage's relationship with the sheriff and the Intelligence Services Bureau are no longer relevant and we have instructed counsel to dismiss the pending lawsuit."

The request for $10 million in damages to the corporation and all the claims and counterclaims were dropped.

"There are no unresolved grievances between the company and the sheriff or any member of his family," Wynn wrote. "The Mirage looks forward to continuing its long history of cooperation with Metro toward assuring the safety of its citizens of Las Vegas and our guests."

In whipping Moran, Steve Wynn had emerged as the preeminent strength in Nevada. He had illustrated a truth once more about his character: With his few close friends, he was fiercely protective; with his enemies, ferociously hostile.

As for Malangone, he was added to New Jersey's lengthy list of excluded persons in July 1993. To New Jersey regulators, he remained a mob guy whose presence in a casino would be an embarrassment to that industry.

In Las Vegas, however, wherever cards were dealt and dice were pitched, Malangone continued to openly gamble.

CHAPTER 13

IMAGE IS EVERYTHING

With the camera rolling, two images of Las Vegas fell into character and performed a bit of shtick. Its story might have been titled, "The Kid and Mr. Sinatra."

The Kid says he owns the joint, but he is clearly awed by the presence of the world's consummate nightclub entertainer.

"Hi, Mr. Sinatra," the kid says. "I'm Steve Wynn. I run this place."

"You see I get enough towels," Sinatra deadpans, handing the Kid a tip.

In another version, the legend pinches the Kid on the cheek. Such a good boy, Sinatra seems to be saying, and so precocious.

———

Commercial persona aside, Steve Wynn hasn't been an awestruck kid for a long time. By using his considerable gift of self-promotion, and perhaps his father's sense of style combined with his grandfather's vaudevillian heart, Wynn has emerged as the shrewdest marketing mind in the casino industry.

Wynn's carefully crafted image starts with a rigorous personal fitness regimen, including weightlifting, and his longstanding—and somewhat obsessive—love of outdoor activity, especially skiing. His broad-ranged athletic pursuits have included rock climbing, running marathons, wind surfing, and golf. Intense workouts and constant dieting help keep him looking more like a lifeguard than the chairman of a billion-dollar casino company.

"His closet is like a department store," Wynn's former professional companion Ron Tucky said. "Everything has its place.

"He's always got these mirrors. He can't pass a mirror without looking at himself. There's not a mirror in the world where this guy, if he knows a mirror's there, he's not going to look at himself. He's an unusual guy with his clothes. He's always, constantly making sure he's perfect. He can't pass a mirror."

Then there's the facelift. It still bewilders some of his longtime acquaintances.

"His facelift changed the shape of his face," one old friend recalled. "It just didn't look natural. He had handsome features, but when he returned from surgery, he didn't look the same. His face was as tight as a snare drum. It was weird. How old was he? Maybe forty-two, forty- three. It's not like he needed it. His face was so tight it looked like it hurt. But he grew into it."

———

Several years later, Wynn and Mirage Resorts executive Mark Schorr had liposuction treatments in New York. Tucky sat by as they snored after surgery, then escorted them back to their suites at the Waldorf Towers. Within minutes of leaving the hospital, the conversation turned from the surgical procedure to a New York-style snack: a pizza on Lexington Avenue.

"They get their stomachs pumped and then they go right out and get a frigging pizza," Tucky said, laughing. "From the surgeon scraping your belly to Mama Leone's. That's my boys."

Wynn's narcissism has not kept him from head-first participation in rugged outdoor sports. Downhill skiing has been a perennial favorite. Because of his poor eyesight and light sensitivity, Wynn, a highly accomplished and aggressive skier, skis with a guide.

On one trip to the family ski lodge at Sun Valley, Idaho, he overshot an expert run and plunged right over the edge of a cliff. He landed on a precipice, and rescuers thought he might be dead or, at the very least, a paraplegic. Once they reached him some sixty feet below the slope, they found him in surprisingly good shape. He was soon back racing again. The often-recounted ski anecdote has come to symbolize his personal style in politics and business.

Wynn has gone through periods of intense interest in activities as diverse as team roping (with former Clark County Sheriff Ralph Lamb), jet skiing, wind surfing, and, more recently, golf.

———

If Steve Wynn's interest in athletic activities has been somewhat eclectic over the years, his obsession with sexual conquests has remained constant. From the most beautiful women in Las Vegas to some downright homely hired help, Wynn's ever-changing circle of celebrity pals and sexual partners were witnessed by Ron Tucky. Over the years, Tucky went from the manager of the downtown Golden Nugget's valet parking to the general manager of the exclusive Shadow Creek golf course. Before quitting the company after a pay dispute in 1993, Tucky accompanied Wynn everywhere as his personal aide.

Tucky found his employer's relentless persuit of the next woman was nothing short of incredible.

"He's always up to something. At the dinner table, in the lounge, whatever," Tucky said. "He's always got something going. I would say 300 [women] a year. Oh, yeah. Boom. That's the over-under. I'd bet the over.... I've seen him go from room to room to room. And go from one to another to another. Three or four a day.

"I was amazed. When I was young and foolish that happened a couple times with me, and the third one I couldn't do any justice to. I was no good. But I said, 'Boy, this guy's something.'"

British journalist David Spanier wrote in *All Right, Okay, You Win* that Wynn "has the kind of magnetism and sexual energy which attract women, and a reputation for dalliance."

Wynn's personal 300 Club includes encounters with Diana Ross and Dolly Parton that are the stuff of legend around the hotel, but not all of his former boss's partners were cover-girl material.

"It doesn't matter if it's Lana Turner or Stomach Turner. When it comes to getting laid, he has no taste at all," Tucky said. "A beast, or a beauty."

Although not every woman fell for Wynn's sales pitch—he managed to alienate actress Sharon Stone during the Las Vegas filming of the Martin Scorsese movie *Casino*.

According to Tucky, Wynn would try to bed nearly every woman he met.

"He'd send [Elaine] home and kiss her goodbye in the casino at 11 o'clock and say, 'Oh, Ron will bring me home later.' And then as soon as she skidaddled out the door to valet, he says, 'Ron, give me this number over here. Go up to Room 1040,' then an hour later it's, 'Ron, let's go over here. I got one over here.' Then, at 2 o'clock, it's, 'Ron, run me home. Talk to you in the morning.'"

Another longtime Wynn associate put it less diplomatically: "A lot of these girls fall for it hook, line, and sinker. It becomes a glamorized form of prostitution down there. You want to keep your job, and you want to keep that needle in your arm that's providing you all that excitement. The rules of society and the rules of morality change once you get inside those gates. It starts right at the top when they see Wynn fucking keno runners and the wives of his friends and the wives of high rollers. As far as the moral code down there, there is none. It's pretty much survival of the fittest."

Although Tucky said he believed women were Wynn's drug of choice, and he had heard all the tales about his former boss's supposed drug use, he never saw him use cocaine.

"I saw him smoke marijuana with Willie Nelson, but that's it," Tucky said.

————

While toying with a handgun, a present from one-time Chicago mob hit man Charlie Baron, Wynn shot a hole in his image as an impeccable physical specimen when he blew off his left index finger. What a fellow whose eyesight is so poor he cannot drive a car was doing playing with a pistol is unclear.

Three hours of reconstructive surgery repaired the mangled digit, which was dangling by a strip of skin, and surgeons removed a 1 ¼-inch piece of bone from Wynn's hip to replace a pulverized knuckle.

Although wild tales of the true identity of the shooter circulated shortly after the 1991 incident, Wynn stuck to his story and even laughed about it later. "My golf swing is one of my biggest worries," he said.

————

His body image and physical feats aside, Wynn and his uncanny gifts for image-making are best illustrated by the Sinatra commercials that defined his casinos as a place apart while establishing his name and face in the minds of millions of viewers.

The scenes would enable potential customers to say, "Look at this, Marge. That handsome young casino owner is as impressed with Sinatra as we are. Why, he's just like you and me." By identifying a friendly face within the cold reality of a casino, customers were sure to be less intimidated by the prospect of entering a world about which most had only read stories.

The commercials were effective, but not merely because viewers remembered the name or smiled in all the right places. The Sinatra spots, and to some extent the advertisements with Dolly Parton, successfully punctured the public's image of the casino operator as a homely dees-and-dose guy with a fat belly, short cigar, long rap sheet, and a hopeless penchant for gold chains, checkered slacks, and white shoes.

In Wynn, the public saw no five o'clock shadow, no mumbling, used-car huckster delivery. He was too fresh faced to be a racketeer, too well dressed to be a dice pimp. He was a fine young man, almost the boy next door.

In those thirty second commercials, Steve Wynn did much to change the face of the American casino industry. And he accomplished the feat without an attorney, accountant, or gaming regulator. In one-half minute, he successfully melded a name and an image that had everything to do with entertainment and nothing to do with that mobbed-up Biblical vice, gambling. As an upscale marketing tool, the commercials were flawless.

"My colleagues and I looked at each other and we said, 'Why not? Who's going to stop us from snatching the business?'" Wynn told a *Newsweek* reporter.

"Suppose I could sell discriminating people on the idea of being involved in an atmosphere almost like a concert in the East Room of the White House. Like a private show with Frank Sinatra. Wouldn't that be fetching? And suppose, as part of the weekend, they could meet him. And we had special parties, and we did the whole weekend. And suppose the service in this hotel was so elegant we could build a special event around our entertainer, and I could take Frank, and Diana, and Kenny, and Willie, and they could be a gift for the weekend. Come for a special weekend—a theme party at the Nugget. That's not the same as the star policy. That's another dimension altogether."

At a $10 million fee for Sinatra plus juicy perquisites over a three-year contract, the commercials were cheap at twice the price.

In 1983, the company's Atlantic City profits rose to $39 million. At $13.79 per square foot, Golden Nugget earned twice as much as the Playboy Casino. Wynn was being heralded as the Lee Iacocca of the gaming industry.

Law enforcement authorities, who had observed Sinatra mingle with the most notorious mob figures in America for more than three decades, were intrigued by his relationship with the wunderkind of the casino industry. In an interview with FBI agents, former mob insider Joe Agosto gave his take on the Wynn-Sinatra connection:

"Agosto advised that 'Fat Tony' Salerno is very close to Frank Sinatra and that Salerno had advised Wynn to secure Sinatra's contract. Sinatra's hotel appearances are known to greatly increase the hotel's revenue. As a result of gaining the Sinatra contract Wynn now owes allegiance to Salerno. Agosto stated that Wynn is in a position to actually have a face-to-face 'sit down' with Salerno but as a practicality would receive instructions through Julie Weintraub and Charlie Meyerson, both of whom are junketeers and known associates of Salerno's. Agosto further stated that in further payment to Salerno, Wynn will be required to place additional associates of Salerno's in key positions at both Golden Nuggets."

The commercials were developed by Lester Colodny and John Schadler through Wynn's in-house advertising agency, T.Y.O.H. (Toot Your Own Horn).

"The use of [Steve Wynn] as a marketing tool and an entertainer were all intentional," Colodny said. "It did not happen that once he came with us we decided that he would be in our commercials. It was a total package."

During the filming of the commercials, Colodny noticed something about his boss. Although it bordered on shameless fawning, Colodny was adamant about Wynn's ability to quickly affect a character and make it work on camera. "You've never seen a man hit the mark the way he does. Never. You'd think he's been doing it for twenty-five years."

That toothy, aw-shucks grin aside, the Kid understood the art of image making as well as any executive on Madison Avenue. He understood the power of Sinatra's name with commoners and high rollers alike. He also knew the object of the game hadn't changed since his father's day: Separate the player from his bankroll, and don't forget to smile.

"Everybody who has ever been in the middle has gone down the toilet," Wynn said. "When I say you have to have a definite identity, you've got to do it completely. The Flamingo Hilton has a definite identity. It doesn't have the world's greatest food. It doesn't have the most wonderful hotel rooms. It doesn't depend on a very exotic, highly trained, and cunning staff of people who know how to handle special kinds of customers. They deal with the average. Average prices, average people, and they've got a good slot program. Circus Circus is the same kind of thing down the scale.

"The Golden Nugget is something else. It's a place that's blatantly elitist. We don't have a sign. No neon. Not exactly subdued, but understated. And it's got the best rooms, the best food, and a highly trained, very personalized staff that's paid to deal with people one on one. It's a place for anybody who enjoys the environment, but it's not priced as a bargain. And it's a machine that has a tremendous amount of energy and costs to operate."

For example, any casino could supply limousine service; Wynn would taxi big players from New York to Atlantic City in plush helicopters, including a Sikorsky S-76 and, later, a Dauphin 2 and a Super Puma Aerospeciale. If Golden Nugget gamblers eventually were bound for the poorhouse, they would travel there in style.

In 1983, the Golden Nugget Atlantic City outcomped the competition, issuing $10.2 million in goods and services—$3 million more than Resorts International, and $7 million more than Harrah's.

Although more than one magazine writer lauded Wynn for his innovative brilliance, the use of celebrities as a casino-marketing tool was hardly a new concept.

Stars and starlets had shilled for casinos since the end of World War II. Ben Siegel, as dapper as he was maniacal, fancied himself as potential Hollywood material when he ventured west to Los Angeles in 1941 on behalf of Lucky Luciano, Meyer Lansky, and their syndicate partners. Although he made a name for himself as the man who built the Flamingo, the first flashy Las Vegas carpet joint, Siegel understood the intoxicating power Hollywood held over players. Wherever Hollywood's elite made an appearance, throngs of fans were sure to follow.

Years later at the Desert Inn, Moe Dalitz developed an exclusive high-stakes professional golf event known as the Tournament of Champions. Golfers are notoriously good gamblers, and Dalitz envisioned Las Vegas as a country club oasis. (Wynn would later recraft that idea and, with unprecedented opulence, develop the $48 million Shadow Creek golf course.) Anyone can deal cards and pitch dice. In an increasingly competitive environment, the whole idea was to give high rollers a touch more dazzle for their dollar.

"'Look, Mr. Casino Operator. You've got the best of this deal,'" Wynn would tell an interviewer in 1984. "'I know it, and you know it, and I accept the terms of that unequal contract, because it suits me. But I expect more from you than I do from a Hilton or a Marriott or some other place where I am just spending an evening because of business. I expect to have my peculiarities catered to, I expect to be overindulged. I am demanding and petulant if I don't get what I want, because I think I have it coming.'"

No person defines the Las Vegas soul in every gambler better than Sinatra. And for a while, the Kid and Mr. Sinatra made ideal pitchmen.

But, as Sinatra has illustrated throughout his career, there is a difference between image and stark reality.

By heaping money, stock, and creature comforts on Sinatra, Wynn was able to present to the world the handsome and glib good Frank. By giving him the run of the Golden Nugget, he also set the stage for the appearance of the mean and loutish bad Frank to appear.

As he had many times during his stormy career in Las Vegas, Sinatra took full advantage and gradually became a classless, mob-friendly bully only too willing to create a scene and threaten the hired help.

———

Sinatra's first encounter with Nevada gaming authorities came in 1963 after the singer was caught catering to Chicago mob boss Sam "Momo" Giancana at the Cal-Neva Lodge on the shores of Lake Tahoe.

Giancana was staying in Chalet No. 50 with his girlfriend, singer Phyllis McGuire, when authorities found him. Sinatra was the principal owner of the North Shore casino and lost his gaming license over the incident, but not before threatening the career of Gaming Control Board Chairman Ed Olsen in phone calls using "vile, intemperate, obscene, and indecent language in an attempt to intimidate and coerce" the state's top casino regulator. Sinatra's friend, Paul "Skinny" D'Amato, allegedly tried to halt the probe by bribing two control board agents, and Sinatra instructed a Cal-Neva casino executive to leave the state to evade a control board subpoena—which wasn't too difficult since the lodge straddled the border, with the hotel side in California and the casino in Nevada.

Headlining at the Sands in 1967, Sinatra ran up $500,000 in debts in the casino and then disappeared over the Labor Day weekend. He reappeared days later accompanied by his teenage bride, Mia Farrow.

But, in his absence, his personal playground had changed. Casino Manager Carl Cohen, who had endured wiseguys most of his life in the gambling racket, cut off Sinatra's credit and damaged the singer's fragile ego.

"I built this hotel from a sand pile, and before I'm through, that is what it will be again," Sinatra announced, failing to mention that he already had reached a performance agreement down the street at Caesars Palace. But that didn't stop him from trashing the hotel, breaking windows, smashing furniture, and threatening employees.

Then he went too far. He entered the Garden Room restaurant and assaulted Cohen with a table.

Cohen, the veteran casino man, responded with one punch, knocking the bobby sox idol's two front caps out. "As far as I'm concerned Carl Cohen is a national hero," a Sands bellman said. "Why should Sinatra be allowed to act like a wild animal?"

———

It was on to Caesars Palace for Sinatra and his throng of loyal fans.

Sinatra and his neighbor, real estate broker Danny Schwartz, had won and collected $2 million from Caesars' baccarat table.

Now, weeks later, Sinatra, doing a solo, was losing it back playing $8,000 a hand. He owed $400,000. He had a handful of whites ($500 chips) but called for another $25,000 anyway. The dealers were under orders: no more chips for Mr. Sinatra.

Never very kind to casino employees, Sinatra's abuse grew as his rage grew.

The pit boss summoned help. Caesars Executive Vice President Sandy Waterman appeared on the scene.

"Frank," he said, "you and Danny won $2 million. You took it with you. Now you owe us. The boys want their money."

Sinatra stood up. He flung his white chips into Waterman's face, at the same time smacking him on the forehead with the palm of his hand.

Waterman turned and ran to his suite. He returned minutes later with a loaded pistol which he pointed at Sinatra.

"Listen you! If you ever lay a hand on me again, I'll put a bullet through your head." Sanford Waterman, ordinarily an iceberg, had lost his cool.

Sinatra didn't lose his. "Aw come off it," he said with a disparaging gesture. "That gun stuff went out with Humphrey Bogart."

Disconcerted by Sinatra's nonchalant response, Waterman's arm lowered just long enough for a Sinatra gofer to strike it. The pistol fell to the floor.

Waterman knew he was in trouble. He turned and ran to the cashier cage, with Sinatra and his wolf pack in hot pursuit.

Sinatra's left arm was in a sling, as the result of some vein surgery.

The cashier door swung open. Waterman tried to close it behind him, but Sinatra clung to it. It smashed back against his left arm and suddenly blood spurted out. Everyone stood appalled, and the drama was over.

Sinatra hurried to his third floor suite, and a gofer went to fetch the house doctor.

It was typical Sinatra stuff. Francis Sinatra may have been the idol of an aging generation of women, but he was no hero to casino dealers. They knew him as noisy and rude. They feared him because they knew he made constant demands that couldn't be met and then insulted them with vile language, often threatening them about their jobs.

Sinatra and Steve Wynn made a great pair.

In typical fashion, Sinatra ran away and sulked, this time in Palm Springs, where he announced he was retiring from show business. Muhammad Ali didn't retire as often as Ol' Blue Eyes.

Sinatra soon canceled his retirement and returned to Caesars. This time, barrel-chested private security guards were members of his entourage. He was 0-2 against casino bosses and obviously planned to let others do his fighting for him.

But it was a wiser Sinatra who returned to Las Vegas in 1974. He became involved in politics, supporting Roy Woofter's successful run for district attorney. He also contributed his time and talent to raising more than $1 million for athletic scholarships at UNLV.

By the time 1980 rolled around, Sinatra's Las Vegas legend had reached mammoth proportions. Given its notorious nature, more than a few people were surprised when he applied with the Gaming Control Board for licensure as a key employee at Caesars Palace. The role he sought may sound familiar: special promotions and entertainment policy consultation. In short, a high-profile magnet to attract high rollers. Sinatra eventually received approval from the Nevada Gaming Commission.

His violent past had been forgiven.

———

But no one should have been surprised by Sinatra's boorish wiseguy act on the evening of December 1, 1983, at the Atlantic City Golden Nugget.

Sinatra, his wife Barbara, and Dean Martin came swaying onto the casino floor of the Golden Nugget, looking for trouble. They approached blackjack dealer Korean-born Kyong Kim and demanded she deal from a single deck of cards. New Jersey casino regulations mandate that all card games be dealt from a six-deck shoe. She either could break the state's strict gaming regulations, and face severe sanctions, or disappoint her famous customer and face his wrath. When she attempted to explain her predicament, the boozy Sinatra snarled, "You don't want to play one deck, you go back to China."

Sinatra got louder, and in the end, the four-person floor crew relented.

A ranting singing legend attracts attention in any casino, and the incident was quickly noted by the Division of Gaming Enforcement. The workers were suspended without pay, and the Golden Nugget was fined $25,000.

New Jersey Casino Control Commissioner Joel Jacobson lit into Sinatra, calling him an "obnoxious bully" for intimidating the dealer and casino floor personnel. Sinatra responded by calling Jacobson a headline-grabbing "parasite," canceling his remaining New Jersey engagements and vowing never to return to Atlantic City. Sinatra's attorney said the singer would not allow New Jersey officials to use him as a "punching bag."

Steve Wynn's marketing coup was turning to mud before his eyes.

———

Ever mindful of protecting his investment, Wynn rushed to Sinatra's side and attacked the media for blowing the incident out of proportion. Although Sinatra and Martin had set foot in Atlantic City casinos before, and could see the dealers using card shoes at every table, Wynn said Sinatra and Martin were unaware of the rules. "They told me that if they had known it was against the law, they wouldn't have done it," Wynn said.

In fact, he said, he met with Sinatra and Martin backstage after their show and asked them about the incident. Wynn told the Casino Control Commission during a September 1984 licensing hearing that the two men were "obviously stunned. Frank spoke up and said, 'I had no idea it was illegal. I've never played any other way in my life. If I had been told, I would have never done it, Steve.' And Martin added, 'It's unbelievable that no one warned us about the law.'"

Equally stunned was commission spokesman Thomas Flynn, who said there was no mention of Wynn's backstage meeting in the official report on the incident or any of the previous testimony. Jacobson again clarified his position on the Sinatra blackjack affair. He told Wynn that the incident, "as each of your employees testified, under oath, with each corroborating the testimony of the others, was Mr. Sinatra's volatile temper and his intimidating, abusive behavior."

Although Sinatra's portfolio as a street-corner bully preceded him, Wynn chose to chastise the media for distorting the incident. Ironically, it was one distinguished member of the media—Doonesbury creator Garry Trudeau—whose week-long lampooning of Sinatra's blackjack incident and his alleged mob associations drove Jacobson to issue a public response: "One post-midnight confrontation on a casino floor should result neither in the execution of a self-imposed exile nor the infliction of a permanent life-time scar."

Less than a year had passed, and Sinatra graciously announced he would return to Atlantic City and thanked Jacobson profusely, not once calling him a parasite: "I cannot help but admire Commissioner Jacobson's forthrightness and want to thank him for having the courage to come forth and put things in their proper perspective. I agree with him it is time to place an unfortunate incident behind us and that it is time for me to return and perform in New Jersey."

Sinatra returned to the Boardwalk.

He managed to keep his front teeth, too.

———

In the new Las Vegas, almost without exception, high play means baccarat. Card for card, baccarat easily ranks as the big money game of chance. At casinos such as the Mirage and Caesars Palace, the bottom line rises and falls on the house's success against high rollers, or "whales" as they are called, in the baccarat pit.

The object of baccarat, or chemin de fer as a French variation of the game is called, is to obtain nine points. Aces count as one point, tens and face cards as zero. A player may bet either with or against the bank, a decision any child can make.

Although baccarat carries with it a mysterious aura—it is, after all, the game of choice of millionaires and James Bond—it is not terribly complex. In baccarat, the house enjoys approximately a 1½ percent advantage.

But pile a fortune in chips on the table and baccarat suddenly becomes a mind game riddled with intrigue and suspense. With millions moving back and forth across the felt table in a single evening and some high rollers remaining at the table for days at a time—and even taking their meals while cards are being shuffled for a new shoe—baccarat is pure adrenaline.

Few can afford the high.

Wynn told a *Forbes* reporter in 1987: "The stories you hear about people losing $2 million, or $4 million, in a weekend, are mostly about Chinese, sometimes Arabs. There's a large group of Orientals from Thailand, Hong Kong, and Japan—maybe a few hundred in that universe—and probably several hundred Mexicans and South Americans. That whole family of foreign players amounts to maybe 1,000. That's 1,000 people known by first and second name at a few high-end casinos. Last week one of them won a million and a half at the Golden Nugget in Las Vegas. He could come back and lose $2 million in a week.

"[High rollers] don't play to make money. They just love to shoot dice. Or play baccarat. It's fun. You should watch those Chinese guys at baccarat. They're all yelling and screaming in Cantonese. They play peek-a-boo with the cards. Why not just turn the damn cards over right away and count them up and see who wins? No—they're having fun. To such a person winning money is good news, but not because he can go out and buy the wife a Rolls-Royce Corniche convertible or a new yacht. Winning is good because now he can play some more with our money. It's inventory."

Of course, barring a one-in-a-million run of luck, the player's inventory usually ends up in the casino vault.

It was a lesson Akio Kashiwagi, nicknamed the Warrior for his aggressive playing style, learned the hard way. Known as a real-estate speculator, Kashiwagi was actually a Tokyo loan shark operating under the broad umbrella of the Yakuza, or Japanese Mafia.

Betting up to $14 million per hour and playing for days at a time, Kashiwagi won and lost incredible sums as a preferred customer at Trump Plaza and the Sands in Atlantic City. He was a privileged player at Caesars Palace, the Hilton, the Dunes, and the Mirage in Las Vegas. He was known from Australia to Stanley Ho's casinos in Macao before he exhausted his bank account, casino credit, and life's options. Kashiwagi broke the bank at the Diamond Beach Casino at Darwin, Australia, collecting $19 million along the way.

When Kashiwagi's luck was good, it was very good. When it went bad, it couldn't have been worse. After losing his money, credit and high roller status, Kashiwagi flew back to Tokyo, where he faced far larger problems. A sarakin moneylender by trade, he also was millions in debt to his Yakuza associates.

Shortly after the New Year in 1992, the Warrior returned to the Kashiwagi Palace near the base of Mount Fuji. It was there his family and police found him, lying on the floor of the kitchen in a pond of his own blood. He had been hacked to death by a samurai sword, his face chopped to a pulp.

It was an object lesson, the Yakuza way, for those who don't pay their debts.

Less dramatic and certainly less bloody was the legend of Ken Mizuno, whose baccarat adventures surpassed even those of the Warrior.

Like Kashiwagi and other Pacific Rim high rollers, Mizuno had a history of Asian organized crime association. Like Kashiwagi, Mizuno was known to move millions of dollars to the United States in part for investment, in part to chase the baccarat dragon.

Mizuno's link to the Yakuza surfaced in Las Vegas in the early 1980s when he attempted to open a gourmet Japanese restaurant, and later a health spa, in the Tropicana Hotel, and as a matter of course needed to apply and be approved for a liquor license.

Investigators searching his background soon began finding traces of the Japanese mob: Mizuno's business associates were friendly with the Yakuza; a member of his restaurant staff catered to a Tokyo crime figure.

The Clark County Commission, which decides who is awarded liquor licenses in Southern Nevada, initially rejected his application for the Mizuno's Teppan Dining gourmet restaurant at the Tropicana. A few weeks later, in a truly Vegas twist, the matter was revisited and Mizuno's application was unanimously approved. Perhaps by coincidence, two of the commissioners who voted in the affirmative were later convicted of accepting bribes.

Mizuno was a hail-fellow-well-met who smiled at the hired help and tipped generously. He was catered to by his personal casino hostess, and he had a locker next to Wynn's at the Mirage chairman's personal golf wonderland, Shadow Creek.

In 1992, Japanese and American law enforcement authorities verified what Las Vegas cops had long suspected: Ken Mizuno's high-rolling lifestyle had its roots in criminal activity.

Mizuno's company sold 52,000 memberships at up to $54,000 apiece for his Ibaraki Prefecture golf course northeast of Tokyo. The memberships were worth $853 million. But the country club was touted as an exclusive course, with Mizuno's Sanki Company promising to sell no more than 2,800 memberships. When more than 4,000 disgruntled members filed suit against Mizuno's 18-hole pyramid scheme, his days as a high roller were all but over.

Las Vegas casino bosses greeted Mizuno's demise with a sincere lament over the lost business. "I hope he gets off. He's good for the town," one local casino owner sighed.

He had good reason to hope: Mizuno alone is said to have lost more than $150 million in Las Vegas and dropped upwards of $75 million in two years just at the Mirage. (By comparison, in 1988 billionaire Kirk Kerkorian purchased the Desert Inn and the Sands hotels for $167 million.)

In the Mirage's first two years in operation, baccarat produced up to 17 percent of its total revenue, with Mizuno and other Asian whales accounting for most of those profits. When Mizuno stopped playing, the Mirage was shaken to its foundation.

From 1991 to 1992, baccarat winnings dropped 24 percent in Las Vegas. In need of greater penetration in the Asian market, Wynn acquired the knowledge the Las Vegas way; he pirated the Desert Inn's Orient gambling experts. The Desert Inn had grown fat by catering to octogenarian Hung Mun triad boss Yip Hon, once the casino king of Macao. Yip was soon seen playing baccarat with both fists at the Mirage.

"A worldwide recession and other factors, particularly in Japan, contributed to a sharp drop in The Mirage's baccarat activity in 1992," the company's 1993 SEC Form 10-K stated. "This was the primary reason for the 24 percent decline in the facility's 1992 operating income, when baccarat accounted for only 9 percent of gross revenues."

But the losses alarmed industry analysts. USA Capital's Tom Hantges asked: "If the flagship on the Las Vegas Strip performs at a loss like this, what message does it send to the construction industry?"

"We've always had an aggressive pursuit of the Asian customers and that has not changed," Mirage spokesman Alan Feldman said after Mizuno's fall. "The high rollers still come primarily from the Far East. There is no need to go through a knee-jerk change in your whole marketing scheme because of a drop in baccarat play. You don't panic. It may just be a slight lull."

For Mizuno, convicted of money-laundering charges in Japan and the United States, the lull in the action could last for decades.

━━━━━━

As the nineties unfolded, Steve Wynn faced something of a conundrum in the family-friendly new Las Vegas.

His wildly successful Mirage had emerged as the symbol of the recession-proof modern Strip, and the construction of his resort was credited with forcing the unprecedented building boom that made Southern Nevada the fastest growing community in the nation.

But, despite the Mirage's success, Wynn found himself being upstaged in a theater of his own creation.

Las Vegas had relied on weekend gamblers from Southern California since the days of Ben Siegel. As air travel improved in the years after World War II, markets in the Midwest and East opened. The ease of travel and increases in meeting space helped Las Vegas become an international convention center. Add to that the ability of a few casinos to cater to the wealthiest players on the planet, and you have a marketing synopsis of Las Vegas gaming.

The family market was all that remained unexploited. Fewer than 7 percent of parents traveling with children came to Las Vegas. But market studies showed that plenty of families were traveling to Orlando's Disney World, Anaheim's Disneyland, and other wholesome theme parks.

And so Las Vegas announced it was going Daffy, Donald, Pluto, and especially Mickey.

First, Kirk Kerkorian unveiled plans for a 5,000-room megaresort complete with a thirty-three-acre theme park on the Strip at the northeast corner of Tropicana Avenue. Betty Boop,

Popeye, and characters from the Wizard of Oz would stroll the grounds and greet the city's newest favorite customers.

Excalibur, a 4,000-room cartoon castle celebrating the Arthurian legend Vegas-style, already stood catty-corner from Kerkorian's big lion.

Circus Circus, which built Excalibur and pioneered the family market in Las Vegas by combining a casino with a carnival midway, also was planning Luxor, a thirty-six-story smoke-glass pyramid casino with the appropriate Egyptian theme, not far from Excalibur.

The action on the Strip, which for so long had been centered near the four corners on Flamingo Road and Las Vegas Boulevard, threatened to move south a mile. Smaller casinos would feature movie theaters, ice rinks, bowling centers, and high-tech arcades.

Steve Wynn's breathless answer to this competition was the announcement of Treasure Island, the Adventure Resort. Wynn stood before a crowd of reporters wearing a pirate's hat, appearing for all the world like an overgrown kid from a Long John Silver's fish and chips restaurant. A Jolly Roger was unfurled, and Wynn went on to explain the virtues of Las Vegas as a Disney-like center for the world's vacationing families. His announcement came days after Kerkorian's and days before the Luxor was unveiled.

"We believe there is more to be done in this market," Wynn told a group of reporters assembled for the Treasure Island announcement.

Markets change, styles change, and so Steve Wynn changed hats. The message was clear in interview after interview: Bring the family. The Las Vegas Convention and Visitors Authority, which spends millions each year extolling the virtues of the city as a place to play, quickly emerged with family-friendly advertising targeted toward the city's essential California market.

No show girls, no smoky slot houses. In thirty seconds, children are depicted splashing in a pool quickly followed by the whole family enjoying a delicious, and surely nutritious, buffet.

"Where else can you afford this much fun?" a friendly voice asks. "Only in Las Vegas."

And only in Las Vegas could a fellow be lauded for his original thinking after so brazenly lifting Disney's Pirates-of-the-Caribbean theme and combining it with a Robert Louis Stevenson story line. But that is precisely what Wynn did, and with substantial success. It helped to have Montreal's famous Cirque du Soleil new-age circus troupe to anchor the resort's family entertainment policy.

"It's not our natural market," Cirque Vice-president Jean David said. "But we came here to help the city change its image."

In exchange for that assistance, Cirque would receive $15 million to perform in Las Vegas year round. To make Cirque's performers more comfortable, Wynn constructed a $20-million theater for the troupe at Treasure Island.

When it came to the stage, illusionists Siegfried and Roy were Wynn's big cats in residence. In the Treasure Island's Siegfried and Roy Plaza stands a gargantuan bust of the two magicians, who also are roommates. The inscription reads, "Siegfried & Roy: Pioneers of Family Entertainment." Perhaps. But, at $70 a ticket, it had better be an upper-middle-class family.

Which set operators who had touted Las Vegas as Disneyland in the desert as hopelessly avaricious hypocrites willing to exploit children for gain. "Give a gambler a good excuse. They'll thank you for it," Benny Binion told Steve Wynn years earlier. By marketing a kinder, gentler Las Vegas, one in which parents ought not to feel uncomfortable about bringing their children on vacation, casino bosses were attempting to give mom and dad a guilt-free excuse to play.

Which made the TV infomercial, "Treasure Island: The Adventure Begins" all the more cynical. Viewers saw plenty of beautiful lights, exploding volcanos, battling buccaneers, and playfully intelligent dolphins, but not once did they catch a glimpse of anything resembling a casino. It recalled Wynn's short-lived ballet, "The Las Vegas Suite," in which the history of the town and its gangster-and-gambler history was depicted in playful terms.

In "Treasure Island," the child accompanying mother and father on a convention is constantly left unsupervised. All the better to fend off pirates, to be sure, but the message is clear: Las Vegas is a safe place for kids to run free while the parents enjoy a little "gaming." Mirage Resorts paid NBC $1.7 million for a one-hour block of time. Coca-Cola pitched in seven figures more for the rights to show commercials between the greater commercial. There was no disclaimer at the outset of the program telling viewers that they were watching an infomercial and not a standard program.

"Gambling" was not once mentioned during the one-hour advertisement for Steve Wynn's world. "Gaming" was uttered only once: "Let's go downstairs and try some gaming. Will you be all right, honey?" mom asks Robby, the preteen protagonist played by Corey Carrier.

Sure he will. He has a friendly pirate on his side, and if all else fails there's always a family of friendly dolphins and Treasure Island's in-house benevolent uncle, Steve Wynn.

"To me, it's more than a hotel," Wynn tells little Robby. "It's a gateway between fantasy and reality."

Nationally syndicated television critic Tom Shales wasted little time in slamming the gate and blasting Wynn's made-for-TV Jolly Roger out of the water.

"It still pays to read the fine print," Shales wrote. "There, tucked among the closing credits of a recent NBC special was the naughty little secret: '"Treasure Island: The Adventure Begins" has been sponsored by Treasure Island Productions, Inc.'"

The Treasure Island that emerged was wedged onto the Mirage parking lot but had no man-made volcano. Its hook is those two ninety-foot ships that do battle every ninety minutes in Mutiny Bay with the pirates eventually prevailing over the British.

"My hero was Disney," Wynn told a *Boston Globe* reporter. "I would be just as happy building theme parks as casinos, but it's been done already....The only reason I like gambling is that it gives me the ability to do what I really love. I love to create environments."

But the problem with the city's family marketing theme was plain: resort operators want parents to bring their children, but the dark, seductive heart of Las Vegas has not changed.

Behind the expansive arcades, motion rides, and a mediocre theme park—and no matter how seductive or homely the commercial image—the city remains an adult playground.

"Gamblers don't like to trip over kids in a casino," Wynn said, aptly summing up the image-versus-reality dilemma of Las Vegas. "...We are spending a little extra money to make our resorts friendly for people of all ages because these days children travel with their parents. But we're not specifically pitching anything to people under twenty-one.

"This is a place for big kids."

CHAPTER 14

A SHADOW OVER SHADOW CREEK

In Las Vegas, with its Dalí-meets-Disney architecture and infinitely hedonistic diversions, Shadow Creek Golf Course embodies the ultimate conceit: a golf course so exclusive it has a membership of one. This verdant mirage sits on 320 acres, carved into the desert like an emerald river north of downtown Las Vegas. Total cost: in excess of $48 million.

The land was purchased for less than $3 million, a relative pittance compared to what the more than 20,000 mature pine trees alone cost. Wynn not only imported the pine trees, he imported the fallen pine needles as well in order to make the course appear mature. The fairways are wide. The greens are large. The wildlife—including wallabies and pygmy deer—and waterfalls are numerous. Tee markers are not the standard oversized blue, yellow, or white balls. They are made of appropriately colored violets. Half the holes feature water hazards dyed a blue found somewhere between Technicolor and Tidee Bowl on the spectrum.

Members for a day need not fret over misplaced clothing or clubs; if necessary, Shadow Creek staff will provide clubs, balls, and shoes—everything but par. Even the driving range balls are Titleists fresh from the package.

Desert conservationists lament Shadow Creek's obscene use of well water—millions of gallons a year to keep green an artificial paradise available to only a few wealthy casino patrons, token Mirage and Golden Nugget employees, and the designated Friends of Steve (a thoroughly transitory status for many).

Wynn's personal shell corporation not only owns the 320 acres Shadow Creek is sculpted on, but he also controls the well that pumps a seemingly unlimited supply of water to his 18-hole Utopia. If might makes right, and Wynn's lawyers generally make that a certainty, then he has nothing to fear from either grousing stockholders or marauding environmentalists.

"No one ever spent this kind of money on this kind of project here; it's going to be famous," Wynn said during the unveiling of the plans for Shadow Creek. "We're not simply cutting a golf course out in the desert, we are going to reshape the terrain."

Critics call Shadow Creek Wynn's perverse abuse of his responsibility to Mirage Resorts stockholders. In fact, Wynn has scolded stockholders who have dared to ask whether they, too, might take a turn on its manicured fairways and satin greens—and get the chance to gawk at the movie stars and professional athletes who frequent the Shadow. Despite his degenerative retinitis pigmentosa, the boss loves golf and has positioned himself as the precious Lord of the Links. Mere investors are unlikely ever to idyll with their idols at Steve Wynn's wonderland.

———

Perhaps only Steve Wynn could own a golf course that qualifies as truly controversial. Conservation concerns aside, Shadow Creek may be the most fretted-over 18 holes in all of America's country club subculture.

"Some, upon hearing these tales of what is either a true dedication to the course-building art or one of the most amazing examples of wretched excess in the history of man, might recall poor Donald Ross having to build a masterpiece like Pinehurst No. 2 in North Carolina with a team of donkeys and a dozen laborers with shovels," James Y. Bartlett wrote in *Forbes*.

"It's the greatest golf course you'll (probably) never play," Michael Konik wrote in *Cigar Aficionado*.

Crossing the gates at Shadow Creek has been likened to entering the Land of Oz. "Everything goes from black and white to Technicolor," one breathless Shadow Creek patron told Konik. "It feels as though you've wandered into some sort of bird sanctuary. There are thousands of them: quail, pheasants, flamingos, chukars, and snow-white swans. They have a wallaby, too. The place really is like a mirage."

Another awed duffer told *Forbes*, "This is the kind of golf course God would design."

"...what Wynn lacks in vision, he makes up for tenfold with ego," Mark Ebner wrote in *Spy* magazine. "In addition to his current favorite sport—blowing up the Dunes Hotel—he is an avid golfer. Of course, it's more fun when you actually build your own golf course, as Wynn did.

"'If Frederick the Great was a golfer, this course would be his,' one travel writer wrote. And Shadow Creek, as it is known, is the despot Wynn's and Wynn's alone. He is the only member, and it's said that he calls it his 'fuck you' golf course.... Shadow Creek may be played only by Wynn's personally invited friends. The fact that there's rarely anyone playing at this top-ranked course may tell us something about Wynn's popularity."

Wynn conceived his personal golf course after being rejected for membership in California's exclusive Vintage Country Club where he had purchased the option on a residence contingent on membership approval. Deemed an inappropriate candidate for membership, he returned to Las Vegas and devised the ultimate payback.

If he lacked the right stuff for that stuffy country club, then he would design and build a course so exclusive that he would be the only member.

And thus Shadow Creek was born.

━━━━━━━━

Shadow Creek was designed with mystery in mind, and Wynn and his staff have seen to it that intrigue surrounds the heavily guarded course.

Tall fences, surveillance cameras, and security personnel separate the invited guests from potential interlopers. Workers are instructed not to talk about either what Shadow Creek looks like or what goes on inside the imposing cyclone fence.

Its guests range from actors Kevin Costner and Joe Pesci to NBA all-stars Michael Jordan and Larry Bird. In fact, Jordan is among a select few Friends of Steve to enjoy a year-round private locker. There is no word on whether Jordan, whose golf gambling losses became a national sports story, has lost any of his millions at Shadow Creek.

Another guest was avid golfer and multimillionaire Asian high roller Ken Mizuno, whose club status became moot after his indictment on tax evasion, fraud, and money-laundering charges in Japan and the United States.

Golfing is limited to a handful of players per day ferried to the course by limousines. With seventy employees at Shadow Creek, including nearly fifty gardeners and maintenance workers, there never are more players than staff. On an average day, as few as four foursomes tee off.

Wynn and course designer Tom Fazio had accomplished what they set out to do: create 18 holes of mystery in a world covered with green places to hit a little ball with a stick. From the moment it opened, Shadow Creek became a 320-acre marketing tool capable of attracting millionaire golf addicts from across the sea.

There are no greens fees. There is no tipping or bribing the starter, caddy, or waiter who will be only too happy to serve you caviar on the course. Players must carry a minimum $100,000 credit line and still must be approved by either Mirage President Bobby Baldwin or Wynn himself.

A stock color photograph of the reclusive golf course is all curious news organizations receive from the Mirage. Players' scorecards feature neither a picture nor sketch of the course. Better to keep the secret of the 7,158-yard layout.

Shadow Creek also exists for a political purpose.

When Wynn became enraged by the Clinton administration's policy making and federal attempts to tax gaming in 1994, he held a breakfast fund-raiser there on behalf of the Republican National Committee and its chairman, Haley Barbour, which raised $540,000—$230,000 from the Golden Nugget.

When Wynn was attempting to woo Connecticut legislators into legalizing gambling, they were treated to a tour of Shadow Creek. The message was clear: Anyone capable of dreaming up a Disneyesque diversion the scale of Shadow Creek surely qualified as something more than a casino owner. On the way to enjoying the park, they were exposed to the marketing expertise of Mirage Resorts. Shadow Creek insider Jerry Weintraub, producer of *The Karate Kid* and a quiet force in the Republican Party through his intimate friendship with former President George Bush, has also strolled the fairways at Steve Wynn's private golf course.

———

After being rated the best new course in the country in 1990, Shadow Creek was ranked the eighth-best course in America in 1994 by *Golf Digest*. The ranking quickly emerged as a point of contention with country club presidents from Pinehurst to Pebble Beach.

Many of the highly well-bred, some would say inbred, leaders of the American country club fraternity were apoplectic at the ranking, which is best on a list of six criteria—shot values, resistance to scoring to scratch players, design balance, memorability, esthetics, and conditioning. A one-to-ten scale is used. The judges are selected by the magazine's editors, which also adjust totals for courses strong on tradition.

"I do not care to have our course involved in a poll that is as easily swayed by elements that have absolutely nothing to do with either the greatness nor the integrity of the course itself," Jack Lupton, chairman of the Honors Course in Chattanooga, wrote *Golf Digest* Editor Jerry Tarde in a letter requesting the Tennessee country club's name be withdrawn from the rankings.

"[I have] first-hand knowledge of Steve Wynn's largesse/generosity heaped upon visiting 'dignitaries' from the golf world....free rooms; free local transportation; no greens fees; meals; balls; even a pocketful of gaming chips," Seminole Golf Club president Barend Van Gerbig sniped in the magazine.

Wynn's response was to offer no response at all. In a *Forbes* article, course designer Fazio pleaded his friend Steve's case. "I told him it wouldn't be fair *not* to have it ranked." What Fazio may not have known was the fact Wynn announced years earlier his intention to make Shadow Creek one of the top courses in the nation.

"It's a one of a kind," Shadow Creek's original General Manager Ron Tucky said.

Tucky, Wynn's former aide-de-camp who has played most of the nation's best courses, would not go so far as to rank it number eight. "That won't be done again. It's wild. It's just beyond golf. I know plenty of people who could afford to build it. But they just don't have the balls. The whole thing is unbelievable."

A scratch golfer who also has played the best courses in America disagreed about Shadow Creek's status.

"Steve can enter a world he knows nothing about and buy his way into the *Golf Digest* Top Ten list," he said. "It's not tough to figure out how it happened. It is a wonderful golf course, but does it belong in the Top Ten? No way. The Top Fifty, maybe. He bought that, too. When you start entering foreign worlds and bowling them over, you're pretty strong. And if he doesn't have it, he starts foaming at the mouth, falls on the floor, and throws a tantrum."

As a casino marketing tool, however, Shadow Creek exploits a weakness common to many multimillionaire high-rollers. No, not baccarat, exotic sex, or designer drugs.

Golf.

___

Along the Pacific Rim, golf-course memberships are coveted treasures traded like blue-chip stock investments. Japanese businessmen commonly pay as much as $50,000 for entrée to Tokyo country clubs. When they go on holiday, they take their clubs with them.

Ben "Bugsy" Siegel recognized the appeal of golf courses with the monied set when he built the Flamingo in 1946. Alas, the veteran killer for Murder, Inc. himself suffered two fatal holes before he could develop eighteen out behind the city's first glitzy resort. "Ben knew there were only so many things that would keep a gambler in town in those days," Siegel's attorney, Lou Wiener, Jr., recalled. "You can't gamble twenty-four hours a day."

Moe Dalitz also recognized the value of a country club setting and incorporated it into the Desert Inn Country Club and the Las Vegas Country Club in Southern Nevada and Rancho La Costa Country Club near San Diego.

The Desert Inn, Dunes, Sahara, Showboat, Stardust, and Tropicana all have used golf courses to market their resorts, attract players, and give customers a refreshing diversion from gaming. Although the courses sucked precious water from the desert, the conspicuous consumption was seen as a necessary part of marketing Las Vegas to the world.

Wynn's Shadow Creek takes that concept, and the notion of security, to the extreme.

———

In January 1994, Donnie Bader found himself an involuntary escapee. The diminutive Las Vegas radio talk-show second-banana and inveterate sports bettor had been unceremoniously dumped as a locker room attendant at Shadow Creek and was steamed about it. So he took time to confide his frustration to *Las Vegas Sun* Sports Editor Dean Juipe, who wrote an entertaining and not entirely serious column on the mysterious shroud surrounding Shadow Creek.

"It's like a concentration camp," Bader said in his satire. "You can't talk about the place, or you'll be fired. Twice a year they hold meetings where they stress just that. It's beyond belief. If you work there, you can't even use the phone or have a can of soda."

Wynn didn't understand or appreciate the humor. The following Sunday on page one of the *Las Vegas Sun* was an apology from Managing Editor Sandra Thompson, under the headline, "Shadow Creek not as depicted."

Acting on orders from upper management, including publisher and Shadow Creek one-time regular Brian Greenspun, Thompson acknowledged that it was silence on the part of the Mirage that created the single-source vacuum in which her sports editor operated.

Then she was careful to mention that more than half of all persons playing the course are regular folks. "The perception is that it's Wynn's personal playpen for high-roller friends. Actually, much of Shadow Creek is an employee perk. Fifty-one percent of the rounds are for non-highly compensated employees of the Golden Nugget and The Mirage.

"... We apologize for [publishing] false perceptions."

Reporters neglected to mention that the Internal Revenue Service and Securities and Exchange Commission frown on company-funded private sanctuaries designed solely for corporate executives and their friends. Making Shadow Creek exclusive might cause an IRS auditor to wonder whether the course was a posh perquisite and therefore a form of taxable income.

With slightly more than 50 percent of Shadow Creek's customers coming from throughout the company, Wynn (on paper) was receiving no more of a perk than a lucky hotel maid or hardworking busboy. Except that, well, those maids and busboys weren't designing mansions on the property for themselves and their closest friends. Wynn was. (The course is, however, made available to members of the University of Nevada–Las Vegas golf team.)

Course rules at Shadow Creek mandate that all players must wear a shirt with a collar, but Steve Wynn has been known to stroll the course bare-chested and in jogging shorts. The regulars, however, are an impressive lot, if not on the golf course, then at least in their chosen professions.

There are 300 lockers in all. Steve Wynn occupies lockers number one and two in the Shadow Creek clubhouse. The locker next closest to him was filled by Las Vegas high-roller and Yakuza mob associate Ken Mizuno, before financial disaster befell him.

Next to Mizuno was the locker of Steve Wynn's brother, Kenny. From there, Mirage President Bobby Baldwin, Rio Hotel Chairman Tony Marnell, PGA tour member Robert Gamez, Mirage officials Bruce Levin and Clyde Turner (now with Circus Circus), former Chrysler Chairman Lee Iacocca, and Las Vegas entertainment legend Vic Damone. Mirage high rollers and celebrity Friends of Steve—including Michael Jordan, Julius "Dr. J" Erving, Willie Nelson, George Strait, Kenny Rogers, Robert Wagner, and Hollywood producer Jerry Weintraub—also have their own lockers.

Of special note is Wynn's longtime friend Kenny Rogers. They became acquainted when Rogers and his group, the First Edition, performed in the lounge at the Golden Nugget in the early 1970s. Despite many hit records and his stardom in Las Vegas, Rogers is less than financially set. That fact has not prevented him from owning a sprawling Georgia estate with its own golf course. Rogers even copied a few of Shadow Creek's holes for his own course.

"Kenny lives like a sheik. He has no money, and he lives like a sheik," Tucky said. "He's upside down all the time. Steve lends him money, and the company lends him money."

One of the oddest pairings Tucky witnessed was Wynn and Donald Trump playing a round of golf with Michael Jackson tagging along.

"That's a real strange animal there," Tucky said of Jackson. "He looked like chalk. If I had money, I wouldn't hang out with him. How'd you like to go to dinner with this guy?"

And Trump?

"They're not friends at all," Tucky said. "Now Trump, there is not a good guy. I've been around people with money, he's not it. People with money don't act like that."

Australian casino giant Kerry Packer, who gambles and stays at Kirk Kerkorian's MGM Grand Hotel and Theme Park, was allowed to tour the grounds but not to so much as swing a club or replace a divot unless he packed his bags and moved himself and his unlimited credit line into the Mirage. Although that carrot has worked with other gamblers, Packer remained at the MGM, where he recently won more than ten million dollars in less than an hour at the MGM Grand baccarat tables.

———

Tucky claims to have introduced Steve Wynn to golf.

At first, Wynn was intimidated by his inability to see the ball after he hit it. By the early 1980s, his retinitis pigmentosa was severely narrowing his line of sight and made him extremely sensitive to changes in light.

"He couldn't see. What we'd do at Shadow Creek, the caddies or I would go out with him and everything, and we always had balls, we always had balls, and we'd be frigging throwing balls and saying, 'Okay, it's a little right.' I'd send a guy out ahead, and he'd throw a ball. I used to call it Walking with Jesus. The balls would be coming out from down below. They'd be coming back on the fairway. I'd say, 'We're walking with Jesus, boys.' Balls would be rolling from everywhere."

Tucky took liberties "so he wouldn't be a volcano....and it's just a way to get in [the clubhouse]. If this guy didn't like something, he'd hit balls into the water on [hole number] 17. Some days he'd hit forty balls. Maybe twenty of them would go in the water. He thought this was fun. I'd just do it to get in and not hear the volcano go off. He's so competitive. Steve, on the practice tee, could put on a clinic. Low fades, high hooks. He could do it on a practice tee."

On the course, conditions changed. So did the result. Wynn's bug-eyed, short-tempered side would emerge. Tucky eventually tired of Wynn's tantrums.

"It's only a game," he said. "A lot of times I'd tell him, 'It's only a game.'...He was too serious."

At Shadow Creek there are PGA rules and winter rules.

But regardless of the season or the prevailing rules, the operating ethic remains the same throughout the year: Wynn rules.

CHAPTER 15

THE POLITICS OF DOLPHINS

Steve and Elaine Wynn spent a few long summer days lounging at Rancho La Costa, after which they sought a diversion and drove to San Diego's Sea World. Famous for its killer whales and comic seal routines, Sea World is one of the most popular tourist attractions in Southern California. But Steve Wynn hadn't come to watch Shamu or clap along with the sea lions.

He was there for the dolphins.

When the Wynns returned home, Steve immediately took to the family's sprawling backyard at their Bannie Lane home. He began marking off the turf, planning a home for the dolphins he insisted he would one day own.

The year was 1983.

Less than a decade later, and over the protests of animal rights groups and the National Marine Fisheries Service, Wynn fulfilled his wish when the creatures became a part of the Mirage's tropical entertainment theme in his creation of a $14 million concrete-

and fake-coral habitat. Dolphins, in the form of commercial and fine art, would become a prominent symbol of the Mirage.

Four pools holding 2.5 million gallons of water are home to eight Atlantic bottle-nosed dolphins, the same sort of grinning mammal featured in the *Flipper* television series. Although everyone loves the king of the sea, few can afford their own private exhibit—and no one can do so legally.

Restrictions on dolphin ownership created an obstacle for Wynn, whose backyard dream by necessity gradually became an "educational" public exhibit funded and sponsored by the corporation. The process took many months and a sharklike lobbying effort that involved not only the superintendent of Southern Nevada's Clark County School District, but also the state's congressional delegation.

Along the way, the Mirage appears to have borrowed from the rhetoric of other successful—and lucrative—dolphin swim programs, especially the popular operation at the Hyatt Waikoloa in Hawaii.

The most compelling part of this story is how Wynn managed to recraft the image of the Mirage as something more than a gambling resort designed to entertain customers as it separated them from their money.

After all, merely emerging as the ringmaster of the Dolphin Circus, Cirque Dolphin they might call it, would send the wrong message to customers who expected more than animal acts and freak shows from the most innovative operator on the Strip. It also would be infinitely politically incorrect and would subject Wynn to the sort of criticism usually reserved for once-popular orangutan trainer and Strip entertainer Bobby Berosini. Berosini's orangutans did amusing stunts, but when it was alleged that cruel and inhumane treatment was used in training them, the act quickly fell out of favor.

Wynn found the angle in education.

The Hyatt Waikoloa had used the education theme to ward off a steady stream of critics who voiced some troubling facts: From 1973, when the government began counting, to 1992, more than 650 dolphins died in captivity, where their average life expectancy was five years. In their natural habitat, however, some dolphins live as long as thirty years.

Dolphin exhibits, supposedly originated in the name of scientific research, had begun swim-with programs years before Wynn's proposal. Like 400-pound faith-healers in slippery suits, true believers are convinced that dolphins—with their special ability to excite and inspire—can help cure children of everything from autism to Down's syndrome.

So, Wynn set out to accomplish his task by employing a tack that had shown previous success.

Wynn enlisted the assistance of highly regarded school superintendent Brian Cram, whose salary was augmented by $100,000 over five years by Mirage Resorts. Cram's assistance and the $20,000-a-year stipend were unrelated, Wynn claimed.

University of Nevada–Las Vegas President Bob Maxson and former Nevada Gov. Mike O'Callaghan joined Cram as part of a Southern Nevada contingent that flew to Washington to lobby on behalf of the resort's saltwater campus annex. Nevada Governor Bob Miller also praised the proposed program. "They are not going to have six dolphins in a Mason fruit jar," a spokesman for the governor said. "Some people back in Washington don't understand this. It will be top rank."

With free admission, and Mirage paying to have Southern Nevada's schoolchildren travel by bus to its facility, the dolphin program promised to be the most exciting field trip of the year for hundreds of young students.

In August 1989, Wynn and his cast of educators stormed a hearing of the National Marine Fisheries Service, a part of the Commerce Department. Wynn stressed that he loved the mammals for themselves, not for their marketing potential. "Dolphins are special and different....Their effect on all humans is overwhelming and unique. How wonderful it would be if all the kids in Las Vegas could experience them."

Cram, the school superintendent, was equally supportive. "Many of our students have never had any experience with marine mammals, and without this project, they probably never will. ...This project will not bring one cent into the casinos....The dolphin project is in fact a gift to the children of Clark County, and it comes from a very public-spirited corporation....I don't feel any responsibility to the Golden Nugget because of any contribution they made to the school district. My impression is, the facility is actually a scientific facility. This isn't an entertainment facility."

In the end, despite criticism that the Mirage was simply buying its way into the dolphin business, the permit was issued.

"We're environmentalists and animal-rights people," Wynn said. "I've stressed this is not a tourist attraction. We want people to see the dolphins in their natural habitat....This is near and dear to my heart. People will be able to watch the trainers and the scientists who will be doing studies on the dolphins. I plan on working with the dolphins. I am so excited about this; I think this will be absolutely wonderful for Las Vegas."

━━━━━

Wynn's argument for maintaining a dolphin habitat was more relentless than compelling.

The dolphins were in captivity already, Wynn argued. They needed a home, and the resort would not charge admission. He never would capture a dolphin from the open ocean; that would be cruel and against his principles as an environmentalist. Why, the Mirage didn't even allow albacore tuna caught in gill nets to be served in its restaurants because those same nets often caught the playful and intelligent bottlenose.

Wynn did not, however, explain how it made good sense to allow dolphins spoiled by captivity to continue to produce offspring, which in turn eventually would have to be shipped to other man-made habitats. But dolphin birth announcements are celebrated at the hotel and featured in Las Vegas newspapers with front-page photographs and playful, pun-riddled cutlines.

None of this hoopla is entertainment, Wynn and his staff assured skeptics—it's education.

"We're interested in education, research, and what we can learn about the dolphins," Julie Onie-Wignall, director of the Mirage marine operations, explained. "One of the goals is to make this as close as possible to [the dolphins'] natural habitat. We have a very good track record with our dolphins. We are considered to be one of the best dolphin facilities in the world."

Not surprisingly, the dolphins—their images emblazoned on company logos—are popular with tourists and students alike. Through mid-1994, more than one million people had taken the resort's dolphin tour, including some 45,000 students per year.

One month after the dolphins arrived in the desert, the resort adjusted its ticket prices from free to up to $5, with students still being admitted without charge.

The price was only the first promise that was cast aside.

Next came the Mirage's assurance that it never would seek a controversial swim-with-the-dolphins program.

———

Frolicking with dolphins is linked to the New Age pet philosophy of one-time scientist John Lilly, whose studies devolved from serious scientific discussion of the mammal's brain waves to the belief that they somehow acted as oceangoing conduits for wisdom-imparting extraterrestrials. Long before E.T. came to visit Earth, Lilly believed Flipper was phoning home.

And dolphin hugging was born.

After Lilly's Hollywood friends, including Kris Kristofferson, Olivia Newton-John and that famous New Age practitioner Phyllis Diller, swam with the dolphin-channeler's prize possessions, a lucrative cottage industry began to take shape.

By 1989, 15,000 people each year were paying $55 each for a thirty-minute dolphin swim session at the Hyatt Regency in Waikoloa, Hawaii. Another 10,000 were taking rides at Dolphins Plus of Key Largo, Florida. A year later, four swim-with programs were in place in the Florida Keys. Their popularity, Greenpeace feared, "increased the demand for the capture of wild dolphins to populate the facilities." Greenpeace experts realized years ago that the Marine Mammal Protection Act of 1972 lacked a provision to regulate dolphins in captivity.

Perhaps by coincidence, the Hyatt program presents itself as educational as well as entertaining. Schoolchildren are given guided tours of the facility, and over the years, a portion of the proceeds from the rides has been devoted to protecting wild dolphins.

———

Are there educational benefits to such a dolphin program?

"Yes, captive dolphins educate, but it's bad education," Ben White of the Sea Shepherd Conservation Society said. "It tells people it is OK to keep these animals and force them to do tricks."

(In June 1994, Wynn handed the Sea Shepherd Society a check for $50,000 to promote goodwill and to support the group's whaling-ship harassment program.)

Desperate parents of autistic and retarded children now wait up to five years for a chance to participate in a dolphin therapy program, which costs as much as $1,800 for a two-week session. Results are the subject of much debate.

Altruistic rhetoric aside, dolphins are a good business investment.

"The trick," said federal marine fisheries investigator Jeffrey Brown, "is for these facilities to slide in as much education as they can while still staying in business."

But are either dolphins or the humans who harass them in any danger?

Contact raises the risk of injury to both, critics of swim-with programs believe. Increased stress and the threat of spreading disease to the mammals are other concerns.

When mature, those grinning, gregarious bottle-nosed dolphins can reach twelve feet in length and weigh 600 pounds. Although often as friendly as Flipper, dolphins also have been known to attack their human playmates. But what's an occasional broken rib or busted spleen in exchange for what former scientist John Lilly considered a supernatural experience?

Male dolphins have also been known to become sexually aggressive with female divers. (A caressing bottlenose nuzzle on the back of the knee is considered foreplay. Divers also have been known to get caught in an "erection roll," which is where foreplay ends and mating begins.)

Younger dolphins are preferred by swim-with programs, which raises a tricky question, namely, what to do with the older mammals?

———

Once the education-only program was in place at the Mirage, it was only a matter of time and politics before the swim-with program opened.

In 1992, the National Marine Fisheries Service attempted to block the Mirage from creating a dolphin program allegedly designed to help autistic children.

Wynn sued.

The legal argument hinged on whether the federal service, which monitors and regulates fisheries-related activity in the ocean, had jurisdiction over dolphins in captivity. The mammals appeared to create a new category, and Mirage attorneys exploited the difference.

In November 1993, Las Vegas-based U.S. District Judge Philip Pro ruled that the fisheries service lacked jurisdiction. His logic was clear: The agency didn't monitor the sales of saltwater aquarium fish at pet stores so it also lacked the power to regulate captive dolphins.

In March 1994, after studies into the effects on dolphins arrived at conflicting results, a congressional subcommittee sided with the Mirage in ruling the National Marine Fisheries Service with all its sea mammal specialists lacked jurisdiction over captive dolphins. That responsibility was thrust upon the Agriculture Department's Animal and Plant Health Inspection Service, the folks better known for scrutinizing the oranges and ferns vacationers haul from one state to another. Its inspectors supposedly have undergone marine-mammal training sessions since 1979.

"While it is true that strict trainer supervision is the key to safer swims, no facility is under any obligation to provide such supervision," said Naomi A. Rose, a marine mammal biologist with the Humane Society of the United States. "The Mirage and the public display industry have succeeded in changing the federal law, currently leaving swim-with programs without any regulatory standards.

"The Mirage claims that the study found nothing to indicate that dolphins are harmed by swimming with humans. In fact, the study found considerable evidence that, in supervised swims, dolphins frequently behave submissively to swimmers—an odd thing, since dolphins are so much stronger and more agile in water than humans. Submissive animals experience persistent stress-related hormonal changes. In addition, there are no contingency plans for those dolphins that 'wash out' of programs because they do not interact well with swimmers. They are often simply isolated and neglected."

Stress from crowds might cause ulcers, and captivity might lead to a shortened life span, but neither fear stopped the Mirage's dolphin lovers from pursuing their ride-with plans.

"These programs don't work," Ric O'Barry, the former dolphin trainer for the *Flipper* television series, said. He now leads the Dolphin Project, which attempts to preserve the mammals in their natural habitat. "Dolphins have been reduced to draft animals. The only way the public should see them is face to face in the ocean.

"Dolphins in captivity don't represent dolphins in our ecosystem. They're reduced to circus performers. If that is educational, then a boxing kangaroo is also educational. And so is a dancing bear chained to a tree.

"Like all amusement park owners, Steve Wynn claims that the dolphins would be 'educational' for people who come to the casino, but the educational value is purely a mirage. You can accomplish the same thing with plastic dolphins."

———

The spread of dolphin exhibits has created a lucrative market for the mammals with prices ranging up to $100,000 apiece for a trained bottlenose. Of the approximately 400 in captivity, about 75 percent were born free. Although they don't risk being eaten by predators, dolphins born in captivity do not always survive. Despite the Mirage's best efforts, two of its baby dolphins died.

Permit or no permit, from the start Wynn vowed that he would be swimming with his bottle-nosed friends. He had had a lifelong fascination with the creatures, he said. Trained by marine mammal biologists in handling the animals, Wynn now regularly wrestles with his dolphins, either in play or as therapeutic exercise.

Although the public at large appears impressed, environmentalists remain critical of Wynn and his motives.

"He's trying to look green, but this is not the way to do it," Mark Berman of the Florida-based environmental group Earth

Island told a *Las Vegas Sun* reporter. "It's hard to believe how they [Mirage] campaigned to gut the National Marine Mammal Protection Act, and they are working as hard as they can to set up these swim programs. If he really wanted to help the environment, he would start a real rehab-and-release program for his dolphins."

(If Wynn is indeed "trying to look green," that image is further tarnished by Mirage Resorts entering into a partnership with the Houston-based Maxxam Corporation, a conglomerate which, among many things, harvests redwood forests in California.)

It cost the Mirage millions of company dollars to construct the dolphin habitat, millions more to staff it, and still more millions to sue and beat the federal government to become a certified desert dolphin oasis. Given Wynn's history of increasingly exotic marketing—Sinatra to Shadow Creek—a high-roller swim program appears ever more likely.

If Wynn can get some of the wiseguy gamblers who frequent the Mirage to willingly swim with the fishes, he will have scored an unprecedented marketing coup.

CHAPTER 16

A GREAT FRIEND, AN ENEMY WHO NEVER FORGETS

Steve Wynn's personalities at times appear to outnumber Elvis impersonators in Las Vegas. Combined, they make up a collective good Wynn and bad Wynn. Whether one encounters the good Wynn or the bad Wynn depends on the circumstance, which can change with dizzying speed.

The good Wynn defines corporate beneficence: His charitable gifts—in 1993, he donated $1 million to the John A. Moran Eye Center at the University of Utah and remains a generous member of the board of the National Retinitis Pigmentosa Foundation—are only outweighed by his superior treatment of the 18,000 employees in the "Mirage family."

Wynn's employee morale programs set an unapproachable standard for the casino industry. In 1982 Wynn awarded 377 luxury automobiles to Atlantic City casino supervisors. In 1983 he showered 5,300 company employees each with twenty shares of common stock whose total value was $1.3 million.

His company meetings are a cross between commercials for the *Power of Positive Thinking* and a heart-to-heart talk with an articulate, charismatic father figure.

Maids and waiters, parking attendants and pastry chefs are all included in Wynn's worker love fest. Employees of the Year from each department are feted at a gourmet dinner ceremony featuring an in-house movie production starring the awardees alongside such luminaries as Madonna and Whoopi Goldberg. Wynn combines the friendly employee-management philosophy with superior customer service and an industry-low 12 percent annual turnover rate. As a whole, the hired help are happy, and in turn they treat the customers better. Improved customer relations translates into revenue at the bottom line.

"The more I do for my help, the more money I make," Wynn once said. "It's the damnedest thing I ever saw. It took me a long time to learn it, but I learned it."

The Good Wynn has plenty of fans.

One of them is John Wilhelm, vice-president of the Hotel and Restaurant Employee International Union.

The Yale-educated Wilhelm was sent by the mob-riddled service workers organization to resolve a citywide labor dispute between resort owners and the union representing 32,000 busboys, waitresses, dishwashers, and maids. Wynn, who signed a four-year contract with the union and did not hesitate to include his new properties in the deal, has made a convert in Wilhelm.

"I think [the employees' superior morale is] a direct result of the fact that Wynn, unlike most executives, practices what he believes," Wilhelm said. "In a service-intensive business, you have to have employees who have a positive outlook toward the company and know their success depends on the company's success.

"He has an ability that I think is unique in Las Vegas and nationally...to capture the imaginations of employees. That probably sounds corny, but I think it's true, and it's a large part due to his personality."

The Good Wynn knows the value of employee relations, which makes some of his critics wonder about the bad Wynn's lightning dismissal of workers and occasional obsession that costs the company a small fortune in attorney fees.

"Steve can be a great friend, but he can also be an enemy who never forgets, who waits until he has his chance to make you regret not paying," Donald Trump adviser Al Glasgow once observed.

Indeed, in Las Vegas, there is no more formidable or mercurial enemy than the Bad Wynn.

———

Wynn is capable of charming both sophisticates and simpletons. He also is capable of becoming obsessed in a finger snap.

The same character who donates sizable sums to charity and lavishes attention on the smallest detail of his resorts also can shred his perceived foes with wicked rhetoric. In the rare cases in which intimidation fails to achieve its desired affect, Wynn is quick to unleash a pack of snarling attorneys handpicked from across the country.

When Wynn, the perfectionist, spotted a burned-out light bulb while walking through his hotel after midnight, his tirade awakened not the graveyard shift maintenance engineer but the head of the entire department at home in bed. When the screaming session was finished, the department chief dressed, drove to the hotel, and supervised the bulb change.

Former Shadow Creek General Manager Ron Tucky said he watched Wynn viciously dress down some employees. Others, himself included, rarely received the verbal assault.

"He'd yell at me once or twice a year. I probably had it coming," Tucky said. "A lot of times he'd be hot at you, and twenty minutes later, he'd be your best buddy.

"He's often in error but never in doubt. When he picks up the phone to holler, he's not in doubt, is he? He may be in error. But this guy, oh, he's never in doubt."

A one-week working relationship between the boss and a prominent gaming industry attorney ended at 3 a.m. when Wynn called the lawyer's home and began hurling invectives.

Rather than shrink and take his ill-prescribed medicine—as other attorneys in the Mirage family had done time and time again—the top-flight lawyer returned fire and severed the relationship. The attorney lost a wealthy client and, potentially, a small fortune in fees, but he maintained his self-respect.

In most cases, Wynn's underlings and opponents are cowered by the onslaught. Those who fight usually wish they hadn't.

But Wynn does not always come away without his own wounds.

Throughout the 1980s Wynn sparred with Donald Trump. Ironically, Wynn was one of many casino operators who helped welcome Trump and his millions to Atlantic City, in part as a means of short-circuiting pending gaming legislation in New York. Getting New York developers interested in the prospects of the Boardwalk helped quench the thirst for various forms of legalized gambling across the state line.

In 1986, when Trump was known as the brilliant bully on the Boardwalk, they shared a symbiotic relationship that helped fuel not only Wynn's Atlantic City exodus but his new Las Vegas project as well.

Acting on a series of tips from Drexel Burnham Lambert analyst Daniel Lee, who confided that Bally's was poorly managed and its stock undervalued, Trump began purchasing blocks of Bally's stock. He acquired $63 million worth of stock—9.9 percent of the company—not through Drexel but through his longtime brokerage house, Bear, Stearns and Company.

With rumors of a Trump takeover rampant, Bally's Chairman Robert Mullane had to act or face the possibility of having his corporation's heart sucked out by Trump. Mullane, whose company, unlike Trump's, had used Drexel in the past, sought the advice of Steve Wynn's allies at Drexel.

Thus was hatched the plan that handed Wynn his first-class ticket back to Las Vegas.

To fend off a takeover run by Trump, Bally's would acquire a second Atlantic City casino. And Drexel just happened to know that Steve Wynn was anxious to sell his Golden Nugget—for the right price, of course. Trump, who already owned two Atlantic City casinos, would be barred by New Jersey law from acquiring another.

With Trump playing the role of the enforcer, Wynn's $440 million deal was done in an unprecedented ten days. His end of the largess included $140 million in cash and stock and the transfer of a $299 million mortgage on the casino. For its part, Drexel sucked up nearly $100 million in fees, including charges from the buyer, Bally's, and the seller, Golden Nugget. Trump, in turn, realized a tidy profit after Bally's bought out his stock for $84 million.

The maneuver was not lost on the Federal Trade Commission, which investigated Trump's relationship with Bear Stearns and eventually fined him $750,000 after it was discovered the brokerage house had allowed him to stockpile blocks of shares in the company's name until market conditions warranted purchase.

Bally's was not so lucky: its stock went into a free-fall from 21 to 1 ⅞. Mullane lost his job. The company was forced into a massive and painful restructuring from which it was still extricating itself nearly a decade later.

Thanks in part to Trump, and for the most part to Drexel and Michael Milken, Wynn had everything he needed to return to Las Vegas in style.

Throughout the 1980s, when Trump was at the top of his media game, he appeared to toy with Wynn. In the 1987 book he coauthored with Tony Schwartz, *Trump: The Art of the Deal*, the Donald left no doubt about his opinion of Wynn after hiring away Steve Hyde from the Golden Nugget.

"Wynn is one of the best gaming guys around, and my philosophy is always to hire the best from the best. After a long-running negotiation, I offered Hyde a bigger job and more money, and he said yes. I think he also liked the idea of working for me, and he didn't mind leaving Steve Wynn.

"Wynn is very slick and smooth, but he's also a very strange guy. A couple of weeks ago, he called and said, 'Donald, I just want you to know that my wife and I are getting divorced.' So I said, 'Oh, I'm sorry to hear that, Steve.' He said, 'Oh, don't be sorry, it's great, we're still in love, it's just that we don't want to be married anymore. In fact, she's right here with me. Do you want to say hello?' I politely declined."

By 1990, Trump's own marriage would disintegrate in a tabloid scandal. (On June 29, 1991 at the Waldorf Towers, twenty-eight years after their first marriage and more than five years after their divorce, Steve and Elaine Wynn were remarried. "Steve just never got around to moving out," Elaine told a reporter. "We regret to say that the divorce just didn't work out," her husband quipped.)

———

The feud between Trump and Wynn, which at times has resembled nothing so much as a couple of toddlers struggling and crying over a toy called celebrity, turned serious with the fight over the employment contract of one-time Golden Nugget President Dennis Gomes.

A former member of state gaming regulatory commissions in Nevada and New Jersey, Gomes had operated the Las Vegas Hilton, Frontier, Aladdin, and Dunes with varying degrees of success when he was approached by Steve Wynn and offered the president's position at the downtown Golden Nugget.

Gomes had an impeccable reputation for integrity in an industry fraught with phony operators. Gomes knew how to make money, particularly for himself. But even more appealing than his performance as a manager were his Asian high-roller contacts. The $620 million Mirage was then under construction and slated to be run by Golden Nugget President Bobby Baldwin. This created an opening at the Nugget. Wynn went after Gomes to fill this opening.

As he had many times before with new finds, Wynn lavished praise, money, and perquisites on Gomes. A $400,000 annual salary and 150,000 shares of substantially discounted Golden Nugget stock would make Gomes comfortable. Even though Gomes would be losing up to two-thirds of the Golden Nugget's work force to the Mirage, Wynn was confident that his new manager would shine.

For a while, at least, Gomes and Wynn spoke the same language. Under the supervision of Gomes, Golden Nugget set record profits in 1990: more than $150 million in the casino, $60 million in nongaming revenue, and a 92-percent hotel occupancy rate. Dennis Gomes had made his new best friend and boss very happy.

But the relationship hit a snag during Gomes' second full year as Golden Nugget president. His incredibly effective marketing to Asian high rollers appeared to be flawed: With a recession in Japan and elsewhere along the Pacific Rim, some of his best customers had begun reneging on their six- and seven-figure casino debts. It was then Gomes said he began to look for a way out of his legal-tender trap.

In January 1991, Mirage Casino Manager Kevin DeSanctis, a close friend of Gomes, quit his coveted position to become president of Trump Plaza. With millions in Asian markers overdue, and Wynn doing his best Norman Bates impersonation, Gomes decided to leave Wynn and follow his friend to Atlantic City. But there was one problem: He was under contract to Wynn until 1992.

Breaking his contract might not have been difficult—Wynn was a volcanic personality and had threatened to fire him many times—but then Gomes did the unforgivable: Without collecting all the outstanding markers, he submitted his thirty-day notice and accepted a top position with The Donald at the Trump Taj Mahal.

Wynn sued Trump for tampering with a contractual agreement between Golden Nugget and Gomes. He sought a preliminary injunction to prevent Gomes from taking the Golden Nugget's trade secrets with him.

Trump responded with a lawsuit of his own, claiming Gomes was repeatedly humiliated by the golden boy. "Wynn directed harsh, bitter, vituperative and abusive language at Gomes," the countersuit claimed. "By this language and conduct, GNLV and Wynn have defamed Gomes and have subjected him to ridicule, personal abuse, and disparaged his abilities as a casino executive."

In his deposition, Gomes cranked a Tommy gun spray of criticism at his former boss. There was enough information and allegation in the public record to inflict substantial bodily harm.

One example: During a meeting, Gomes said he was shocked by Wynn's seemingly irrational outburst, during which the boss "started becoming very upset with a casino executive, and....his eyes bulged, and he started screaming at the top of his lungs and banging his head on the table."

Although few of the remarks covered new ground—Wynn's tyrannical outbursts and allegations of his drug use and link to reputed cocaine trafficker and mob associate Louis Cappiello were more than a decade old—Gomes made the most of his opportunity to tar his former employer. He alleged that Wynn commonly referred to African-Americans specifically and casino workers generally as "niggers," Catholics, of which Gomes was one, as "mackerel-snappers," and Asians as "chinks."

And that was only the nasty start.

For all his work ethic, Gomes sniped, Wynn was never too busy to pursue the Golden Nugget and Mirage cocktail waitresses and even sent limousines around to the homes of the crème de la crème of the female flesh—married or not—in what Gomes called a "chronic sexual harassment of female employees." Gomes said he resented playing matchmaker for Wynn's libido.

"I was worried the [sexual harassment complaints] could possibly impact me because I was aware that if, as an executive, you didn't do anything about sexual harassment that you were aware of, that you could be the person liable for that," Gomes said.

More than the emotional outbursts, Gomes said he feared Wynn's corporate decision-making would land both of them in trouble with authorities. Wynn used Golden Nugget plumbers, electricians, painters, and carpenters for renovation projects at the family's Bannie Lane home at company expense, according to Gomes. A security guard was used as a Wynn family valet, picking up dry cleaning and refueling the Mercedes.

"In addition, the Golden Nugget's chef and food and beverage director would prepare elaborate catered dinners for personal parties at Wynn's home without billing Wynn for the cost of preparation," the suit alleged.

Although such reputed transgressions might not appear serious to newspaper readers and daily viewers of the Trump-Wynn soap opera, if proven true, they established a violation of Wynn's fiduciary responsibility to Golden Nugget stockholders. Such violations were the kinds that could cost a corporate chairman his position or even send him to prison. After the fact, Gomes said he wanted no part of it.

"I was worried that I could get into the same kind of problem that Leona Helmsley's executive did, and I believe he went to jail," he testified under oath.

Wynn denied everything. "I did not direct Gomes to get the phone numbers of any cocktail waitresses, and I did not engage in any sexual harassment of female employees," Wynn said in his deposition. "I deny any statements or insinuations made by Gomes or anyone that I am a person of racial, ethnic, or religious prejudice or bias.

"Dennis Gomes lied in his deposition. At trial, we will prove he lied."

The hearings on the case bore a closer resemblance to a barroom brawl than an orderly display of motions and writs. Wynn hired savvy defense attorney Morton Galane to do his rabbit punching. Galane, who represented entertainer Wayne Newton in his multimillion-dollar defamation trial against NBC News, was given to ear-splitting outbursts, machine-gun rhetoric, and extended diatribes.

Trump countered with formidable former federal prosecutor Donald Campbell, who savaged Galane and his client in something akin to a courthouse stiletto fight. Galane and Campbell called each other names for weeks and argued over everything from deposition questions to each other's personal demeanor. Clark County District Court Judge Lee Gates lost control of the courtroom and wound up recusing himself from the proceedings on a technicality. When Judge Nancy Becker, a highly regarded jurist on the county bench, relieved Gates, the shouting only grew in intensity with Becker filling in as a capable third.

The case predictably never reached trial but was settled out of court in an agreement sealed by both parties.

However, word quickly circulated that Trump had been forced to cough up the court costs, which had reached approximately $1 million between the two warring parties. Wynn's advocates used the fee payment as proof that the golden boy had prevailed.

"Trump is not the kind of person who can do you any harm," Wynn told a writer for *GQ* magazine. "Donald's a cartoon character, a perverse exaggeration."

Wynn fought other skirmishes with lesser-known adversaries, all of which showcased his pugnacious and vindictive nature.

There was, for example, the clash with former Las Vegas city councilman Steve Miller.

As a city councilman for a single elected term, Steve Miller was known as a glorified gadfly who attracted crowds with his populist rhetoric and who had the dangerous tendency to shoot from the lip. An unsuccessful run for Las Vegas mayor had left him on the outside looking in at city hall.

But Miller wasn't finished roasting his critics. He became a drive-time radio talk-show host at Southern Nevada AM station KLAV and unleashed a relentless assault on all those he considered to be corrupted by city hall. To a small audience of senior citizens, Second Amendment advocates, and fellow city hall critics, Miller blasted the mayor, select council members, local newspaper reporters, and Steve Wynn, whose outspokenness and high profile made him impossible to resist.

When Wynn attempted to persuade Connecticut legislators to the tax benefits of casino gambling in their state, Miller was there on the air regularly criticizing him, using as ammunition the issues raised in Wynn's earlier fight with Sheriff John Moran. Miller nipped at Steve Wynn like a gnat and drew a predictable swat.

Wynn's attorneys were unleashed, the radio station's license threatened, and Steve Miller—his fiery crusade snuffed out like a two-bit Tiparillo—offered an abject retraction.

"After review of the tapes of the 'Steve Miller Open Line,' I must agree with Mr. Wynn that the statements I made impugning his integrity and reputation were reckless distortions of fact, false accusations, and character assassinations—not only against Mr. Wynn, but also other public officials and individuals related to or associated with him," Miller said on the air. In an interview, he said he would consider returning to the radio talk-show format, "only if Mr. Wynn would allow me to in the future."

Miller also penned an apology to Wynn, scribbled on a paper grocery sack.

━━━━━━━━━

The inability of Steve Wynn to suffer critics reached the level of absurdity with Jim McGaughey, who himself had been described in absurd terms in the local press.

A veteran assemblyman representing a section of rural Clark County, McGaughey had taken up the cause of ousted UNLV basketball Coach Jerry Tarkanian, who resigned under pressure after nineteen winning seasons and one NCAA National Championship.

Tarkanian, whose program over the years had been accused of all manner of NCAA violations, had sought revenge against Wynn-backed university president Robert Maxson.

For his part, McGaughey formed a legislative committee to attempt to get to the bottom of the so-called conspiracy to force out UNLV's beloved Coach Tark. Along the way, he called into question the role of key university boosters—including Steve and Elaine Wynn—in ushering Tarkanian into retirement.

McGaughey was at best a harmless flea on an elephant's back, but Wynn, who hates to be criticized, vowed to do what he could to get McGaughey voted out of office. A letter to McGaughey's constituents critical of their assemblyman's performance backfired on Wynn, who instead of being viewed as a seeker of truth was seen as a know-it-all and a bully.

McGaughey easily won reelection.

━━━━━━━━━

For Mike Flores and his father, Paul, the decision to challenge Wynn did not have the happy ending of the McGaughey tiff, but, instead, proved costly.

Owners of the thirty-six-unit Villa De Flores apartment complex just off the Strip, the father and son found themselves at odds with the most powerful casino operator in Nevada when construction of the Mirage began in 1990. Villa De Flores was left the only piece of independently owned real estate in the immediate area.

With the small swimming pool in its courtyard, the Villa's studio and one-bedroom units—squat, homely two-story buildings—sat near the site of a planned Mirage coliseum for concerts and championship fights and did not exactly blend in with Wynn's tropical theme. Flores was interested in selling but for more than the $1 million offer Wynn had made for the one-acre complex. With the Mirage being touted as a $620 million resort, and his stucco outpost amid a sea of parking lot netting him approximately $100,000 per year, Flores figured he had room to negotiate—or seek another buyer.

When Flores balked at early offers made on behalf of Wynn through Las Vegas attorney Michael Mushkin, the golden boy called him "the schmuck with the apartments."

Flores replied by going up the street to the Imperial Palace, where owner Ralph Engelstad—who does not conceal his dislike for Wynn—allowed one of his top executives to secure an option on the property: The terms were $1 million down with an agreement to pay another $5 million at the close of the purchase.

Clearly Engelstad meant the move to irritate Wynn, who had been one of the Imperial Palace owner's staunchest critics during what became known in Las Vegas as the Der Fuhrer Furor. In that flap, Engelstad had been ridiculed for holding a birthday party honoring Adolf Hitler and fined $1.5 million by the Nevada Gaming Commission for conduct that impugned the image of the state's largest industry.

Believing Flores was negotiating in bad faith, Wynn responded, "He made a mistake because now I won't buy his piece at any price. NOT AT ANY PRICE."

Villa De Flores is today a stucco island behind the Mirage and Treasure Island resorts surrounded by a desert of parking spaces.

Wynn also butted heads with boxing's dominant promoter, Don King, over the soul of a one-fight heavyweight phenom named James "Buster" Douglas.

A native of Columbus, Ohio, Buster Douglas fought a losing battle with a weight problem and staggered through a tepid professional career until one night in Tokyo when he faced an undefeated Mike Tyson.

A 42-to-1 underdog, Douglas was fighting only days after the death of his mother. Tyson was battling managerial problems, the constant threat of litigation, and a strain of the flu. Douglas stopped Tyson in the tenth round of their bout, making worldwide headlines.

Wynn seized the moment and made Douglas an offer that seemed too good to be true: $60 million in cash and 100,000 shares of company stock for a conditional two-fight contract. Douglas signed without getting a down payment. To consummate the deal, however, Douglas had to sever his contract with King that granted Tyson a rematch.

Douglas sued King. King sued Wynn and Douglas. Wynn went on the offensive.

"The day of exploiting a fighter shamelessly is over," Wynn proclaimed. "Why should a fighter give up money to the promoter when he can go straight to the site?...We don't make a living out of taking a piece of a fighter's purse."

But Don King did not become known as The Don of boxing for nothing. If Steve Wynn wanted to dabble in King's arena, he would pay the $4 million price.

With King waiting in the wings, Wynn proudly promoted the Douglas-Evander Holyfield championship at the Mirage. In addition to court costs and King's ransom, Wynn would spend at least $40 million to bring off the championship.

Although warned repeatedly by boxing insiders, Wynn had not counted on the fallibility of Buster Douglas.

When he should have been training, Douglas was spotted eating enormous quantities of food. Room-service waiters lost their breath running meals to Douglas's suite. Holyfield, always in great shape, stopped "Buffet Buster" in the first round.

In a November 1990 issue of *Forbes*, Wynn claimed to have more than recouped his investment thanks to $10 million from the gate, $15 million from pay-per-view television sales, another $10 million foreign broadcasts and closed-circuit deals, and $10 million more at the gaming tables. The Mirage normally won approximately half that much in the casino on a given weekend.

How that $45 million figure offset Wynn's enormous expenses, court costs, and Douglas's $60 million sweetheart deal is anyone's guess, but *Forbes* was impressed by Wynn's version.

Then there was the tangle with Jack Bona, a real-estate investor with ties to mob conduit Morris Shenker. As a result of his tussle with Wynn, Bona spent twenty-three months in what only can best be described as debtor's prison for failing to hold up his end of a purchase agreement with the Atlantic City Golden Nugget.

Before hooking up with Shenker, Bona had been a small but prosperous San Diego real estate and condominium developer. After getting to know Shenker, Bona gained entrée to larger loans and bigger deals.

In April 1983, Bona purchased 51 percent interest in the foundering Atlantic City Dunes and immediately set out to expand the project. He attempted to have the sites of the President Hotel and President Motel vacated, and that August paid $2 million for an option on 2 ¼ acres of real estate owned by Golden Nugget Atlantic City. In total, Bona would be required to pay $18 million for the Golden Nugget land.

It quickly became apparent that, for all his big plans and long list of potential investors, Jack Bona was in over his head. Shortly after picking up the Golden Nugget option, he filed for protection under Chapter 11 of the bankruptcy code, in effect locking up the real estate for four years.

The deal had all the earmarks of a typical Shenker production: Find a willing front, announce big plans, raise capital, generate massive construction debt, and then shrug when the bills come due. Shenker pulled the ultimate shrug when after two decades of being chased by the IRS, FBI, and SEC, he was indicted on bankruptcy fraud and tax evasion in February 1989. He died before facing trial—owing the IRS $66 million.

Wynn was apoplectic over Bona's bankruptcy filing.

He dispatched a team of attorneys from the offices of Greenberg and Margolis—the same Martin L. Greenberg who was a former state senator and New Jersey powerbroker with top connections in the governor's office—to make someone pay. Morris Shenker was, by then, nowhere to be found; and Bona really was broke.

That didn't stop Wynn's attorneys from relentlessly pursuing Bona in court. They evoked a 300-year-old legal philosophy dating back to the time the first Pilgrims landed at Plymouth Rock, which enabled a judge to incarcerate a deadbeat in England, and Bona was jailed for failing to pay his debts.

No bail was set; Bona was not charged with a crime. Golden Nugget attorneys claimed Bona had secreted approximately $30 million in illicit cash and that a few months in the slammer would refresh his memory.

Months turned into two years before Atlantic City Judge John Callinan scrutinized the case, became appalled at the malicious actions, and wrote a lengthy opinion that resulted in Bona's release.

By the time Bona was freed, Steve Wynn had sold the Atlantic City Golden Nugget.

Billy Walters was the one who got away.

As a golf hustler and sports bettor, William Thurman Walters is a real estate and golf course developer, ranked among the more successful men in America, and a Las Vegas legend.

However, even though he is a high-rolling gambler, he is not welcome at the Golden Nugget, Mirage, or Treasure Island despite his habit of wagering hundreds of thousands of dollars in a single evening. His banishment stems from an 1982 incident that occurred at the Golden Nugget in Atlantic City when Walters legally exploited a roulette wheel and Wynn and won $3.9 million in a single twenty-four-hour period.

On a previous trip to Atlantic City, Walters had gambled away $1,047,000 playing blackjack. Wynn was a most gracious host and invited Walters to return to try his luck again. Walters, in turn, switched from blackjack to roulette and lobbied Wynn to remove the double zero from the wheel to make the game more European and, in effect, a closer bet. With eighteen red and eighteen black numbers on the wheel, the presence of the two zeroes gave the house a decided edge over the player on any given spin. Wynn agreed, although who knows what the gaming officials would have said about that. Meanwhile, Walters spotted something in the wheel that Wynn did not.

Upon his return, Walters played at a fevered pitch for hours. More than a day passed before Billy Walters quit the table, having won $3.9 million from the casino.

Wynn, who had spent the day golfing, returned to find one of his biggest customers flush with Golden Nugget winnings. He was livid. Instead of inviting Walters for a return trip, he banned Walters from all Wynn casinos.

Then Wynn set out to find what Walters had done to the wheel. Surely he had rigged it to give himself an edge. Or, perhaps it was a Golden Nugget insider. A dealer, maybe. Or a friendly pit boss. It was no use. Smooth-talking Billy Walters had talked himself into a nearly four-million-dollar payday at Steve Wynn's expense.

———

About himself and his reputation for being a mercurial wielder of power, Wynn has commented only obliquely. He seems to feel above such restrictions as normal good manners. Once, when he was sitting at a table in one of his restaurants and a young reporter asked him a question he didn't like, he responded by flinging the glass table lamp to the floor, smashing it into smithereens.

"If a man has learned anything by his forties, it better be softness," he told a *GQ* writer. "I've come to love a guy of power and means who doesn't have to show it. That's the most potent combination. My father had it naturally, but I had to learn it."

To a different writer he added this observation: "You know where a temper comes from? Being able to get away with it. I'm a self-made brat. I'm like everybody else: I want to get away with it if I can.

"I've been indulged."

EXPANDING THE EMPIRE

At the south end of Miami Beach, where Collins Avenue dead-ends into Biscayne Street, an enigmatic German entrepreneur named Thomas Kramer began buying real estate for cash in 1992.

Within two years, Kramer had spent $100 million for forty-five acres of land and numerous buildings—approximately half the available land in the South Pointe neighborhood. With no apparent source of income, he'd paid a fortune for some of the choicest property on the billion-dollar sand bar.

During a brief honeymoon with the Florida press, Kramer crafted his personal legend. The son of a wealthy Frankfurt stockbroker, Kramer made his first trade from a pay phone as a fourteen-year-old boarding school student and, by seventeen, he'd earned his first million.

Kramer was an international playboy who married Catherine Burda, daughter of a German publishing giant. The marriage so angered the father that he reportedly mounted a media smear campaign against Kramer, making father and son-in-law a favorite subject of the German tabloids. Kramer's plan to corral investors for a sweeping purchase of East German real estate after unification was torpedoed by Burda, and Kramer wound up declaring bankruptcy in Germany with $1.1 million in liabilities over assets.

Somehow, while most investors were losing vast fortunes in the stock market crash of 1987, Kramer managed to generate $30 million from commodities and fortuitous deals. He later survived a fraud and tax investigation in Germany before cutting his losses, repaying a $1 million debt, and, in 1992, turning up in Miami Beach.

Between real estate purchases, Kramer revealed an amazing propensity for offensive behavior and managed to enrage just about every minority group in Miami Beach.

In an interview, Kramer said the city's slums would virtually disappear once Fidel Castro was ousted and Miami's Cuban population was returned to Havana. In another instance, he fondled a woman's breasts, was sued for sexual harassment and settled out of court.

Approximately two years, forty-five acres, numerous buildings, and $100 million later, the fog lifted.

It was then the public learned that the highly liquid, highly offensive Thomas Kramer had entered into a partnership with Steve Wynn.

———

It wasn't just any association.

Together, Kramer and Wynn were a cross between the Dynamic Duo and twin *enfant terribles*. Kramer was Miami Beach's most notorious lout; Wynn was the controversial grinning face of the gaming industry. Between them, although they attempted to remain in the background, they became the featured villains in the anti-casino movement's advertisements.

Announcing their association in the Portofino Group in February 1994, the two immediately faced a dilemma: Kramer's acquisitions made an ideal setting for a proposed $600 million Mediterranean-themed resort but were not among those recorded in the Proposition for Limited Casinos. Even though by late March it had spent thousands and had collected more than half the signatures necessary to put the initiative on the ballot, at Kramer's prodding, the pro-casino group threw out the signatures and began campaigning anew—this time with the Portofino project in the South Pointe Redevelopment Area written into the script.

"We think South Beach is one of the most exciting places in the world, and we're thrilled about the prospect of bringing a dynamic entertainment facility of this kind to South Florida's residents and tourists," Kramer said, neglecting to mention that gaming initiatives had failed twice before in the state.

But it was no time for skepticism: The casinos were coming. Casino companies began pouring millions into a lobbying and image-making effort: Boyd Gaming, owners of the Stardust, Sam's Town, and the California Hotel in Las Vegas, led the way with $2.4 million. Kramer and Wynn, contributing $1.5 million apiece, easily topped the big spenders.

Even though thirty of the proposed forty-seven gaming sites were to be located at the state's struggling parimutuel dog and thoroughbred tracks and jai-alai frontons, opponents' attention immediately focused on the other land-based casino sites—especially the Kramer-Wynn South Pointe property.

The two were easy targets for critics. Anticasino television spots struck at the heart of the gambling industry's image problem: "Why are a notorious casino kingpin and a foreign developer bankrolling the casino campaign? Because Amendment 8 not only legalizes casinos in Florida, it mandates that a casino be built on their private land project." For his part, Miami Beach Mayor Frank Gelber called Wynn, "America's casino don."

The election was a debacle for the gaming industry. As it had been in 1978, the casino proposal was trounced by a resounding

62 to 38 percent landslide. Casino industry executives were stunned. Despite spending an estimated $16.7 million—easily the most expensive political campaign in the history of Florida—the defeat was so devastating that some pundits wondered whether the measure might have had a better chance had the industry stayed out of the campaign.

———

The Florida debacle was only one of several rebuffs Steve Wynn would receive as he attempted to expand his gambling empire. The next blow came from Connecticut.

If ever a state figured to swallow its pride and embrace Wynn's casino plans, it ought to have been Connecticut. Mired in recession, increasingly ravaged by inner-city blight, Hartford and Bridgeport resembled nothing so much as a couple of strung-out economic junkies desperately searching for a job and tax-revenue fix. Both cities were projected to run multimillion-dollar budget deficits.

In a three-year period beginning in 1989, Connecticut lost 155,000 jobs statewide. The potential employment and economic infusion from two large-scale casinos were enough to make the politicians swoon: 22,000 jobs and $200 million in annual state tax revenues if Mirage's proposed casinos in the two cities were approved.

Wynn would spend $2 million lobbying Connecticut's legislature and citizens. He would enlist the assistance of his chief Nevada allies, including University of Nevada–Las Vegas President Robert Maxson and Las Vegas City Manager Bill Noonan.

Oddly enough, the Connecticut casino story begins not in the middle of the city but on the tribal lands of the Mashantucket Pequot, a tiny tribe of native Americans who, more than 200 years ago, were all but driven into extinction by the British. With the expansion of the Indian Gaming Regulatory Act of 1988, the

Mashantucket Pequots suddenly emerged in February 1992 as a force in the industry. The tribe's Foxwoods High Stakes Bingo and Casino near Ledyard, run by a team of gaming experts and native Americans, was dollar for dollar the nation's most profitable casino. Several former Golden Nugget executives, including ex-president Al Luciani, were directing the tribe's success.

The $60 million Foxwoods casino, with its 2,600 employees, attracted nearly 500,000 customers in its first month of operation and grossed approximately $500,000 per day. Even without the use of slot machines, Foxwoods was the Indian gaming ideal: a quality operation in an excellent location. With plans to expand the casino, add three hotels and a golf course, the industry impact of Foxwoods was felt as far away as Atlantic City.

Slightly more than a year after it opened, Foxwoods posted a profit of $20.4 million in a single month. By comparison, Mirage Resorts grossed $409 million in its first year of operation but netted only $30 million before taxes.

"There's an understated elegance to the place," tribal spokesman Bruce MacDonald said. "It's not tacky, it's not chintzy. It has windows. You don't have pulsating neon. It's not as tough on the eye as most casinos."

The native American success story impressed Las Vegas. In less than a month, Wynn and Mirage Resorts appeared at the Legislative Office Building in Hartford to make their pitch. If the Indians could gross $200 million per year without slot machines on the reservation without the best amenities, then there was no telling how much an operator with Steve Wynn's skill and experience could generate. At least, that was the idea when Wynn's road show hit Connecticut in late 1992.

Wynn, a Connecticut native who was making a strange sort of homecoming, didn't help matters by proclaiming to the legislature and the state's residents that, "[Connecticut] is boring. There's nothing to do here. I don't think that comes as much of a revelation." What they needed, he decided, was a complex featuring entertainment suitable for the entire family: Movie theaters, bowling alleys, fine restaurants, and affordable buffets.

And, of course, a Steve Wynn casino.

"I can't be responsible for everybody's perception of casinos," Wynn proclaimed before the Connecticut Association of Chief Financial Officers. "And although I am trying to sell, for lack of a better word, a casino, that word dominates every move I make. When I try to explain that it's not what I do for a living, that it's not the business I'm in, people with another point of view say, 'Sure, he's trying to sugarcoat it, he's trying to camouflage himself.'

"Well, I don't even know how to deal blackjacks or craps."

Citizens groups and the Foxwoods lobby had a field day with Wynn's biography and the sordid history of Las Vegas casinos, their case bolstered by criticisms hurled by former Las Vegas politician-turned-radio talk-show host Steve Miller, who, before being forced off the air, read damaging news reports about the Mirage.

Connecticut residents, who had long since legalized many other forms of gambling, including lottery and pari-mutuel wagering at horse tracks, dog tracks, and jai-alai frontons, were slow to warm up to Wynn. "I felt as if I was an extra in a *Godfather* movie," the Reverend Howard Stewart of Hartford told a reporter. It was precisely the impression Wynn had tried not to make.

The Mashantucket Pequot Indians weren't about to get massacred again. Their lobby cut to the heart of the matter by offering $100 million for the exclusive rights to operate slot machines at Foxwoods and found an ally in Connecticut Gov. Lowell Weicker, Jr. The guarantee, which eventually rose to $113 million, was built into the state budget. (The Indians could afford it. By 1994, Foxwoods was grossing approximately $600 million.) If the gaming-expansion bill passed, then the Foxwoods guarantee would be canceled.

Mirage's New City Development eventually countered by announcing that it was willing to raise the stakes and match the

Foxwoods group figure, but in the end—with nowhere nearly enough votes to override Weicker's promised veto—the gambling-expansion bill didn't come up for a vote in the legislature, and the Indians prevailed.

Despite a relentless political press, flashy video presentations, the promise of two $350 million resorts, and an impressive lobbying effort by Mirage's Connecticut point man and New City Development President Richard "Skip" Bronson, the outcome was the same dismal turndown suffered in Florida.

———

Canada was next on Wynn's expansion agenda.

In February 1994, word surfaced out of British Columbia that Wynn's Mirage Resorts had entered into a casino partnership with VLC Properties of Canada to build a resort in Vancouver skirting Burrard Inlet.

The $750 million resort, to be called Seaport Centre, would feature a 1,000-room hotel with a 270,000-square foot convention facility on a twenty-four-acre waterfront plot. The promise of 11,000 new jobs, a $190 million annual payroll, and $256 million in total annual tax revenues initially made the project appealing to the Vancouver development community.

But there was the usual catch: Casino gambling was illegal in Vancouver; Wynn not only would have to sell the Canadians on his company and character but also on the whole casino industry.

It would not be an easy sell. Canadians might accept Lotto, and a good percentage of Vancouver's vast Asian population might find its way to back-room card and dice games throughout the city, but the thought of glittery casinos in their sparkling city, with its fresh air and low crime rate, struck many residents as appalling.

On first blush VLC seemed the ideal partner for Mirage. After all, the British Columbian provincial government held a 16 percent stake in the firm. Entering into a partnership with the same officials who ultimately would be responsible for approving casino gambling and licensing applicants likely would make it easier for Mirage to spread north of the border.

For his part, Wynn was the picture of confidence. Opponents wouldn't stand a chance. "If your government says, 'Go—do it and do it your way,' a billion dollars is not too high a price to spend on this development....I am talking about quality, building the finest, integrated recreation and entertainment complex in the world....It's happening in other cities of the world, and here we are at Mirage at the top of our game. This is an industry whose time has come and here we are, middle-aged and feeling good—and surf's up."

The Mirage team wasted no time accentuating the positive for the Vancouver media.

The casino's job generation would have a strong impact on Vancouver's 9.8 percent unemployment rate. The company's on-the-job training program is second to none. The average annual salary for all Mirage employees in 1993 was $33,584, not including a $10,000 medical and dental package. The work force is one-third minority based, and Mirage's 12 percent annual turnover rate was approximately one-third that of other Las Vegas casinos.

Not mentioned was the known downside to casinos: the jobs that gradually would be lost; the racetracks or handful of charitable bingo operations that would be out of business; the individually owned restaurants, pubs, and hotels that would be destroyed because they couldn't match a resort's prices; the crime wave that might be triggered by a gigantic cash business and swarms of tourists; the up to 7 percent of the population that would develop a compulsive gambling problem.

For its part, the *Vancouver Sun* flatly hated the idea of a mega-casino in its city. Suave Steve Wynn and his advance team had failed to make the right impression.

"There's a word for resorts where a fake volcano erupts every few minutes and stuntmen on a replica pirate ship and frigate reenact a battle. The word is tacky," the *Sun* proclaimed in an editorial. "The charms of the 'pleasure palaces' with which Mirage Resorts Ltd. has graced Las Vegas are lost on us, although clearly not on the thousands who flock each year to these 'destination resorts,' which offer their clientele endless slot machines and gaming tables, Vegas-style shows, lagoons, golf courses, a white tiger display, etc., etc., etc. Opines Mirage chair Stephen Wynn, marketing guru extraordinaire, worshipper of Walt Disney (this explains the pyrotechnics): 'Las Vegas exists because it is a perfect reflection of America.' We think not, but to each his own poison.

"...So far, Mirage's marketing of Seaport Centre Vancouver— casino, cruise ship terminal, hotel and convention center—has been reminiscent of the snake-oil salesmen who once blew into town. Jobs! Money! Housing! Fun! Something for everyone! Why, Mirage even employs the old 'run-me-out-of-town-if-I-cross-you' trick: 'If we screw up, you must have the right to kick us out without the right of appeal,' Jim Ritchie, a company vice-president, told a reporter. Thanks for the advice, but let's pass on the flagellation offer and remember what the snake-oil salesmen called their audience: rubes."

The VLC-Mirage partnership initially appeared to have the inside track with the provincial government through a labor-friendly alliance with the Liberal Party. But even VLC's formidable influence and the support of local unions did not mitigate the reality that, unless the public warmed to the idea of casinos in their neighborhood, the legalization issue was controversial enough to end the careers of its backers. The Friends of Steve at the provincial government went underground. The Seaport Centre juggernaut was grinding to a halt.

In July 1994, the *Sun* revealed that Wynn and politically connected VLC Chairman Jack Poole had been negotiating the resort proposal in secret several months before the federally-owned Vancouver Port Corporation announced that it was accepting ideas from developers. Intriguingly enough, early discussions included a cruise-ship terminal and convention center but made no mention of a casino. Government insiders knew about the Mirage plan and had said nothing.

Meanwhile, Wynn's relationship with the media had long since gone cold. His big idea was crumbling before his eyes, and his personality continued to get in the way of business.

"Steve Wynn has a PR problem: Himself," *Sun* columnist Elizabeth Aird wrote in early June 1994. "Mr. Mirage swanned into town this week, acting for all the world like a messiah misunderstood by us ungrateful wretches who just can't appreciate the blessings he wants to bestow upon us.

"....Wynn looks like the California guys you see on re-runs of *The Rockford Files*, except he doesn't wear jewelry, not even a wedding ring. His only adornment is a gold watch with a black alligator-patterned strap. His feet were bare inside buff leather loafers. He was wearing beige stretch pants that looked polyester but surely couldn't be, and a black sweatshirt with an insignia on the front.

"Mr. Wynn can't seem to bear it when anyone fails to appreciate the great gifts he wants to give this city.

"...Do we want to buy into Steve Wynn's vision of heavyweight prizefights, Disney-style extravaganzas, mass-market tourist shows aimed at grabbing the biggest possible audience? Is that what we want for our children? If the French can consider Euro-Disney a cultural invader, why can't we take a lesson in cultural backbone from them?

"Steve Wynn is as incomprehensible a creature as I've met in a long time, and the objections he's hearing from Vancouver people seem every bit as incomprehensible to him. There is no good reason to bridge the two solitudes."

Just five months after Mirage's promising Vancouver announcement, Mirage had worn out its Canadian welcome. "The project's backers have tried every trick in the book to drum up public and political support for the casino and none of them has worked," the *Vancouver Sun* stated in an editorial.

With the public overwhelmingly opposed to the casino proposal at the Seaport Centre, the governmental entities were forced to heed the people.

———

Of all Wynn's big ideas, the licensing attempts of Mirage subsidiaries in the Midwest held fleeting promise.

His push for a casino spot near Houston remains far less than certain. His casino development agreements with the Sac and Fox nation in Kansas and the Puyallup tribe in Washington state were quickly moved to the back burner.

Wynn also bombed in West Dundee, Illinois, in a fizzled partnership with Arlington International Racecourse. Mirage Resorts was one of several Nevada casinos to be stopped short of carving out a deal in Chicago. Wynn's effort in St. Louis in 1994 quickly was replaced by potentially more lucrative markets.

Beyond the United States, his attempt to enter the lucrative Australian casino market met with defeat. More promising was his 50-percent partnership with British casino operator Max Kingsley and a group of Asian investors in the Casino Iguazu in the far northeastern tip of Argentina, near the famed Iguazu Falls.

But for the deal to work, the Argentine government would have to expand its gambling statutes to include ownership by American companies, something for which Wynn and his partners were willing to lobby. According to Buenos Aires newspaper accounts, that effort included enlisting the presence of no less than former President George Bush to help smooth the transition on behalf of Mirage. Bush, who had been spotted playing the Shadow Creek golf course, through a spokesman denied the reports.

For once Wynn was not at the center of controversy, but an Argentine casino was another idea whose time had not yet come.

"This spread of gaming, the complexity of new jurisdictions, and the issues raised are going to put a new requirement upon fellas and ladies like myself," Wynn told a *New York Times* writer. "A requirement to be very circumspect. To learn how to think dialectically, on a number of levels besides just operational. We're in the political business now."

What was wrong? What was causing setback after setback, rebuff after rebuff?

"In Las Vegas, he's the king. There's no question," a vice-president of a gaming corporation said. "There's no question. He's obviously a charismatic, very bright, and very creative guy. But he overpowers people. Somebody like Steve comes in, and he scares them. It's too slick. It's too Las Vegas. In Vancouver, he was almost a caricature of Las Vegas. Here he comes with his perfect suit, perfect hair, and perfect teeth."

Another casino industry executive, who has observed Wynn's road show, said, "Steve's basic position is, 'Here's what I'm here to sell. If you don't like it, you're an idiot.' That tends to offend some people.

"Wall Street eats out of his hand through his marketing. Gaming analysts kiss his ring. But what are the results? The company spent $11 million in R and D [research and development] in 1993, and what does it have to show for it? He'll never admit it, and his underlings will never tell him, but he's the problem. For all his bluster and outward confidence, he still wants to be accepted as a mainstream corporation. It's not going to happen. The only way Mirage is going to do anything outside Nevada is if he stays in the background. That's not going to happen, either."

Another longtime Las Vegas casino executive, whose company has ventures pending in several jurisdictions, said, "Steve has poisoned the well so many times. He can say what he wants, but it's just true. He gets up and lets everyone know how smart he is and how ignorant they are."

Circus Circus executive Mike Sloan has watched Wynn rise from liquor distributor to the most dynamic force in legalized gaming.

"Steve is a remarkable guy," Sloan said. "He's one of the most gifted people I've ever known. We should be grateful he does have a few shortcomings. To the extent he's learning to control [his emotions], he's going to become a formidable player in other jurisdictions."

Until then, Wynn finds himself landlocked in Las Vegas: at the center of the gaming universe but a million miles from international acceptability.

CHAPTER 18

THE VEGAS KING

Steve Wynn's influence in nearly every aspect of Southern Nevada life may be difficult for occasional Las Vegas visitors to appreciate. His strength in the community transcends the fact that he heads a $1.7 billion corporation which employs nearly 20,000 workers. Although he has failed to still all the voices of discontent and occasionally mistakes bullyboy tactics for political strategy, Steve Wynn in Las Vegas truly is king.

Wynn's Shadow Creek golf course is allowed to consume as many millions of gallons of water as necessary to keep it tropical because Wynn owns rights to water pumped from the same aquifer that services hundreds of other lesser mortals who must conserve according to a strict summer schedule or face a citation.

Wynn is capable of putting a halt to proposed monorail projects that do not suit his vision of the future of the Strip, no matter to what degree that they might alleviate choking traffic.

With his superior vision and battalion of attorneys, Wynn changes the course of streets and sewer lines almost at will. And woe unto the lowly politician who crosses swords with him.

Where other casino operators have been content to influence elections through campaign contributions, Wynn has developed his own political machine capable of affecting the outcome of races ranging from the Clark County Commission to the House of Representatives.

Wynn's political fund-raising skill has sent shock waves all the way to Washington, where his outspokenness about President Clinton's tax policies upstaged Nevada's Democratic congressional delegation.

The influence of Wynn pervades Southern Nevada's education system, where Elaine Wynn has established herself as one of the most powerful forces at the University of Nevada–Las Vegas and the Clark County School District.

Unlike his casino industry predecessors, Moe Dalitz and Howard Hughes, who possessed formidable influence but allowed others to stand in the public eye on their behalf, Wynn is up front at every press conference and nearly every commission meeting. The effect has made him the most recognized face in Nevada and the American casino industry.

In 1992, *Fortune* magazine listed Wynn as the year's most highly compensated executive in corporate America. His salary and benefits, including lucrative self-awarded stock options: at least $34.2 million. That year, after paying down its junk-bond mortgage notes, Mirage Resorts netted only $28.4 million. A *USA Today* study of executive stock options conducted by CDA Investnet listed Wynn as the sixth highest paid boss in the nation with $35.7 million in exercised options alone. His stock options were exercised at an average price of $8.75. In March 1993, each of those shares was worth $32.55.

Wynn called the magazine article misleading, telling stockholders that the figure was arrived at by estimating the value of decade-old stock options that had come due. Wynn was one of hundreds of corporate executives who beat the Clinton administration's proposed tax changes by cashing out their stock options before the end of 1992.

"I haven't gotten a nickel of that money," Wynn told his fellow shareholders. "They are just valuing my options, and I don't get options every year. It would have expired in March 1993, and I would lose if I had not exercised that option."

Wynn's $285 million personal net worth placed him just off the list of the 1994 edition of the *Forbes* 400 Richest Americans. His friends, brothers Michael and Lowell Milken, were worth a combined $810 million. Las Vegas gaming industry rival Bill Bennett, who earlier in the year had relinquished the chairman's seat at Circus Circus, was worth an estimated $515 million. Jeremy Jacobs, son of Emprise Corporation founder Louis Jacobs, whose company was convicted of concealing ownership in the mob-riddled Frontier in the deal that brought Steve Wynn to Las Vegas, was worth more than $450 million. But no executive made more in 1992 than Wynn.

Along with money have come the trappings of wealth and the perquisites of heading a billion-dollar corporation.

In addition to the relatively modest ranch home on Bannie Lane in Las Vegas, Wynn owned a ski chalet at Sun Valley, Idaho, next to his mentor, E. Parry Thomas. He was also building a $10-million mansion on the grounds of Shadow Creek.

Friends and rivals might match or even better his personal wealth, but none approach the unprecedented hold on Southern Nevada politics and business that Wynn enjoys.

Even if he has to struggle for respect elsewhere, Steve Wynn reigns over Las Las Vegas as its undisputed monarch.

———

But it takes more than money to maintain the throne. It also takes plenty of influential friends and the ability to force political change.

Where previous Las Vegas casino operators limited their campaigning to the amount they contributed to candidates, Wynn has crafted a different course by creating his own in-house campaign central complete with maps of political districts, phone banks, and constant public-opinion polling. Favorite candidates not only receive cash contributions, but, perhaps more importantly, gain access to his polling and political telemarketing.

For one so accustomed to issuing orders to underlings like lightning bolts from Mount Olympus, Wynn has taken a decidedly softer tack in shaping public opinion—especially with the highly opinionated seniors whom Mirage Resorts courts with its "Silver Voice" newsletter.

The "Silver Voice," circulated to Southern Nevada's burgeoning retirement population, features tips on everything from ballot initiatives to apple muffins. Whether it qualifies as a service to the community or a prime example of Wynn's growing and maturing political power base is a matter of perspective. One thing is certain: Much like recreational activities that have captured his fancy over the years, Wynn treats politics as a blood sport for which he has shown a hard-hitting talent—and a growing, if sometimes misguided, killer instinct.

"Mirage Resorts takes its role as a corporate citizen very seriously. Throughout the year, we are happy to provide services to our community through support of seniors, veterans, the homeless, and many other volunteer projects," one issue of the "Silver Voice" boasted. "At election time, our 19,000 employees are very active in the election process. Virtually all of our employees who are eligible, register to vote. They educate themselves about the candidates and issues that affect our country, our state, and our local community. They back up their involvement with strong participation at the ballot box."

Properly motivated, Wynn's more than 19,000 employees are capable of swinging almost any political race in the state.

Wynn was therefore given much credit in the Las Vegas media for helping promising Republican congressional candidate John Ensign defeat Democratic incumbent James Bilbray in the GOP Massacre of 1994. On the other hand, he was unable to assist Hal Furman in knocking off Democratic incumbent Richard Bryan in the U.S. Senate race.

Wynn collected nearly $1 million for the Republican cause. He also developed a habit of calling up Nevada's congressional delegation and issuing his strong opinions on the direction in which the Democrats ought to vote on key issues. Although he denied he was attempting to threaten Nevada's senators, the muscle flexing was obvious, and the message was received: With a burgeoning political machine at his disposal, no one dare take Steve Wynn lightly.

Even Wynn's $1 million contribution in 1993 to the John A. Moran Eye Center at the University of Utah is not without its political spin.

Wynn's donation toward the Michael M. Wynn wing of the Moran center came after he withdrew a similar contribution to Johns Hopkins University whose administrators failed to follow precise instructions on the manner in which the donation was to be used. Moran, the chairman of the Dyson-Kissner-Moran Corporation of New York, had recently been named the finance chairman of the national Republican Party.

Wynn-backed candidates have managed to succeed at all levels, but his machine occasionally misfires. His success rate remains spotty. It may be a sign that the much-maligned voting public may not be ready to sell out to muffin recipes, election tip sheets, blanket phone polls, and rhetoric worthy of a sword-wielding political pirate.

———

Wynn's life may be filled with uncanny coincidences and far-fetched twists of fate, but the men who comprise his inner circle of protectors and attorneys provide one of its most perplexing puzzles. Many are the same men who, as state gaming regulators, federal prosecutors, and local and federal law enforcement officials, have held his future in the industry in their hands.

Foremost is former Nevada Gaming Commission Chairman Frank Schreck, one of Nevada's most effective powerbrokers. An attorney for major players in the gaming industry, Schreck also is a chief Democratic Party fund-raiser.

In Nevada, few politicians survive more than one campaign without the blessing, and the financial backing, of the state's largest industry. Schreck has managed to remain with a foot in each world for years. By the time he was thirty, the Nevada-born Yale graduate had emerged as one of the state's leaders in the Democratic Party. As a gaming commissioner, he led a unanimous vote to approve Steve Wynn's casino license at the Golden Nugget.

Schreck's clients enjoy an uncanny success rate before Nevada's Gaming Control Board and Gaming Commission. Members of both bodies are appointed by the governor, the same person for whom Schreck helps raise millions of dollars in casino-industry campaign contributions. In Nevada, with its politics so inseparably intertwined with the casino industry, such relationships are relatively common. Only on rare occasions are they criticized.

Wynn also hired career FBI man James Powers, who ranks among his earliest corporate executive trophies.

Powers became the special agent-in-charge of the bureau's Las Vegas office in 1977, after his predecessor retired in the wake of charges of misconduct by several Southern Nevada-based FBI agents. Those agents were disciplined for accepting complimentary favors from the casinos and for grooming uncomfortably close relationships with mob associates. Powers was sent in to write a new chapter in the FBI's flawed history with the Las Vegas casino industry. Instead, he joined Steve Wynn.

After being defeated for reelection in 1979, former Clark County Sheriff Ralph Lamb joined Wynn as a security director at the Golden Nugget.

Lamb, who had survived numerous federal investigations ranging from organized crime influence within the department to income tax evasion, appeared well suited to handle security at the downtown casino. He was intimately familiar with "half wiseguy" characters Louis Cappiello and Neil Azzinaro. A lifelong Nevadan, Lamb also was well acquainted with the sometimes-tricky nuance of measuring the caliber of reputed hoods.

Wynn hired former gaming commission member Clyde Turner and former control board Deputy Chief Ron Tanner.

In Atlantic City, former New Jersey State Police Captain Joseph Petuskey was hired as director of security. Sabino Carone, a twenty-five-year FBI veteran, became director of surveillance. Al Luciani, who helped draft the Atlantic City casino act as an attorney with the New Jersey Division of Criminal Justice, later became president of the Golden Nugget before leaving the corporation after a dispute with Wynn.

Wynn would acquire the political expertise of former Organized Crime Strike Force prosecutor James Ritchie, whose involvement with the casino industry spans three decades. Ritchie was one of the Justice Department's most promising young prosecutors when he made the decision to enter private practice in Washington. On the way, he was named to the Commission on the Review of the National Policy Toward Gambling.

Of all the federal authorities to join Wynn's entourage, Stanley Hunterton had perhaps the most promising career of all.

An award-winning strike force prosecutor with the Justice Department's Detroit and Las Vegas offices, Hunterton ranked as one of the country's biggest mob busters. He was a key prosecutor in the casino-skimming and hidden-ownership case against Allen Glick's Argent Corporation and in Detroit prosecuted the case that led to the ouster of mob interests at the Aladdin. Hunterton also supervised the insider-trading investigation of the Golden Nugget. Although a grand jury was convened, the inquiry did not result in an indictment.

In 1984, Hunterton left the Department of Justice to accept a position as deputy chief counsel of the President's Commission on Organized Crime. He served on the commission sixteen months, inviting his friend and future client, Steve Wynn, to testify on behalf of the casino industry in matters pertaining to Golden Nugget high-roller Anthony Castelbuono's laundering of small bills at the Atlantic City casino. Hunterton later resigned from the commission and entered private practice, where Wynn became his biggest client.

———————

Nowhere in Southern Nevada has Steve Wynn's presence been greater than at the University of Nevada–Las Vegas.

In the name of remaking the image of Las Vegas, Steve and Elaine Wynn embarked on a plan to make UNLV a respected center of higher learning. On the way to turning the state university into the Harvard of the West, they managed to ignite a firestorm that consumed the careers of controversial college basketball coach Jerry Tarkanian and an auditorium of lesser figures.

The sordid tale begins in 1972 with the hiring of a new basketball coach at UNLV. Southern Nevada athletic boosters, seeking respect for the maligned college known to many as "Tumbleweed Tech," believed that the fastest way to national prominence was through athletic success.

The boosters, a group which included the most powerful and politically active members of the Las Vegas community, found their man in Tarkanian.

At the University of California, Long Beach, Tarkanian had gained a national reputation for winning despite being unable to recruit the best athletes in the country. He also had become known as a rule-flouting iconoclast who was the bane of the NCAA's existence.

Tarkanian's teams won from the outset, but his reputation as a rebel without a rule book persisted. As he built his program into a national powerhouse with one hand and fought the NCAA with the other, Tarkanian was for a time the darling of the Las Vegas social scene. His teams packed the convention center and later the Thomas and Mack Center. He was featured on local television commercials hawking everything from cellular phones to gold jewelry.

In the front row of every Rebel home game sat the biggest names in Las Vegas society. Among them: Irwin and Susan Molasky, Dr. Elias and Jody Ghanem, and Steve and Elaine Wynn, sometimes accompanied by one or more of their famous friends from the entertainment industry. Of all the showrooms, lounges, discos, and restaurants in Las Vegas, this was the place to see and be seen. It became known as Gucci Row.

Then came the recruitment of Lloyd Daniels.

Daniels was born in 1967 to a mother who died when he was only three years old. He was raised by his grandmother in the East New York section of Brooklyn but lived on the street. By 1986, Daniels' ability with a basketball had gained mythological proportions on the playgrounds of New York. Daniels not only had been featured in *Sports Illustrated*, but he was the principal subject of John Valenti's stirring book, *Swee' Pea and Other Playground Legends.*

At a sleek 6-feet-7, Daniels was the consummate street-ball legend: a player capable of dominating at guard, forward, and even center, a sleight-of-hand artist whom experts readily compared to Magic Johnson. And Lloyd Daniels was not yet out of high school.

Nor was he about to graduate any time soon.

As superb as he was on the court, Daniels was at a total loss in the classroom. Only his athletic skill kept him in school. He bounced around through four high schools in three years, racking up superlative statistics in every category but attendance and

grade-point average. Daniels rarely attended class, had a reputation for drug abuse and petty theft, and showed no interest in
learning. "I ain't allergic to no school," Daniels once said. "I just
don't want to go."

Daniels was sought after in 1986 by dozens of universities but
chose to attend UNLV. Runnin' Rebels recruiting coordinator
Mark Warkentien moved to obtain legal guardianship of Daniels,
who took remedial-reading courses at UNLV and, later, attended
Mount San Antonio Junior College.

Daniels was dyslexic, read at a third-grade level, and, worst
of all, showed no interest in bettering himself for any reason other
than gaining academic eligibility. It took plenty of assistance,
including earning two credits for playing on the school's basketball team, but after a year, Daniels managed to muster just enough
credits to qualify as a junior-college transfer student to UNLV.
On paper, Lloyd Daniels was a university student—even if he
couldn't read the paper.

Once he moved to Las Vegas, Daniels quickly reacquired his
Brooklyn street-running habits.

In February 1987, Tarkanian's grand experiment exploded.
Daniels, the student-athlete, the next Magic Johnson, was
arrested outside a North Las Vegas crackhouse after attempting to
buy $20 worth of rock cocaine. He was rounded up along with
fifty-three others. Daniels stuck out in a crowd. "You're ruining
my career," Daniels told a television cameraman, who captured the
star recruit in the floodlights.

Tarkanian moved swiftly, dropping Daniels from the program
before he had dribbled a basketball in an official practice, but it
was too late.

As if Daniels didn't carry enough personal baggage to campus,
he also traveled in the company of self-described commodities broker Sam Perry, who was no more a trader in pork bellies than
Daniels was a Shakespearean scholar. In reality, Lloyd's friend Sam
was Richard "Richie the Fixer" Perry, a mob bookmaker with two

convictions for sports fixing, including the Boston College basketball point-shaving scandal of the late 1970s. Perry surfaced when he posted a $1,500 bail for Daniels.

"Lloyd Daniels shocked everybody," Wynn told *Shark Attack* author Don Yaeger. "When we found out that they had tried a scheme of making the guy a guardian, everybody said, 'Whoa.' The manner in which it was handled was disrespectful of the university and the university's obligations that it voluntarily and freely assumed as a member of the NCAA system.

"The recruitment and the treatment of Lloyd Daniels was flagrantly out of line with the obligations that we had to assume. I just thought this was crazy. I didn't understand what anybody was thinking. For them to go out and adopt a guy and think that it was okay and then proceed to do things under the flag of a ward, of a legal guardianship, it was preposterous. It was spitting in the face of the NCAA. We looked real, real, real stupid. He looked stupid. We looked like we were sneaky and dumb. ...To do that while you're an official of the athletic program, if Jerry [Tarkanian] didn't understand the rules chapter and verse, he should have.

"We're at a level of accountability here that you can't escape. If we're looking like we don't respect our commitments flagrantly, if we look stupid, it's embarrassing. We looked stupid."

Investigative pieces surfaced about Tarkanian's basketball program. Most were written by *Los Angeles Times* reporter Danny Robbins. Some were written by Las Vegas journalists. From the players' fancy cars and clothes to Tarkanian's trading of his 220 complimentary game tickets for services in the community, nothing was sacred. A program that had been protected by powerbrokers from the casino industry to the Metropolitan Police Department suddenly found itself exposed.

Tarkanian resigned effective at the end of the 1991-92 season after photos of sports-fixer Perry playing basketball and sharing a hot tub with three Runnin' Rebels surfaced in the *Las Vegas Review-Journal.*

Even before Tarkanian left the campus, the university administration was caught authorizing a secret videotaping of the Runnin' Rebels in an illegal practice. The video camera was positioned in an air-conditioning duct and appeared to capture the team being led by then-UNLV assistant coach Tim Grgurich in a practice prior to the NCAA-mandated time.

Although the footage confirmed the suspicions of Tarkanian's critics, the videotaping outraged much of the Las Vegas community. It didn't matter that university counsel Brad Booke, UNLV president Bob Maxson's in-house lawyer, accepted responsibility for authorizing the taping. The damage was done. The good guys were acting like bad guys in this soiled morality tale.

It proved a turning point for University Regent Shelley Berkley, who went from being a staunch supporter of the president to an ally-by-default of the Tarkanian camp.

"The videotaping was an affront to academics, an affront to decency, and it was stupid on top of everything else," Berkley said.

When she dared to speak her mind to a newspaper reporter, Berkley said she received a threatening phone call from Elaine Wynn.

"If you supported Bob [Maxson]," Berkley said, "you were one of them. There was no give or take. I was one of those who were totally intoxicated by Bob. We won the national championship that April. The money was pouring into [Wynn's private University Foundation]. The '91 session of the legislature went extremely well for UNLV. Those foundation board meetings were social events; I couldn't wait to go. When I became a regent, I thought I was going to be schmoozing with the foundation people, cutting ribbons, and drinking a piña colada with Elaine."

Gradually, Berkley said she began to realize who actually controlled the university.

"I thought, 'Who's in charge here?' He's our employee. Bob worked through the foundation and largely through Elaine. Elaine was the foundation. Who was going to argue with success? But it was all being dictated to us, and I thought, 'There is something wrong here.' It also became clear that Bob was serving two masters. His real master was the foundation board."

The foundation provided a home for the president, generous spending accounts, and exquisite perquisites.

"[The regents] were just inconveniences that he just needed to pat on the head. I would say they [foundation board members] were his patron saint. It gave him an incredible amount of clout that was not commensurate with the role he was playing. We had no control over the president. This was a good deal for Bob and the Wynns. And they were Machiavellian enough to appreciate it. Elaine established the foundation mechanism. It was infantile when she took it over. What they received in return was of tremendous benefit to the Wynns."

During a foundation awards dinner, at which Elizabeth Dole was the keynote speaker and Elaine Wynn was honored for her generous support of the university, Berkley said she looked across the jammed banquet room at the Mirage and saw a group of twenty Connecticut legislators taking in the scene.

They were in Las Vegas as the guests of Steve Wynn, whose subsidiary was lobbying hard for the passage of legislation legalizing his company's casino projects. They couldn't help but be impressed by the status honorary Ph.D. Elaine Wynn enjoyed as the guiding light of higher education in Las Vegas. Combine that sight with the letters and phone calls by the university president lauding the Wynns' generosity, and it painted a compelling portrait of concern for UNLV and the community.

"I realized that the money that the Wynns donated to UNLV was small potatoes in comparison with what they received on that night alone," Berkley said.

With Tarkanian gone, there was the matter of a replacement to consider. With plenty of lobbying help from Steve Wynn, Villanova Coach Rollie Massimino was the choice of UNLV president Bob Maxson.

Massimino had led Villanova to its only national championship and enjoyed a national reputation as a coach whose players earned their college degrees. "No Rebel player will ever embarrass this university [again]," Massimino announced at his opening press conference, immediately offending Tarkanian sycophants throughout the valley.

It wasn't long before Massimino had to eat those words. By the end of his first year, it was discovered that his best player, Isaiah "J.R." Rider, had taken a seminar for credit in premenstrual syndrome in order to gain eligibility. Rider, who enjoyed the services of an academic tutor, was later found to have turned in plagiarized homework.

Rider's academic shortcomings did not prevent him from being a first-round NBA draft choice and signing a multimillion-dollar contract with the Minnesota Timberwolves. They did, however, help paint Massimino and the Maxson administration as hopeless hypocrites.

Massimino would be well compensated while at UNLV with a five-year guaranteed contract. His announced annual contract was worth $386,000, including salary, personal appearances, and television and radio. His Nike shoe deal was worth another $200,000.

Unknown to the public, a large segment of which had made a daily sport of scrutinizing every move made at the university in the wake of Tarkanian's departure, Massimino had quietly signed a supplemental contract with the Wynns' private University Foundation to "perform other and different duties to enhance and promote the growth, reputation and development of the University, consistent with and in furtherance of the goals and objectives of the Foundation."

The foundation, which later changed its name to the Varsity Club, heaped cash and benefits on the new coach. While the public believed Massimino was being paid $386,000 per year, his secret contract called for him to receive from $350,000 to $600,000 per year in additional remuneration. By comparison, Tarkanian had been criticized for making $600,000 per year.

The subject of Massimino's contract wound up before the Nevada Commission on Ethics where the former Villanova coach testified, "They structured it, they said this is the way we can do it, it was fine, there was no debate, no major discussion in any way."

In November 1994, the commission made the call: "The Commission concludes that the Supplemental Contract between Roland Massimino and the Foundation, and later between Mr. Massimino and the Varsity Club, violated the Code of Ethical Standards...in that the Supplemental Contract provides for the payment of Mr. Massimino of private income from a private source for the performance, at least in part, of duties that were already required of him as a public employee."

The ethics commission did not find Wynn culpable. He was an academic and athletic booster, not a state employee. The commission did, however, find his fingerprints all over Massimino's recruitment and secret supplemental contract.

In the end, the commission vilified Maxson and university counsel Brad Booke, both for violating the state's ethical standards. Massimino, whose Varsity Club friends were suddenly absent from his side, found himself clawing for a way out of town. His contract was bought out for $1.88 million.

Of all Massimino's transgressions, failing to win a high percentage of his games proved perhaps his greatest sin. Although he won 60 percent of his games as UNLV's coach, attendance at the Thomas and Mack Center plummeted. Revenues for basketball, which had long supported the rest of the athletic department, dropped sharply. By the time he left UNLV, well compensated to be sure, Massimino's reputation as an academically oriented coach was ruined.

Tarkanian was the winningest coach, by percentage, in college basketball history, but key boosters, including Steve and Elaine

Wynn, decided that he projected the wrong image for the university and that he had to go. The community was put through a meat grinder in the process.

In the wake of Massimino's ouster, Tarkanian's loyal assistant, Tim Grgurich, left his job with the Seattle SuperSonics to become UNLV's new basketball coach. Millions of dollars had been spent. Several careers had been ruined. The bloodied Tarkanian had prevailed and took his seat behind the UNLV bench for the team's first home game.

Steve and Elaine Wynn, who quietly canceled their $2-million endowment for the retired university president and received only minimal criticism from the largely intimidated Las Vegas media, were not in attendance.

———

But even Steve Wynn, with his ferocious reputation and millions, is not immune from the dark heart of Las Vegas, as he found out in a bizarre episode involving his daughter Kevin.

On July 26, 1993, Kevin Wynn was returning from a dinner date at the Mirage with her family and friends to her condominium on Crooked Stick Way in the exclusive Spanish Trail community west of the Strip. It was approximately 10 p.m. when she pulled her white Audi into the garage.

Spanish Trail is a gated, guarded development that is home to many of Southern Nevada's wealthiest citizens. Kevin Wynn, a tall, attractive twenty-six year old with long blonde hair and the older daughter of the most visible man in the gaming industry, worked in the logo development department of a company named Atlandia Design.

Entering through the garage into the kitchen, she flipped on the wall light and turned toward the living room.

Two masked men, one tall and one short, grabbed and easily overwhelmed her. Chaos followed. Her eyes were taped. The short man began talking nervously.

"You didn't see us," he said. "You didn't see us. You don't know what we look like."

"What do you want?" she gasped, shaking.

"We want money."

"What money?"

"We just want the casino's money."

In that moment Kevin Wynn realized she had not interrupted a burglary in progress. She had been the intended target.

"Please don't hurt me. Please don't hurt me," she said. Then she began to sob.

A phone call was placed to the Mirage. Steve Wynn was paged. His daughter's captors demanded $2.5 million in untraceable currency. It was the kind of money the public presumes a man of Wynn's substantial means can with a finger snap pick up from the casino cage.

In reality, withdrawing that much cash from a casino cashier cage even the size of the Mirage, which grossed $721.8 million in 1993, would be immediately noticed. Draining the cash on hand would halt operations at one of the biggest gambling operations in the world. Although Wynn said he was "frightened beyond description and very confused," he also was angered by the request from the man on the phone, who called himself Voss.

"You can't do that, it will cause a complete stir," Wynn told his daughter's kidnapper. So Voss compromised.

The kidnappers, in a second phone call, agreed to settle for $1.45 million.

Kevin Wynn and her father exchanged only a few words.

"Don't worry, honey, I'm gonna take care of this," Wynn told his daughter.

"I love you, Dad," she said.

"I love you, too," he said.

Wynn was told by the man on the phone that he would be under constant surveillance at the hotel. He was instructed to drive from the Mirage to Sonny's Saloon, a bar located on Spring Mountain Road just north of the resort. Again Wynn balked. With his degenerative eye disease, he said he couldn't drive at night. His personal valet, Albert Oaks, would deliver the cash, Wynn said. The kidnapper agreed.

Instead, Wynn managed to signal hotel security agent Charles Price. He would pose Price as the driver, informing him of the instructions as they moved through the Mirage's crowded tropical atrium. Price drove the car and made the ransom drop at a spot between a convenience store and Sonny's Saloon.

———

At the condominium on Crooked Stick Way, the short man was giving orders and feeling confident. He had been watching Kevin Wynn for weeks. He knew her work hours, where she lived, who her friends were. He knew her Audi's license plate—BIONDA—was Italian for blonde. He had been referring to her as "blondie" to his accomplice. He'd even burglarized her automobile and removed her garage-door opener in preparation for this night. He had bragged to his friends that he had pulled similar jobs, and that he had run drugs from Chicago. He viewed himself as a wiseguy just one score away from the big time and his obsession—a Ferrari Testarossa. Steve Wynn's daughter would make his dream come true with piles of money to spare.

Kevin Wynn was escorted to her bedroom and ordered to disrobe. She reluctantly complied, removing her jumpsuit. While in her bedroom, her abductors stole an estimated $180,000 worth of her jewelry.

Wearing only a bra and panties, she was positioned on the bed next to the tall man and heard the click of flashbulbs as the short man took snapshots of her in a compromising pose. Dark glasses covered her eyes, which were taped shut. She was made to appear a willing participant in the pictures. The photos would be used as insurance to prevent her father from going to the police, the short man said. If Steve Wynn contacted the authorities, copies of the photographs would be sent to the *National Enquirer.*

With the ransom calls completed, Kevin Wynn was led from the bedroom to the garage. She was forced onto the floor of her Audi and covered with a quilt. The vehicle was driven at a leisurely pace. From the voices, she believed the tall man was black, the short man white.

As time passed, Kevin Wynn began to fear the worst.

"I thought they were driving me out into the desert somewhere," she said later. Instead, she was taken to the overflow parking area of McCarran International Airport.

It was there her assailants left Kevin Wynn, telling her she would be watched constantly and instructing her not to move.

"I hope this money does you good," she said to the tall man. "Isn't it a shame that we're born into different situations, and this has to happen?"

A few moments later, the small man said, "It was nice meeting you."

"Under different circumstances, I might have said the same thing to you, but I'm very scared right now," she replied.

With Mirage President Bobby Baldwin driving, Wynn followed the kidnappers' instructions and turned into the parking lot shortly after midnight. They spotted the Audi and recovered the frightened young woman.

The exchange had been made: $1.45 million for Kevin Wynn.

From start to finish, the ordeal had lasted two-and-a-half hours.

———

By morning the local and national news media were featuring the story.

"Casino Mogul's Daughter Kidnapped and Freed," a *New York Post* banner headline blared. National television tabloid programs feasted on the story of the casino man's beautiful daughter.

Just as quickly, armchair experts began speculating as to the kidnappers' motivation. Money was one obvious reason, but was it too obvious?

Was Steve Wynn laundering money from his own casino?

Were the ghosts of the New Las Vegas's mob past returning to haunt the golden boy of legalized gaming?

A weekly Las Vegas tabloid, the *Casino News*, fueled the money-laundering speculation. The mob talk was abundant, as was the chatter about what Wynn would do once he got his hands on the kidnappers. Former Nevada Governor Mike O'Callaghan raised such ominous speculation in his *Las Vegas Sun* column.

The FBI was called in.

The first break in the case came almost immediately. The telephone used to place the follow-up call to the Mirage was located outside the 7-Eleven convenience store adjacent to Sonny's Saloon. The same pay phone had been used earlier in the evening to call the Sacramento residences of Ray Marion Cuddy, Jacob Sherwood, and Anthony Watkins. Shortly after the investigation began, Cuddy's twenty-two-year-old son, Jason Cuddy, was located in Las Vegas and questioned extensively about his father.

Follow-up interviews located a taxi driver who identified a man fitting Cuddy's description at the pay phones at approximately the time the call was made to the Mirage.

At McCarran International Airport, surveillance cameras had recorded Cuddy's 1986 Volkswagen Rabbit, including its license plate, entering the parking lot at 11:28 p.m. and exiting twenty-two minutes later. Earlier that evening, an airport surveillance camera also recorded Kevin Wynn's Audi entering the airport's overflow lot. Cuddy's accomplice, Jacob Sherwood, had left a palm print and fingerprint on the parking-lot ticket.

Then Cuddy did something really stupid.

Less than a day after he had abducted the daughter of the most powerful gaming figure in the New Las Vegas, Cuddy strolled into Newport Motors, a Southern California auto dealership, and picked out a $196,000 red Ferrari Testarossa. If he was going to be a millionaire, and for the time being he was just that, then he planned to look like one. He would buy only the best ostrich-skin cowboy boots, even if they did cost $2,000 a pair.

He opened several checking accounts at banks throughout the Newport area in a crude attempt to launder the mounds of cash. He kept nearly $200,000 in the trunk of his car. And he kept a pistol with him, too.

Six days after the kidnapping, when he returned to the dealership to pay off the Ferrari, police and FBI agents nabbed Ray Marion Cuddy.

"It's hard for me to call [Cuddy] a mastermind," FBI agent Tom Griffin deadpanned.

"They left a paper trail...that would choke a goat," Assistant U.S. Attorney Jay Angelo said at the trial.

━━━

Testifying at the trial were seventy witnesses, including the victim and her father. Kevin Wynn was questioned by the defense only briefly. Steve Wynn was not crossexamined. Elaine Wynn and Kevin's sister, Gillian, sat in District Judge Lloyd George's courtroom and at times were accompanied by gambling patriarch Jackie Gaughan, whose own family had once experienced a hostage ordeal.

Perhaps the most baffling aspect was the fact the trial took place at all.

Considering even a small part of the evidence—Cuddy nailed with the money and Sherwood's finger and palm prints on the parking lot ticket—the two men were headed for a long fall. Despite this, they rejected a plea-bargain offer that would have meant a twelve-year sentence. Their recalcitrance was not lost on the judge, prosecution, FBI agents, or Steve Wynn. "It was just two guilty people taking a shot," Assistant U.S. Attorney Tom O'Connell said.

Case agent Mike Growney, who retired days after the kidnapping trial ended, went further still: "In twenty-four years as an FBI agent, the greatest obscenity I've ever seen is Cuddy and Sherwood, knowing the facts of this case, forcing Kevin Wynn and her family to relive twice that night of horror and degradation."

In the end, Steve Wynn, who has had so much to say on so many subjects, kept his comments brief.

"The family is relieved that our daughter's ordeal is...coming to an end. We have been a part of the trial process and have witnessed in person the behavior of the men who conducted this miserable affair.

"After waiting for an explanation of some sort, which was not presented at trial, we are unable to understand why these cruel and calculating criminals chose to make Kevin, her mother, and the rest of the family relive that experience.

"Now Cuddy, Sherwood, and Watkins can face the grim reality of the hard life in federal prison. We will resume our lives, but we will do so with deep personal understanding and compassion for victims of violent crimes."

Steve Wynn would resume his life but increase the security around him and his family. The family's home on Bannie Lane in the upscale Scotch 80s neighborhood could be made only so safe. Wynn began construction of a mansion at the Shadow Creek golf course.

The course, home to high-rolling golfers and friends of Wynn, features a high fence, constant security patrols, and surveillance cameras. Wynn also hired former Cincinnati FBI boss Al "Slick" Tolen as a security supervisor, an experiment that fizzled after a few months. Mirage sources privately lamented that Tolen enjoyed his job of fine-tuning the security at Shadow Creek, but he liked golfing there even more.

Wynn would keep a closer watch on his family even as he kept running scared into the future.

RUNNING STRONG INTO THE FUTURE

October 17, 1994. Steve Wynn was back in the news doing what he does best: announcing a new resort-to-end-all-resorts in Las Vegas.

Less than a year after the Dunes was collapsed in a brilliantly choreographed cloud of dust, a new Las Vegas resort was being heralded as the next wonder of the world. This one would make the sparkling Golden Nugget look like a service station, The Mirage and Treasure Island look like cardboard cutouts. Never given to understatement, Wynn declared that it would be the "single most extravagant hotel ever built on Earth."

Called Beau Rivage, French for "beautiful shore," it would be an $800-million, forty- six-story, 3,000-room resort sculpted on a seventeen-acre island moored in a shimmering fifty-acre lake that surrounded the jewel with stretches of beautiful shore.

At a press conference, Wynn recapped the growth of his company from a downtown casino without hotel rooms into a $1.7 billion corporation with four Nevada properties, 8,151 rooms and suites, 240,500 square feet of casino space, 7,110 slot machines, and nearly 20,000 employees. With the Golden Nugget downtown and the Mirage and Treasure Island on the Strip, Wynn had twice raised the level of competition. And once again he was about to raise the stakes.

Even Nevada Governor Bob Miller was on hand to praise Wynn's latest coup. "I think that all of us realize that that success in large part, and almost to the extent of exclusivity, comes from the creative genius of Steve Wynn," Miller said. "And that creative genius has enabled our community to have destination resorts which have reshaped gaming in Nevada and gaming throughout the world."

"The secret, in my view, of Steve Wynn's genius—and he is a genius—has to do with the employees," Culinary International official John Wilhelm said. "I don't think it has to do with the bricks and the mortar...These properties open so well, run so well, are so financially successful. When the companies grow, they [employees] grow, too....All of us in the union are excited about not only this new project, but we're excited about the fact that if you work for this company, you can feel good and you can feel confident about your future."

"Nevada's future will be determined by Nevada. Not by Texas, Alabama, Florida, New Jersey. Our future depends on what we do," Wynn told his audience. "It is a living testimony, in the most absolute unequivocal terms, of the success that even in a regulated industry that individual entrepreneurial spirit coupled with a partnership with an enlightened government can make just about anything happen."

To accommodate his new project, an enlightened county government has allowed Wynn to build a forty-six-story resort on an island in the desert; to reroute an asphalt artery, Harmon Avenue, and a major sewer line; and to intrude a 540-foot building into the Federal Aviation Administration-certified air space at McCarran International Airport.

In Steve Wynn's sophisticated world of marketing, almost anything can happen.

And his competition knows it.

———

Only weeks after the Beau Rivage announcement, Wynn's image machine shifted gears once more. Wynn said his visits to Lake Como near Milan in Northern Italy had enchanted him. He decided to change the name of his new project from Beau Rivage to Bellagio, a small town near Lake Como.

Translated, Bellagio means "elegant relaxation."

This, explained Wynn, was precisely what he had in mind for his latest, greatest-ever casino-resort creation.

———

"People love to bad-mouth Steve because he can be extravagant and showy. But just about everything he touches turns golden, and no one is going to deny that," Binion's Horseshoe President Jack Binion said years earlier.

Added Henry Gluck, president of Caesars World, "You have to separate the ego from the accomplishments. We don't care what he says or does as long as he brings in business to the city."

Harrah's executive Claudine Williams marvels at Wynn's business acumen.

"I sit back as a person who has pawned her ring to get money on an old piece of ground, and I think it takes something special inside a person to do the things he's done," she said. "My God, we should be thankful to have someone with his creativity. He has somewhere amassed the knowledge of how to raise the funds. I have a great deal of respect for Steve. I really think everybody in the state, whether they approve of everything he's done or not, should be damn glad he did it. He didn't do it as easily as everybody thinks he did....I know how hard this business is. A lot of people hate you if you've got two dollars. They don't know how hard this couple [Steve and Elaine] worked to get them. People think they've always been rich. These kids worked...Egos are bad when they get out of control, but without an ego, I don't think you could do much of anything."

Barbary Coast and Gold Coast owner Michael Gaughan, who had worked with Wynn two decades earlier at the Golden Nugget, said, "He's probably about the most creative guy I've been around. He hates day-to-day operations, but his eye for detail is fantastic. He probably overspends, but Steve has never done anything second rate. He's the only gaming guy outside of Resorts International who probably ever made a killing in Atlantic City. I think Steve overspends, but he does have a knack. Probably in gambling right now, Steve might be the Number One guy."

Circus Circus executive Mike Sloan: "The conventional wisdom was that the Mirage couldn't make it. That's absolutely proven to be false. His success in Atlantic City was spectacular. For better or worse, he's the poster boy of American gaming."

———

In careworn downtown Las Vegas, Wynn is also the driving creative and political force behind the Fremont Street Experience, a $64-million "celestial vault" under construction over one of the most recognizable thoroughfares in the world.

With downtown's casino profits faltering and its customer base dropping, Wynn enlisted the help of architect Jon Jerde to attract new customers to Fremont Street. The answer was to construct a computerized canopy above Glitter Gulch, outfit it with lasers and thousands of synchronized lights, and flip the switch on a Vegas-style Disney light show.

"Better to see the hookers and avoid the panhandlers," one cynic suggested.

The porous canopy, designed to provide shade during the day and special-effects light shows after dark, will shelter retailing kiosks and feature events to draw tourists downtown. The addition of a 1,600-vehicle parking garage will ease congestion and approximately 38,000 square feet of retail space will add to the experience.

"The Golden Nugget's share of the development cost of the Fremont Street Experience is $3 million," Mirage Resorts' 1993 Form 10-K to the Securities and Exchange Commission states. "The other major participating casinos are contributing similar amounts, bringing the casinos' total contribution to $18 million. The balance of the $63 million total development cost will be principally provided by city redevelopment funds and the Las Vegas Convention and Visitors Authority."

With Kenny Wynn supervising the design and construction, the Fremont Street Experience is set to open in late 1995.

Culminating a great year for Wynn, in November 1994 he was named the Hotelier of the World by *Hotels* Magazine, a publication circulated to more than 150 countries.

It was a gracious Steve Wynn who accepted the honor. "This award is made possible because of the dedication of our employees who share a commitment to keeping our promise of making our guests' visits to Las Vegas memorable."

———

None of these triumphs have sated Wynn. His appetite for investment is becoming as diverse as it is ravenous.

Despite numerous setbacks outside Nevada, Wynn wisely took advantage of a changing political climate in New Jersey and his friendship with Republican Governor Christie Whitman. Wynn flew to Trenton to applaud her State of the State address—and the pending casino deregulation—to announce in 1995 his interest in returning to Atlantic City, the "slum by the sea" he had raced to escape eight years earlier.

The investigation of Steve Wynn by the New Jersey Division of Gaming Enforcement was something of a lampoon.

Midway, Governor Christine Todd Whitman of New Jersey was Wynn's guest in Nevada.

Were the investigators going to embarrass their Governor?

No way.

A man being interviewed by an investigator was surprised and amused by the delicate tone of the questions.

"Listen," he said. "This investigation is just an exercise, isn't it. This is a done deal, right?"

The investigator nodded.

In a matter of months, the once-snarling New Jersey Division of Gaming Enforcement proudly announced that its exhaustive investigation of Wynn and his Mirage Resorts associates had developed nothing that would prevent it from recommending licensure. Investigators discounted the damaging New Scotland Yard report and did not revisit the findings of their own 1986 report raising questions about the organized crime ties of employees of the Atlantic City Golden Nugget.

The investigators based their recommendations in part on the twenty-two affidavits of former law enforcement officers, who swore they knew of no connection between Wynn and the mob. The fact that some of the officers were receiving compensation was not made public.

In late June, the Casino Control Commission unanimously voted to license Wynn and welcome him back to Atlantic City, where he announced plans for a $600-million megaresort on a 178-acre tract of real estate.

With his ego in check, and his attorneys billing overtime, Steve Wynn is finally poised to expand his immensely popular casino resorts outside Nevada. After one appears, others are sure to follow—presuming he can continue to run ahead of his critics.

The ability to play the gracious host to presidential candidate Bob Dole in 1995 at Shadow Creek only accentuated Wynn's image as a man capable of operating politically at every level of government. Dole, a Kansas Republican who was an outspoken critic of the amorality of Hollywood, enjoyed the generosity of Wynn and a select group of supporters at a luncheon that raised $500,000.

Wynn and Dole have more than a conservative agenda in common. They also enjoy the services of imagemaker Sig Rogich, the former Las Vegas advertising executive who helped craft media perceptions for Presidents Reagan and Bush.

And Wynn continues to look for new venues to conquer. He is a member of an international investment group, H.N.V. Acquisitions, which was believed to be headed by Michael Milken, whose former Drexel Burnham Lambert clients willingly followed the man who had financed their futures in the 1980s with junk bonds.

With Milken as its most notorious investor, the group in 1994 began bidding hundreds of millions of dollars for real estate and office buildings throughout Europe. Among Wynn's fellow partners: media magnate Rupert Murdoch and cellular-technology developer Craig McCaw.

Milken's conviction on federal securities fraud charges might have banned him for life from working for a United States brokerage firm, but nothing prevented him from making personal investments or from offering his expert advice to friends. His felony conviction also did not stop him from amassing a mountainous investment portfolio, including his 1994 partnership to acquire Heron International, a London-based company that held twenty-two office buildings throughout Europe. For its part, the Gaming Control Board did not appear concerned that Wynn was conducting business with the most notorious white-collar criminal of his generation.

In October 1994, Wynn joined the board of directors of International Cablecasting Technologies, a publicly traded company which programs, markets, and distributes Digital Music Express, a leading digital audio service that provides commercial-free music to local cable television systems.

"Steve Wynn will be a tremendous addition to our board," ICT's Chairman and Chief Executive Officer Jerr Rubinstein said.

As the country moves closer to entering the information superhighway, the DMX system—known as the HBO of radio—is bound to grow geometrically in popularity.

It was a long way from Anne Arundel County to the cutting edge of digital audio music distribution, but Wynn's business interests have grown and diversified.

Nothing illustrates that more clearly than his joint venture with director Steven Spielberg, former Disney Studios chief Jeffrey Katzenberg, record industry honcho David Geffen, and Chicago-based restaurant magnate Larry Levy in *Dive!*, a submarine-themed eatery located at the Fashion Show Mall on the Strip. Spielberg's quest for the ideal submarine sandwich led him to open the first *Dive!* in Los Angeles.

Another potential diversification for Wynn was probably nothing more than a bargaining chip. In June 1995, Nevada Power Company, the state's largest electrical utility, secretly applied to the Public Service Commission to sell power to Mirage Resorts at a multimillion-dollar discount. Its reason: Mirage had threatened to drop the utility and produce its own power through a technologically advanced cogeneration process.

If the requested discount smacked of an instance of corporate extortion on the part of the state's biggest casino player, Nevada Power appeared only too happy to accommodate.

Rushing to keep Mirage as a customer not only promised to cost residential customers more money, but it opened the way for other resorts to obtain similar discounts.

▪▪▪▪▪▪▪

Dozens of photocopies of the New Scotland Yard report surfaced wherever Mirage Resorts lobbied for a casino. Politicians and reporters received copies for their consideration, all mailed anonymously.

It was obvious that someone didn't like Steve Wynn.

Wynn dispatched private investigators to the East Coast to obtain affidavits from retired organized crime officials willing to refute the report's contents.

Two dozen affidavits, many with similar wordage, and all with the same sentiments, were thus acquired. These were sworn to by former cops and retired FBI agents, some of whom worked or had worked for Wynn and his attorneys.

A typical example: retired FBI agent John J. Danahy swore that he read the report and said that, in his opinion, it contained considerable innuendo from unidentified sources of unstated reliability and unverified information.

The others were almost identical in tone and conclusion.

Wynn's bloody battle with the British report seemed to have ended in June 1995, when, despite the report, he received unanimous approval for a casino license in Atlantic City.

Relying heavily on the affidavits, the New Jersey Casino Control Commission referred to and then totally discounted the dusty 172-page accusation-filled New Scotland Yard report and welcomed Steve Wynn back to Atlantic City.

Said Commission Chairman Bradford Smith: "In summary, considering the entire record before us, there is simply no basis to afford any credence to the allegations in the purported New Scotland Yard report concerning a relationship between Stephen Wynn and organized crime."

At Wynn's request, "certain portions of the record" were sealed from public view.

Amen!

Although he is unlikely to match or exceed elsewhere the immense success and influence he has enjoyed in Las Vegas, and his attempts to expand into other jurisdictions have been mostly unsuccessful, Wynn remains the single most important image-maker in Las Vegas history. With his resort creations and attempts to portray himself as a sparkling clean businessman with an Ivy

League education, Wynn has changed the shadowy face of Las Vegas forever.

But as Wynn scores victory after victory, his greatest nemesis may perhaps turn out to be the Disney dice-dealer image he has created.

Las Vegans remember Moe Dalitz and Benny Binion with fondness not merely because of their generosity and colorful personalities but because both held no delusions about their place in society's big picture. Despite Dalitz's impressive record as a developer and Binion's love for the ranching life, they were neither contractors nor cowboys but gamblers proud of their calling.

In his breathless attempt to turn gambling into harmless entertainment and remake himself as the son of Walt Disney, Wynn appears to have forgotten that his roots are not in the Magic Kingdom but in East Coast bingo halls and the carpet joints of Sin City. Despite the best wishes of profile writers, he is not simply an adult version of that precocious ten-year-old who gazed in amazement on the Strip's neon precipice so many years ago.

Legalized gambling, clearly the latest American phenomenon, can now be found in forty-eight of fifty states. It has arrived disguised as increased tax revenue and easy employment in some areas, as part of a sophisticated must-see theme resort in others. Although riddled with scandal and organized crime, gambling has swept across America and established itself firmly in the national psyche from sea to shining sea. The process has been an evolutionary one in which Wynn has played a major role by reshaping the Biblical vice into a widely accepted form of recreation.

"Steve has a different impression of the impression the world holds of gaming," one of Wynn's longtime casino allies said. "He thinks he's John D. Rockefeller. But we're not U.S. Steel. And we never will be. We'll always be thought of as an industry on the edge of propitious behavior."

Said another decade-long acquaintance, "It starts at the basest level of sexual gratification. He's the most powerful and interesting man in town. He definitely thinks he is Walt Disney. Walt Disney and Hugh Hefner."

"He just really forgot where he came from," one of the city's old-school casino operators said. "He knows how to use people. He knew who could help him. If you couldn't do him any good, he didn't need you. One of these times, his hotheadedness is going to get him in trouble."

With his palace at Shadow Creek completed, Steve Wynn in early 1995 moved behind locked gates into his personal playland. A state-of-the-art security system would keep out undesirables, and a $17,000 German shepherd attack dog, which responds to commands in German, was sure to heed his master's voice. The dog had barely settled in at Shadow Creek before it bit the hand that fed it. Wynn's cuts required several stitches.

Michael Milken, Mirage President Bobby Baldwin and Golden Nugget President Barry Shier were rumored to have lots there. Wynn had designed a special corporate tax break for the lots surrounding the fantasy golf course, had spent millions on construction and hundreds of thousands just to raise the grade of the lot and improve the view.

Wynn is more successful than ever.

And more isolated.

For, despite all the wealth, influence, women and fawning executives, Wynn's life had become very much like Budd Schulberg's own Sammy Glick:

"He would still have to send out frantic S.O.S.'s to Sheik, that virile eunuch: Help! Help! I'm lonely. I'm nervous. I'm friendless. I'm desperate. Bring girls, bring scotch, bring laughs. Bring a pause in the day's occupation, the quick sponge for the marathoner, the recreational pause that is brief and vulgar and titillating and quickly forgotten, like a dirty joke."

In the end, there is no such thing as a benevolent dictator, and good kings are the stuff of Arthurian legend. Beyond his hedonistic excesses and insatiable pursuit of acceptance in markets outside Nevada, Steve Wynn remains an accomplished gambling man with imagination, ambition, money and a gift of gab. These have made him the latest Vegas king.

In a society brimming with players great and small, with souls just itching for a piece of the action, those gifts ought to be enough to keep Steve Wynn running strong into the future.

THE RUNNER
STUMBLES

In the wake of the publication of *Running Scared*, Wynn's publicity machine worked overtime to promote Mirage Resorts and its chairman. There was plenty to praise. Company profits were soaring: up 26 percent to a reported net income of $206 million in 1996.

Although few in the media were watching closely, 1996 also marked the first year that the addition of new properties failed to grow gaming profits. Instead, industry publications buzzed with the news that Wynn was planning grandiose casino projects in Atlantic City, Biloxi, Mississippi, and on the former site of the Dunes Hotel on the Las Vegas Strip.

In the middle of it all, he took time out to appear on the syndicated Don Imus radio program, and went so far as to host the Imus show at the Mirage. As ever, Wynn's favorite object of ridicule was Donald Trump: "No one has ever equaled his record. Three failures. Three bankruptcies. No one has ever done that in the gaming business."

In March 1997, Mirage Resorts was listed by *Fortune* magazine as the second-most admired company in America behind Coca-Cola. Later that year, *Men's Journal* published a gushing profile of Wynn, and Charlie Rose devoted an hour of his nightly public television program to praising the man he unabashedly called his dear friend, and whose company happened to be his sponsor on Las Vegas Public Television.

At a Mirage Resorts stockholder meeting in May, Wynn promised greater profits to come with the development of the $1.6 billion Bellagio on the Strip, the nearly $700 million Beau Rivage in Biloxi, and the proposed $2 billion Le Jardin Palais development in association with the Boyd Group and Circus Circus Enterprises (later called Mandalay Resort Group) on an H-shaped 178-acre tract of land lining a marina in Atlantic City. Wynn appeared poised to reshape the American casino skyline to his personal vision of opulence.

"This group's been together a long, long time, and I think we're finally getting the knack of it," Wynn boasted to a reporter. At that moment in time, was there any doubting him?

Mirage Resorts was not the only casino company on a roll in Las Vegas and looking to expand. Under a dynamic new leadership, Circus Circus Enterprises joined Wynn, Donald Trump, MGM Grand, Harrah's and others in the hard sell of legalized gambling in Detroit, a market with a billion-dollar revenue potential.

In a move that infuriated some voters, Las Vegas Mayor Jan Laverty Jones flew to Detroit on a Mirage Resorts jet to deliver a sales pitch for the casino industry while ignoring the fact that the downtown area in her own jurisdiction had grown increasingly careworn. Once voters approved casino development for the dilapidated downtown Detroit area, Wynn pushed hard for one of the licenses, but found himself aced out early. He eventually withdrew from the competition and refocused his efforts on his plan to return to Atlantic City.

If he was the least concerned about competition from Donald Trump, the reigning boss of the Atlantic City Boardwalk, Wynn didn't show it: "Outperforming Donald Trump in Atlantic City is child's play," he boasted, "All his properties together have never made a dime."

Casino industry observers noted that during his licensing in New Jersey, Wynn had clearly benefited from his relationship with Circus Circus and the Boyd Group, companies already approved for licensure in jurisdictions outside Nevada. They would be his partners in the biggest development in the history of Atlantic City.

Or would they?

Initially, Mirage Resorts had agreed to work exclusively with Circus Circus. The two companies had already successfully developed the Monte Carlo on the Strip, and the H-tract site would be an ideal follow-up. But only hours before the final bid was to be submitted for the acreage, Wynn phoned Circus Circus Chairman Mike Ensign and told him he wanted to purchase the land alone.

Although reportedly furious with Wynn, Circus executives maintained their composure and remained in the deal. According to Pete Earley's *Super Casino: Inside The 'New' Las Vegas*, "it would be the last time the Circus Circus officers would rely on their personal relationship in a business deal with Wynn.

"After the bid was approved, Boyd Group joined the partnership.

"After conferring with Clyde Turner, Ensign and William Richardson, Schaeffer sent word that Circus Circus was willing to pay $40 million toward Wynn's expenses. But from this point on, Schaeffer announced, the company wanted all of the details of its dealings with Wynn drawn up in a formal contract. "There would be no more handshake deals."

Little had changed physically in Atlantic City in the decade since a series of investigations and licensing hearings had led Wynn to sell the Golden Nugget to Bally and vow never to return. Indeed, he had often used BOTH Atlantic City's lack of redevelopment and Trump as the butt of his jokes. But in the mid-1990s a dramatic change occurred in the way New Jersey's casino regulators approached their role. Regulations to ensure that casinos were not infiltrated by organized crime began to be relaxed.

A damaging report generated by investigators about Wynn and his company were shelved, and Wynn was poised for a dramatic return to Atlantic City as the developer of a large parcel of real estate once used as a city garbage dump. He planned to create a casino district apart from the Boardwalk, and he added the political muscle needed to see that plan come to fruition.

By 1996, Wynn had not only reacquainted himself with the New Jersey political structure by befriending Governor Christie Whitman, then touted as a possible nominee for Vice President, but had contributed to the campaigns of local politicians, the kind whose votes could control the destiny of the H-tract site.

Atlantic City Mayor James Whelan became an unabashed supporter of the project despite the fact that a state-funded roadway leading to it would displace dozens of residents and cost $330 million, only $55 million of which Mirage Resorts was obligated to pay. Known officially as the Atlantic City-Brigantine Connector, the 1.8-mile arterial was portrayed in the press as an example of a state enamored of a single casino mogul over the interests of its own citizens.

One of the most vocal of those citizens was Lillian E. Bryant, whose family had owned its home for more than 30 years before she received the state's ultimatum: take the money, or else.

"Steve Wynn must have something good on these people," she told *Philadelphia Inquirer* columnist Steve Lopez. "The state is bickering about having to pay $200 million for public education by an order of the Supreme Court, but they'll spend $300 million to build a private driveway for a billionaire."

On Wall Street, news of Wynn's Atlantic City progress was reflected in a steadily rising stock price. Mirage Resorts shares hit $30 in late 1997 as word spread of the coming of Wynn's ultimate Las Vegas palace, Bellagio, and a scaled-down vision of opulence in Biloxi, Mississippi called Beau Rivage.

Company lawyers and lobbyists carved their way through the New Jersey political structure. Approval of the tunnel project also put unprecedented pressure on Boardwalk casino owners, chiefly Donald Trump, who made no secret of his contempt for Wynn.

Then Wynn pressed his bet. On September 9, he filed a massive federal antitrust lawsuit in New York against Trump and Hilton Hotels, alleging the two parties had conspired, through sham law-suits and unethical political influence, to prevent Mirage Resorts from entering the Atlantic City casino market. Publicly, the lawsuit was greeted with the same tiresome claims and counterclaims that had been a given in the perennial Wynn-Trump feud.

Unlike the previous litigation against Trump over casino executive Dennis Gomes' contract a few years earlier, Wynn clearly saw the lawsuit as a way to silence his chief critic forever. It was with that level of zeal that Wynn's attorneys and private investigators approached the defendants. It was with that knowledge that Trump prepared to defend himself.

In October, Trump Resorts attorney Kevin Smith hired Manhattan investigative firm William Kish International, whose namesake was a retired FBI agent with a wide network of contacts and a knowledge of the background of Wynn's own hand-picked security director, former FBI agent Tom Sheer. The war was on.

But Wynn was used to fighting battles on many fronts. While his attorneys and investigators fought the Trump lawsuit, he was busy flying to Europe to spend millions on the art of Cezanne, Matisse, Van Gogh and others to hang on the walls of the Bellagio Gallery. Although some stockholders were shocked, their voices were lost in the chorus of praise for Wynn's upscale vision of Las Vegas and his $1.6 billion addition to the local skyline. For good measure he acquired the tacky Boardwalk Casino and three other parcels of Strip real estate near the Bellagio for another $135 million.

Each side worked to develop damaging dossiers on the other. The difference between Trump and Wynn was clear: While Trump's flaws and foibles were mostly the stuff of tabloid headlines — he was the subject of numerous authorized and unauthorized biographies — Wynn had been investigated for far darker issues, and had spent a fortune to keep his background out of the public eye and away from media scrutiny, as was proven by his hometown litigation in Las Vegas against *Running Scared* publisher Lyle Stuart over one sentence in a book catalog advertisement.

Kish in February 1998 hired West Coast private investigator Louis "Curt" Rodriguez, a former Los Angeles cop and IRS and U.S. Customs Service operative, to collect information on Wynn and Mirage Resorts. There was plenty to do. Months earlier, Mirage Resorts marketing host Laura Choi had been arrested in Korea, convicted and jailed for currency violations.

In attempting to collect casino markers, Choi violated Korean law by smuggling currency out of the country and failing to declare it in the United States. In the midst of a financial crisis, South Korean authorities took the violations seriously. Although Mirage was certainly not the only Las Vegas casino company to break the law — the Tropicana and MGM Grand would commit similar money laundering infractions — the Choi case was fully exploited by Trump.

The Nevada Gaming Control Board investigation only complicated matters for Wynn and his crew of executives and attorneys. During the state inquiry, Agent Raelene Palmer interviewed Mirage legal counsel Bruce Aguilera in late January 1998. At the time, Choi was still locked in a small jail cell in Seoul.

Wynn's company denied she was sent to Korea to collect casino debts and that they'd abandoned her. In that conversation, Palmer asked Aguilera whether he had spoken to Choi about her return to the United States. Aguilera told the agent he had not spoken with

Choi. Aguilera's apparent deception later returned to haunt Wynn and Mirage Resorts.

In August, the Gaming Control Board filed a 12-count complaint against Mirage for violating state regulations, including those rules intended to track money laundering and other currency transaction violations, and took special notice of Aguilera's alleged lie to the gaming agent.

Mirage settled the complaint three days later with a $350,000 fine that was spun by the company as being "made for the purposes of avoiding litigation and economizing resources." Although Aguilera did not admit lying to the agent, the Mirage neither admitted nor denied the state's claim, but "acknowledges that clear and convincing evidence likely exists to substantiate this count."

By then, however, a six-figure fine and a little corporate embarrassment were the least of Mirage Resorts' concerns. In their relentless pursuit of Trump, Mirage operatives had secretly drawn private investigator Curt Rodriguez into their camp to act as a double agent.

———

Meanwhile, the gaming industry press remained focused on the coming of Bellagio, which promised to bring unprecedented taste to the Las Vegas market. Visitors would be able to dine at a different gourmet restaurant each night for a week. Julian Serrano of San Francisco's famed Masa's, Sirio Maccioni of Manhattan's Le Cirque, and Allesandro Strada of Mary Elaine's at Arizona's Phoenecian Resort were swept into Las Vegas with the fanfare that traditionally accompanied the arrival of Elvis or Frank Sinatra.

Add to that the prospect of a Broadway-caliber musical in the showroom along with Cirque du Soleil's $100-a-ticket "O," and the Bellagio promised a memorable experience for those able to afford it. Wynn was so confident that he could successfully leave the vast mid-level gambling market to lesser operations that he bragged that Bellagio would blow away all competition.

Although the Mirage set Strip performance records after its 1989 opening, at $1.6 billion, Bellagio was still a Titanic-sized risk. The Strip had added more than 40,000 hotel rooms since the Mirage's debut a decade earlier. Not only had the ensuing years increased competition for the well-heeled gambler market with the opening of Sheldon Adelson's Venetian, Mandalay Resort Group's Mandalay Bay, and Park Place's Paris, but an economic recession throughout much of Asia had made it more difficult to attract the high-rolling, multimillion-dollar mostly-Asian gamblers known as whales. Not only was it more difficult to get them in the door, but the hard times made it even more challenging to prod the whales into making good on their gargantuan gambling debts.

If Wynn saw the trouble signs, he never let on. On the contrary, his bravado only increased as Bellagio climbed skyward.

When asked about the Bellagio's marketing by an industry journal, he scoffed:. "You can't compare anything at Bellagio with what we did at Mirage. We're 10 years more sophisticated. We have a goal that is at least 11 times more ambitious. We have employed unlimited amounts of capital to achieve it. And to be quite frank with you, we have an attitude about this hotel.

"...Bellagio is designed to be an alternative to Paris, as a weekend getaway.

"...So we speak about Bellagio in a quiet, reserved and unexaggerated voice. It's the greatest hotel ever built in any century. Everybody is going to know this as soon as it opens, but we won't say it. We'll let others say it. When you've got what we've got, you don't have to say anything. We've got an attitude. We do newspapers a favor by giving interviews. This hotel is bigger than the publicity. This hotel is bigger than the media."

Not that he stopped courting the media entirely. As Bellagio came closer to opening, Wynn grew doubly irritated with anyone who questioned his vision.

"We ask Wynn if all this doesn't make him a little nervous in the face of the recent gambling slowdown," *Forbes'* Seth Lubove wrote. "He treats the question with contempt. 'It slowed last year,' he snaps. 'One year.' He glances at his German shepherd, who is loyally dozing by his desk. Despite the slowdown, Mirage's occupancies and average daily room rates climbed last year, and its earnings rose 26 percent to $206 million, $1.06 a share."

But the Bellagio, coupled with the Beau Rivage in Biloxi, more than doubled the Mirage Resorts' debt load to nearly $2 billion. All the confidence in the world couldn't change the fact that Wynn was betting the house. How could anyone believe that a 3,000-room hotel could offer the same amenities and service as the world's truly posh, five-star palaces, most of which offered no more than a few hundred rooms? Wynn spent several hundred million dollars of stockholders' money on artwork, and was not in the mood to suffer his investors' complaints.

Wynn decided that if he built it, they would come. Although few of his executives would raise the issue and risk experiencing one of his withering verbal assaults or head-banging tantrums, it was obvious Wynn was confusing the public's tastes with his own.

Adding gourmet restaurants and upscale shopping experiences to the city's surf-and-turf and t-shirt traditions made some sense because, if properly marketed, both ideas contributed to the bottom line. But flying to London with Paul Anka or another celebrity pal on the Concorde to bid on a Matisse at Christie's struck many investors as a shameless waste of corporate assets.

If Wynn possessed a love of art, he did not make it public until the Bellagio project. As he retold the story to an interviewer, the idea for using expensive paintings to develop an elegant theme at his ultimate resort, "... just popped into my mind. What a great thing! I could have a Caravaggio behind the front desk."

His first purchase was Renoir's "Young Women at the Water's Edge" at a cost of $12.5 million. As plans for Bellagio took shape, Wynn went on a buying spree with the company checkbook, spend-

ing millions for one painting after another. He bought several with
his own money too. Even for those familiar with his life's many
obsessions, Wynn's fascination with art collecting was by far his
most expensive hobby.

Finally, his docile stockholders began to speak up and a murmur
of disapproval grew in the investment community.

In a few months he'd put together a collection for Bellagio and
for himself with a combined estimated value of $300 million. It
was considered by some to be one of the finest private collections
west of Chicago. Renoir, Monet, Matisse, Van Gogh, Cezanne. They
were all there in huge letters on the Bellagio's marquee.

Wynn not only had decided to acquire the art, but he would use
these famous names to market his hotel and casino. Wynn's new
obsession with art reminded some observers of his fascination with
dolphins a decade earlier. A few recalled that he once considered
putting a dolphin pond in the backyard of his home, only to encounter a tangle of federal regulations.

To get the dolphin program approved for the Mirage, Wynn enlisted the services of several prominent Las Vegans. Now he took a
similar route to protect his personal art collection from being taxed
as property under Nevada law. It became known as the "Show Me
the Money" bill at the 1997 Nevada Legislature and vividly reflected
Wynn's political power.

Thanks to top lobbyist, attorney Harvey Whittemore created a
legal loophole which allowed buyers of publicly displayed art val-
ued at more than $25,000 to avoid paying tax. The art had to be on
display at least 20 hours each week and 35 weeks each year. Legislators from both parties who didn't know a Renoir from a rental car
rushed to embrace the bill.

All but State Senator Joe Neal and a handful of iconoclasts at the
Legislature. Neal charged that Wynn's tax loophole would cost the
citizens of Nevada upward of $18 million. Neal reveled in his battle
against the casino giant. Wynn's attorneys argued that since Wynn

was already a licensed art dealer, he would have been exempted from the tax.

Then Wynn went further. He not only was free to claim millions in exemptions on sales and property taxes, but in addition he was going to charge a $10 admission to the Bellagio Gallery of Fine Art, thus turning the arrangement into a potential moneymaker for himself and Mirage Resorts. But the Nevada Tax Commission ruled that the personal property deduction wouldn't apply if Wynn charged admission to view the art.

It wasn't as if he weren't already making a hefty profit. Wynn arranged to lease his personal art to the company for $5.2 million a year. Despite Neal's relentless criticism and the obvious favoritism being shown the state's most politically active casino boss, the tax exemption not only became law but was later modified to allow Wynn to charge admission to the gallery.

The $300 million Bellagio art collection served as more than a lesson in how the wealthy and well-connected avoid paying taxes. It was the centerpiece in the resort's greater theme, and Wynn's personal testament to the belief that the public would gladly pay a high price to enjoy a superior experience, as defined by gourmet restaurants, spacious suites and exposure to artistic greatness. Even if Venetian's owner, Sheldon Adelson, could brag that his rooms would be larger than those at Bellagio, Wynn was creating a standard by which all others would be judged.

Skeptics abounded.

Wrote Robert Hughes in *Time*, "Economic meltdown in Asia, collapsing hedge funds in Connecticut, mass layoffs at brokerage houses, a falling market for expensive cigars and Ferraris—yet there goes the Bellagio, sailing into the teeth of the gathering global gale, with 3,000 of the highest-priced rooms in Vegas and something like $300 million worth of works of art nailed to its mast."

Although he called Bellagio a "visionary achievement," Bear, Stearns' gaming industry analyst Jason Ader cautioned that the new resort would cannibalize business from the Mirage. He said, "Inadequate long-haul aviation service continues to bedevil the city, as does the absence of high-rolling Asian gamblers [as well as] and the addition of massive new room supply, which totals more than 18,000 rooms, post-Bellagio."

Wynn proved skeptics wrong before. Said one impressed analyst, "the back of the house at Bellagio is nicer than the front of the house at Circus Circus."

Wynn said, "The Las Vegas resort scene is going to have to deal with ... Bellagio's main-stream, hard-core elegance. My theory has always been that if you build houses of bricks, people can huff and puff all they want."

But something was amiss.

For all their cockiness, Wynn and his number one executive, Bobby Baldwin, had underestimated the negative impact of Bellagio on the Mirage. The high room rates Wynn had bragged about were immediately lowered, in some cases to under $100.

Wynn's prohibition on non-hotel guests bringing anyone under age 21 onto the property offended droves of tourists. His command that no baby strollers be allowed on any Mirage Resorts property was seen by some as an unreasonable rule made by a man who himself once tripped over a baby carriage. Mirage Resorts went out of its way to make it clear the Bellagio was for well-heeled tourists, not weekend slot players from California or lowly locals.

Within weeks, the company was rewriting its marketing concept, lowering its room rates, revising previous statements that Bellagio would rival five-star resorts with a fraction of its 3,000 rooms. It paid the price for its hyperbole in the backlash of customer criticism on the Internet as well as the letters-to-the-editor page complaining about cold cups of coffee and Bellagio's overpriced buffet.

For all its glory, art masterpieces, fancy shops, its gourmet restaurants operated by award-winning chefs, its flower-filled arboretum, and its water show spectacle in the man-made Lake Cuomo, Bellagio was foundering at the bottomline. As fragrant and pleasing to the eye as Bellagio was, it wasn't doing what Steve Wynn properties had always done best: generate superior cash flow for the casino.

If Bellagio was biting into the Mirage's place in the Las Vegas market, the nearly $700 million Beau Rivage managed to overshoot the blue-collar gambling market in Biloxi. The company propensity for arrogance and hyperbole offended area residents, as had its demand that employees work long hours. The local gamblers, it seemed, were more comfortable at Biloxi's less fragrant and less pretentious casinos.

As 1998 ended, Steve Wynn had almost doubled the Mirage Resorts debt load by creating two stunning palaces that weren't returning the nearly $2.2 billion investment fast enough. With time, he might be able to turn them around, but his competition wasn't standing still. Adelson's Venetian, despite its construction delays and labor disputes, was every bit as posh as Bellagio.

At the Mandalay Resorts Group, Glenn Schaeffer and Company unveiled the shimmering Mandalay Bay, which savvy industry observers called "90 percent of Bellagio at half the price." With its themed nightclubs and tropical atmosphere, Mandalay Bay was something the stuffy Bellagio could never be — upscale and fun.

Things became truly crowded when Park Place Chairman Arthur Goldberg opened Paris, barely a croissant's throw from Bellagio. The Paris, too, improved the breed of local resort without losing its sense that visitors weren't looking for European culture when they came to Las Vegas. They wanted a good time, and Bellagio was just a pretentious mausoleum by comparison.

———

The price of Mirage Resorts stock dropped, but Wynn continued his art purchases. Inside the hotel, workers quietly added a bank of nickel slot machines in an attempt to catch the eye of the low-roller crowd and perhaps to try to change Bellagio's image as a stuffy resort for the upper classes.

But it would take more than a revamp of the casino floor to change Bellagio's fortunes. In their attempt to become known as the undisputed king of all high-roller hotels, Mirage executives had showered promotional perquisites on their best players.

A *Forbes* study of the gaming industry's biggest companies found that Mirage Resorts reported a $233 million promotional budget in 1999. By comparison, MGM Grand spent just $97 million. Mirage's suffering bottomline translated into a 63 percent drop in after-tax profits to $58 million for 1999.

In April, at a time when even his closest associates believed his mind should be focused elsewhere, Wynn filed a new lawsuit in federal court in Las Vegas against Donald Trump and his companies.

The lawsuit claimed that Laura Choi and Paul Liu, a senior vice present of Asian marketing at the Mirage, had both conspired with the enemy and stolen trade secrets when they spoke with representatives of Trump. The fact that at the time of Trump's initial contact with Choi, she was still in jail in Seoul after being abandoned by Mirage, was not highlighted in the complaint.

"What will be revealed will demonstrate the most outrageous misconduct, the most flagrant violations of law and decent behavior in the history of the resort hotel industry," Wynn proclaimed. "The behavior of Trump Hotels and Casino Resorts and its agents will be a chronicle of activities demonstrating a complete lack of integrity."

In a way, Wynn was right. But, in the end, it was his own behavior that was questioned most.

Kish International, on behalf of Donald Trump, paid Rodriguez $88,000. But Rodriguez lost his enthusiasm for gathering evidence against Wynn when he was told he could make more money working for Wynn as a double agent than against him.

In a brief filed in federal court, Trump attorney Donald Campbell wrote, "From February 1998 through August 1998, Rodriguez performed various investigative services on [Trump Hotels'] behalf. In so doing, Rodriguez developed information regarding Mirage's illegal business practices as well as impeachment material concerning Mirage executives.

"For example, Rodriguez reported that a Mirage executive engaged in the subornation of perjury in an effort to satisfy jurisdictional requirements for the filing of a lawsuit against a Las Vegas reporter in the State of Kentucky. Additionally, it was a matter of public record that Mirage paid $350,000 to settle a Nevada Gaming Control Board Complaint alleging, in part, that Mirage's legal staff had obstructed an official investigation involving Laura Choi."

Future documents filed with the court by Campbell would establish that the identity of the Mirage executive who had suborned perjury was none other than Steve Wynn.

From an affidavit filed by Trump investigative specialist William Kish:

"Although Mirage and Rodriguez state that it was Trump Hotels that caused the FBI to investigate Mirage, that is absolutely untrue. The Mirage was already the subject of an intensive investigation by the FBI which we learned was conducted under the name of 'Operation Snake Eyes.'

"Mr. Rodriguez personally lodged a complaint with the FBI against the Mirage. To explain, during July of 1998, Rodriguez informed me that the Mirage was aware that he was doing investigative work for Trump's counsel. On almost a daily basis, Rodriguez claimed that his life was in danger. As support for this claim, Rodriguez cited many events he had uncovered during his work for Trump's counsel. He also reiterated several recent events in which he had personally become the subject of illegal acts by Mirage's agents. Among these events were the following:

"A. his roommate's automobile had been broken into and material stolen from the interior;

"B. his roommate's car had been tampered with in such a way as to make his tires blow out at high speed;

"C. his home had been broken into, records taken, and illegal electronic surveillance equipment had been installed, and

"D. he was the recipient of harassing telephone calls."

———

But it got much worse. In his secret capacity as an undercover operative for Mirage Resorts, Rodriguez signed a $10,000-a-month consulting agreement with an attorney in Wynn's stable named Barry Langberg to work on behalf of Wynn's interests. As part of the agreement, Wynn and his company agreed not to sue Rodriguez for any previous actions.

Rodriguez began meeting secretly with Mirage officials as early as October 1998. After making his confidential deal, he turned over confidential documents to Mirage officials in what Trump's lawyers called a violation of law. From January to April 1999, Rodriguez recorded 20 conversations with his sponsor, William Kish, Trump Organization security chief Joseph Guzzardo, former Mirage Resorts Korean marketing executive Paul Liu, and many others in an effort that in court documents was called "Operation Seoul Train."

Mirage corporate security boss Tom Sheer, a retired career FBI agent who had once headed the Bureau's New York office, filed a complaint against FBI agents Hanford and Stowe with the Office of Professional Responsibility, which found no wrongdoing on the part of the agents. Stowe later was promoted to the No. 2 position in the FBI's massive Chicago office, and Hanford became the head of the organized crime unit in the Las Vegas office. What had become less certain was whether Sheer, who had sided against his federal fraternity brothers, still managed to keep his contacts with the local office.

———

While early negative reports from Bellagio and Beau Rivage sent shivers down the spines of some industry analysts, Wynn hustled to counter the growing concern over the future of his company

In late April of 1999, the investment community did something uncharacteristic. It reacted negatively to Wynn's idea. Had the golden boy lost his touch? Mirage Resorts stock fell nine percent in a single trading day. It was a portent of things to come. Arthur Goldberg, who makes no secret of his dislike for Wynn, later got his wish and added Caesars Palace to Park Place's formidable string of resorts.

Wynn who'd made a half-baked attempt to acquire Caesars, now found himself the hunted rather than the hunter by the best shot in the gaming jungle. In late August, Mirage stock tumbled to $12, and Wynn received worse news when billionaire Kirk Kerkorian began buying up massive blocks of the clearly undervalued shares. By Labor Day, Kerkorian had accumulated approximately 10 million shares, or 4.9 percent of the company's stock, and appeared on the verge of a hostile takeover.

The sudden stock purchase reminded casino industry insiders of the often-told story about how, during a Mirage board meeting, Wynn had questioned Kerkorian's abilities in the wake of the opening of the MGM Grand. It appeared Kerkorian had answered the criticism with the devastating understatement that had become his trademark. Those who had challenged Kerkorian rarely realized they were in a fight, until they found themselves being helped to their feet from the canvas of big business.

Later in the year, Kerkorian sold his shares, not only proving that he was capable of adding Mirage Resorts to his list of acquisitions, but pocketing $20 million in profit in the process. The sale came at a time the *Wall Street Journal* called Mirage Resorts ripe for takeover. It was becoming all too clear that Wynn's reign as the enfant terrible of the casino crowd was coming to an end.

Not that he had become a pushover. He railed against a growing number of negative press depictions, and succeeded in killing a lengthy investigative article by Robert I. Friedman for the S.I. Newhouse-owned *GQ* magazine. Ironically, as publisher of the *Cleveland Plain Dealer*, earlier, Newhouse had killed an unflattering story about Teamsters President Jackie Presser at the request of mobster Tony Salerno's attorney Roy Cohn.

Friedman, an investigative reporter and organized crime authority, has expertise that brings him lucrative book and movie contracts, as well as death threats. During one investigation of the influence of the Russian Mafia in America, Friedman was forced to go into seclusion after the FBI informed him a contract had been taken out on his life.

What had Friedman unearthed that would so alarm Wynn that the casino man and his attorneys would actively lobby to halt its publication?

Newspapers reported the political intrigue behind the killing of Friedman's story, but the details contained in the article remained unpublished. Friedman received his full writer's fee and was free to sell the story elsewhere with the unspoken threat that wherever he went one of Wynn's legal pitbulls would follow.

Wynn was portrayed in a somewhat unflattering light in Earley's *Super Casino*, a study of the thriving Mandalay Resorts Group and Mirage Resorts. Earley mentioned the New Scotland Yard report and the money laundering controversy involving Wynn and mobster Anthony "Tony Cakes" Castelbuono without drawing litigation from Wynn. The portrait ran in counterbalance to the glowing portraits of Wynn as a visionary developer in David Thomson's *In Nevada* and Andres Martinez's *24/7*.

A more dramatic sign of trouble came in early September when Mirage Resorts Chief Financial Officer Dan Lee suddenly quit, "to explore other business interests." Behind the scenes, Lee was said to be fed up with Wynn's art-buying binge even as the company's stock was plummeting. Officially, Lee's resignation had nothing to do with the fact Mirage stock had dropped from $26.38 per share in May to $11.75 by the time of his departure.

Wynn denied Lee's departure had anything to do with a reported argument they'd had over his purchase of Cezanne and Matisse artwork for $95 million at a time stockholders were losing their shirts.

Wynn's public statements reflected a man living in denial. "The principal drive at our company is at the hotel level," he told a reporter. "Our Chief Financial Operator position is a little less dynamic than others."

Wall Street analysts and gaming insiders immediately speculated that Wynn's future projects were in jeopardy. They noted that, for all Wynn's contacts in the financial world, it was Lee who had assembled the financial packages which allowed Mirage to continue to expand at extremely favorable interest rates. Lee gave Wynn tremendous credibility, and now poker champion-turned-casino president Bobby Baldwin added CFO duties to his job description. For all Baldwin's talents, the move only served to further shake investor confidence.

And it gave Trump an opportunity to gloat, "It's too bad [Lee] left, but there seems to be a lot of bad things happening to Steve Wynn and Mirage. I've always said Steve Wynn is a lightweight, and now I guess I'm being proven correct. I don't think he can get the financing to build in New Jersey anymore."

Trump knew far more than he was admitting, for behind the scenes his litigation with Wynn grew more vicious. By November 22, 1999, the 10th anniversary of the opening of the Mirage, the company's stock dipped to the $13 mark. Wynn's empire was on the verge of collapse and so was his reputation as a masterful operator.

As if to illustrate the point, that month his trademark charm and broad-brush platitudes about the future of the gaming industry betrayed him during a pitch before a group of influential Wall Street bankers. He attended ostensibly to pump up investor interest in Mirage Resorts and to assure skeptics that he hadn't made a critical mistake by spending so much on Beau Rivage and the art-adorned Bellagio.

Wynn devoted part of his presentation to announce the coming of "Miss Spectacular," a Jerry Herman musical that would be created especially for Bellagio.

"Miss Spectacular" would be presented in the spirit of Herman's "Hello, Dolly!" and "Mame." Alas, Wynn didn't stop there. Inexplicably, he started to lip-sync the tape-recorded songs that he played for the analysts.

"People were shaking their heads in disbelief," one eyewitness told the *New York Post*. "They couldn't get out of that room fast enough to phone in their sell orders."

Behind closed doors, Wynn was losing battles on two fronts. Just days into the New Year, filings in Las Vegas in the federal lawsuit between Wynn and Trump told the sordid story of the hiring of Curt Rodriguez, the sleazy surreptitious recordings, the subornation of perjury in the unsuccessful defamation suit in Kentucky against this book, and a long list of transgressions that promised to stain Wynn's image for the rest of his career.

It would not be easy for any Mirage Resorts executive or associate to explain away the use of briefcases with hidden tape recording devices, a recorder concealed inside a jockstrap, microcassette tapes the size of postage stamps, and a transmitter hidden inside a clock radio. Not to mention the illegal surreptitiously recorded phone calls that had been made to federal agents.

Nevada magistrate Judge Lawrence Leavitt had set an evidentiary hearing for February 22, 2000, but after a 24-hour delay the hearing was called off. The case had been settled. Both parties signed confidentiality agreements, but it was clear Trump had trumped against his bitter rival. Wynn tried in vain to suppress the fact that Trump wasn't obligated to pay him a penny.

As usual, press accounts merely scratched the surface of what had been the most vicious civil action in the history of the gaming industry, one which some observers believed had helped open the door for Wynn's departure from Mirage Resorts.

As if on cue, Kirk Kerkorian's MGM Grand appeared like an invading army on the horizon. It made a $4.4 billion offer for Mirage Resorts. The takeover was friendly, insiders smiled, and inevitable. Wynn managed barely a peep of protest before rejecting the $17-per-share offer as insufficient, but then Kerkorian's crew upped the deal to $21-a-share, or $6.7 billion.

In 12 days, perhaps the most sweeping deal in legalized gaming history was signed. Although Wall Street insiders called it "the 12-Day War," Wynn had been unable to put up anything resembling a fight.

———

Why had a man who had drunk so deeply of the intoxicants of the corporate structure suddenly acquired such an aversion to stock options and first-class perquisites? Had the Trump suit, with its allegations, ranging from money laundering to perjury, rattled him that much? Had he finally gone too far by allowing his own subordinates to run amok in a desperate attempt to destroy an enemy?

Or had his personality, which had attracted investors to him in the first place, become so mercurial that the Wall Street banking community lost its faith in him?

Writing for the *Wall Street Journal*, Andres Martinez wrote, "In the end, no matter who winds up controlling Mirage Resorts, it will emerge from this saga eager to play by Wall Street's house rules — one of which is that you don't trust a madly brilliant artist for whom money is no object to run a publicly traded company."

In *Business Week*, Ronald Grover wrote, "The game he'll miss is called perks galore, and few know how to play the angles better than Steve Wynn. Shareholders paid the bills for a $10 million condo he used in New York, a $3 million home in Atlantic City ... and a $40 million MD-80 aircraft that happens to be bigger than the one

that ferries Donald Trump around. Oh, yes, and none of this includes the $5.2 million Mirage Resorts paid the chairman last year
to rent various works of art he collected so that the company could
hang them on the walls of its Bellagio casino."

The press compared Wynn and Kerkorian. The latter's low profile and aversion to the media had wrongly branded him a recluse
in many stories. In fact, the opposite was true. When in Las Vegas,
Kerkorian was known to frequent local restaurants with old friends.
He never traveled with an entourage, avoided chauffeurs and drove
himself around town.

But the two men were most dramatically different in the way
they ran their hotels. Kerkorian was the quintessential delegater of
authority, unlike Wynn who had his fingerprints on every detail.
Kerkorian never accepted a free meal, drink or plane ride on the
company. For nearly 30 years Wynn hadn't lived any other way.
When Kerkorian attended a fight at the MGM Grand Garden Arena,
he bought his own ticket and never sat in the front row. MGM
Chairman Terry Lanni said in an interview that the only perk he
could recall Kerkorian ever accepting was a cup of green tea during
a company board meeting.

Steve Wynn might have litigated against little people, terrorized
his enemies and struck fear in the hearts of local politicians, but his
bullying ways only made him look more foolish next to Kerkorian's
understated style and formidable billions.

The political community, which had benefited from his largess
and done his bidding, responded to his departure almost as if the
death of a benevolent king had occurred. Former Governor Bob
Miller gushed, "I think that without question he has been the greatest
visionary in the history of Las Vegas. He's done more to modernize,
to upscale it than any single individual."

Some of the farewells were more gracious than others.

State Senator Joe Neal, who had gone to war at the Legislature
over Wynn's art tax exemption, said: "He frightened a lot of politi-

cians with that power. Frankly, I believe MGM will be a better corporate citizen."

Steve Miller, the former City Councilman and Las Vegas political gadfly, who had been forced to apologize to Wynn a few years earlier, seized the moment to attack his old adversary: "The influence peddling he has displayed in the state of Nevada ... has caused him to fall from favor not only of his fellow Nevadans but observers outside." To Steve Miller, Wynn would be remembered "as a blowhard and a manipulator and a corrupter of politicians."

In short order MGM Grand began combining Mirage Resorts' strongest executives with its own crew of top guns. The result would be the most formidable assembly of talent in the history of the casino industry.

MGM Grand officials then let it be known the company intended to sell off Bellagio's $300 million art collection. At the same time, gaming industry sources spoke of a plan to turn the $48 million Shadow Creek golf course, which at one time had been touted by a Mirage spokesman as a country club with a membership of one, Steve Wynn — into a revenue-generator, possibly by selling memberships as well as home lots not far from Wynn's own mansion.

Days after making final its acquisition, MGM Grand announced it had sold eleven of the company's paintings for $124 million. Wynn purchased three of the paintings.

But the clearest sign that a more responsible management team was in place came when it was also announced that the millions generated from the sale of the art, 547 acres of real estate near Shadow Creek, land in the Poconos and Texas, a $3 million home in New Jersey, a $10 million apartment in New York, and a $40 million MD-80 jet — an estimated $250 million in all — would go toward paying down the debt MGM Grand incurred during the acquisition. MGM Grand would also save more than $5 million a year Mirage Resorts was paying Wynn to lease his art collection for the Bellagio gallery.

Wynn, meanwhile, reinvented himself once again. Now he was a man too independent for Wall Street and its quick-buck mentality. He made good on his rumored purchase of the Desert Inn for $270 million, and overcame higher bids on the property from investment groups offering less cash. He appeared re-energized by the prospect of building a new mega-resort project.

Within days of the purchase, Wynn announced he would close the Desert Inn, tear it down and build a sparkling megaresort in its place that would be like nothing Las Vegas had ever seen before. The move would also force the buyout and removal of dozens of residents of the Desert Inn's golf club estate homes and put 1,500 employees out of work.

Wynn's personal tastes and personality had so permeated Mirage Resorts that he'd had a hand in choosing everything from the waitress uniforms to selecting the company's spokesperson — himself — for commercials and in-house advertisements.

Only hours after MGM Grand officially closed the deal and took over the company, Wynn's voice vanished forever from the scented air at Bellagio as well as the rest of his former properties. For whatever success Wynn might enjoy in the future, it would be hard to imagine anything rivaling his prior Las Vegas run.

Steve Wynn had become a ghost in his own machine.

BIBLIOGRAPHY

BOOKS

Adams, James Ring, *The Big Fix*. New York: John Wiley & Sons, Inc., 1990.

Adler, Jerry, *High Rise—How 1,000 Men and Women Worked Around the Clock for Five Years and Lost $200 Million Building a Skyscraper*. New York: HarperCollins Publishers, Inc., 1993.

Bailey, Fenton, *Fall from Grace—The Untold Story of Michael Milken*. New York: Carol Publishing Group, 1991.

Barrett, Wayne, *Trump—The Deals and the Downfall*. New York: HarperCollins Publishers, 1992.

Brownstein, Ronald, *The Power and the Glitter—the Hollywood-Washington Connection*. New York: Pantheon Books, 1990.

Bruck, Connie, *Master of the Game—Steve Ross and the Creation of Time Warner*. New York: Penguin Books USA Inc., 1994.

Bruck, Connie, *The Predators' Ball—The Inside Story of Drexel Burnham and the Rise of the Junk Bond Raiders*. New York: Penguin Books USA Inc., 1988.

Demaris, Ovid, *The Boardwalk Jungle*. New York: Bantam Books, Inc., 1986.

Demaris, Ovid, *The Last Mafioso*. New York: Bantam Books, Inc., 1981.

Dombrink, John, and Thompson, William N., *The Last Resort*. Reno, Nevada: University of Nevada Press, 1990.

Drosnin, Michael, *Citizen Hughes—The Power, the Money, the Madness: In His Own Words, How Howard Hughes Tried to Buy and Sell America*. New York: Bantam Books, Inc., 1986.

Gerber, Albert B., *Bashful Billionaire—A Biography of Howard Hughes*. New York: Lyle Stuart, Inc. 1968.

Hess, Alan, *Viva Las Vegas—After-Hours Architecture*. San Francisco: Chronicle Books, 1993.

Johnston, David, *Temples of Chance—How America Inc. Bought Out Murder Inc. to Win Control of the Casino Business*. New York: Doubleday, 1992.

Kornbluth, Jesse, *Highly Confident—The Crime and Punishment of Michael Milken*. New York: William Morrow and Company, Inc., 1992.

Kwitny, Jonathan, *Vicious Circles—The Mafia in the Marketplace*. New York: W.W. Norton & Company, 1979.

Lacey, Robert, *Little Man—Meyer Lansky and the Gangster Life*. Boston: Little, Brown and Company, 1991.

Levi, Vicki Gold and Eisenberg, Lee, *Atlantic City: 125 Years of Ocean Madness*. Berkeley, CA: Ten Speed Press, 1979.

Levine, Dennis B., and Hoffer, William, *Inside Out: A True Story of Greed, Scandal and Redemption.* New York: The Berkley Publishing Group, 1991.

Linn, Edward, *Big Julie of Las Vegas.* Greenwich, CT: Fawcett Publications, Inc., 1974.

Messick, Hank, *Syndicate Abroad.* London: Collier-MacMillan Ltd., 1969.

Moldea, Dan E., *Dark Victory: Ronald Reagan, MCA, and the Mob.* New York: Viking Penguin, Inc., 1986.

Moldea, Dan E., *Interference: How Organized Crime Influences Professional Football.* New York: William Morrow and Company, Inc., 1989.

Morrison, Robert S., *High Stakes to High Risk—The Strange Story of Resorts International and the Taj Mahal.* Ashtabula, Ohio: Lake Erie Press, 1994.

Neff, James, *Mobbed Up—Jackie Presser's High-Wire Life in the Teamsters, the Mafia, and the FBI.* New York: Bantam Doubleday Dell Publishing Group, Inc., 1989.

Nelson, Willie; Shrake, Bud, *Willie—An Autobiography.* New York: Simon & Schuster, Inc., 1988.

O'Donnell, John R., *Trumped! The Inside Story of the Real Donald Trump—His Cunning Rise & Spectacular Fall.* New York: Simon & Schuster, Inc., 1991.

Pileggi, Nicholas, *Wise Guy: Life in a Mafia Family.* New York: Simon & Schuster, Inc., 1985.

Pollock, Michael, *Hostage to Fortune: Atlantic City and Casino Gambling.* Princeton, New Jersey: The Center for Analysis of Public Issues, 1987.

Puzo, Mario, *Inside Las Vegas.* New York: Charter Books, 1976.

Rappleye, Charles and Becker, Ed, *All American Mafioso—The Johnny Roselli Story.* New York: Doubleday, 1991.

Rubin, Max, *Comp City—A Guide to Free Las Vegas Vacations.* Las Vegas, Nevada: Huntington Press, 1994.

Schulberg, Budd, *What Makes Sammy Run?* New York: Random House, 1941.

Shawcross, Tim, *The War Against the Mafia—the Inside Story of a Deadly Struggle Against the Mob.* New York: HarperCollins Publishers, 1995.

Sifakis, Carl, *The Mafia Encyclopedia.* New York: Facts On File Publications, Inc., 1987.

Solkey, Lee, *Dummy Up and Deal.* Las Vegas, Nevada: GBC Press, 1980.

Spanier, David, *All Right, Okay, You Win—Inside Las Vegas.* London: Secker & Warburg Limited, 1992.

Stein, Benjamin J., *A License to Steal—the Untold Story of Michael Milken and the Conspiracy to Bilk the Nation.* New York: Simon & Schuster, Inc., 1992.

Stewart, James B., *Den of Thieves.* New York: Simon & Schuster, Inc., 1991.

Stone, Dan G., *April Fools—An Insider's Account of the Rise and Collapse of Drexel Burnham.* New York: Donald I. Fine, Inc., 1990.

Stuart, Lyle, *Casino Gambling for the Winner.* Secaucus, NJ: Lyle Stuart, Inc., 1980.

Stuart, Lyle, *Lyle Stuart on Baccarat.* Secaucus, NJ: Lyle Stuart, Inc., 1984.

Stuart, Lyle, *Winning at Casino Gambling.* New York: Barricade Books Inc., 1995.

Turner, Wallace, *Gamblers' Money.* New York: The New American Library, 1965.

Valenti, John, *Swee' Pea and Other Playground Legends—Tales of Drugs, Violence and Basketball.* New York: New York Newsday, Inc., 1990.

Venturi, Robert; Brown, Denise Scott; Izenour, Steven, *Learning from Las Vegas.* Cambridge, MA: The MIT Press, 1993.

Yaeger, Don, *Shark Attack—Jerry Tarkanian and His Battle with the NCAA and UNLV.* New York: HarperCollins Publishers, Inc., 1992.

MAGAZINES

Across the Board, Dec. 1992, *A World of Mirrors*, Benjamin J. Stein.

Allure, Jul. 1993, *Vegas*, Judy Bachrach.

Architectural Digest, Sep. 1992, *The Villas at the Mirage in Las Vegas*, Joan Chatfield-Taylor.

Atlantic City, Oct. 1984, *Romancing the Nugget*, Jonathan Z. Larsen.

Barron's, Apr. 3, 1989, *The Junk King Under Siege.* Kathryn M. Welling.

Barron's, Feb. 19, 1990, *The Biggest Scam Ever?*, Benjamin J. Stein.

Business Week, Feb. 18, 1985, *Rapid American's Juggling Act*, Aaron Bernstein.

Business Week, May 13, 1985, *Liquor Makers Try the Hard Sell in a Softening Market.*

Business Week, Apr. 29, 1987, *Drexel's Clients Are Rallying 'Round Milken*, Chris Welles.

Business Week, Dec. 10, 1990, *Milken is Taking the Fall for a Decade of Greed*, Chris Welles and Michele Galen.

Casino Journal, Nov. 1988, *Steve Wynn.*

Casino Player, Dec. 1994, *Mirage Resorts Announces Plans for Beau Rivage*, Sergio Lalli.

Cigar Aficionado, *A Secret Golf Course*, Michael Konik.

The Economist, Sep. 9, 1990, *By His Friends.*

Far Eastern Economic Review, Sep. 6, 1990, *The King of Macau*, Jonathan Friedland.

Financial World, Mar. 1, 1982, *Boardwalk Beauty.*

Financial World, Jul. 26, 1988, *The Ten Worst Managed Companies in America.*

Forbes, Apr. 14, 1980, *Upstart on the Boardwalk.*

Forbes, Oct. 13, 1980, *The Invisible Enterprise*, James Cook.

Forbes, Oct. 27, 1980, *The Invisible Enterprise, Part 3, Casino Gambling: Changing Character or Changing Fronts?*, James Cook and Jane Carmichael.

Forbes, Apr. 6, 1985, *Bye-Bye, Love Couch*, Jeffrey A. Trachtenberg.

Forbes, Jan. 26, 1987, *Wall Street's Hottest Hands*, Dyan Machan.

Forbes, Jul. 13, 1987, *A Chat With Michael Milken*, Allan Sloan.

Forbes, May 28, 1990, *Can Steve Wynn?*, Joel Millman.

Forbes, March 4 1991, *Step Right Up, Folks*, Laura Jereski and Jason Zweig.

Forbes, Dec. 9, 1991, *Enter Wynn*, edited by Edward Giltenan.

Forbes, Mar. 16, 1992, *My Story—Michael Milken*, James Michaels and Phyllis Berman.

Forbes, Apr. 13, 1992, *The Milken Letters.*

Forbes, Aug. 31, 1992, *Where's the Truth About Milken?*, James W. Michaels.

Forbes, Dec. 6, 1993, *The Pied Pipers of Vegas*, Lisa Gubernick.

Forbes, 1994 Edition, The 400 Richest People in America. *Inherited Talents*, Frank Wolfe.

Forbes, Mar. 14, 1994, *The Golf Bag*, James Y. Bartlett.

Fortune, Nov. 10, 1986, *Biggest Mafia Bosses*, Roy Rowan.

Fortune, Jun. 20, 1988, *Fast Stepping At the Predators' Ball*, Stratford P. Sherman.

Fortune, Nov. 7, 1988, *Michael Milken, Philanthropist*, Terence Pare.

Fortune, Jun. 14, 1993, *What CEOs Make.*

GQ, Sep. 1990, *Mr. Lucky*, Neal Karlen.

Gaming and Wagering Business, Nov. 5, 1994, *Mirage Partners With Brits and Asians to Open Argentine Casino*, Bruce Handler.

Gaming Industry Weekly Report, Alan R. Woinski, Feb. 11, 1995.

Golf, Dec. 1992, *Las Vegas Golf and Gambling in a Neon Gomorrah.*

Hartford Courant Magazine, May 17, 1992, *Wynnings*, Joel Lang.

Hotel and Motel Management, Jun. 19, 1989, *Milken Remains Las Vegas Hero*, Sergio Lalli.

The Insiders' Chronicle, May 16, 1983, *Insider Shorttakes.*

Insight, Jun. 12, 1989, *The Friends of Michael Milken.*

International Gaming & Wagering Business, Mar. 1, 1995, *Treasure Island: Fantasy by Design*, Jeff Burbank.

Jet, Apr. 12, 1993, *Michael Jackson May Start Cable Network With Ex Junk Bond King.*

Jet, Jun. 20, 1994, *Investors Group Files Suit Against TLC Beatrice International.*

LV, July 1986, *Steve Wynn Running Scared Straight Ahead*, Scott A. Zamost.

Los Angeles Business Journal, Feb. 19, 1990, *Geller Examined Milken Funds.*

Los Angeles Business Journal, Feb. 19, 1990, *Kirkland: His New Broom Begins to Sweep.*

M. Inc., Oct. 1990, *Family Man*, Kim Eisler.

Meetings & Conventions Magazine, Jun. 1993, *A Wynn-Win Situation*, David Migdal.

Nevada Casino Journal, Mar. 1989, *Zelma Wynn*, Sergio Lalli.

The Nevadan Today, Feb. 12, 1989, *Elaine Wynn: Poised and Powerful.*

New Republic, Aug. 28, 1989, *The Friends of Michael Milken*, Mark Hosenball and David Ellen.

New York Magazine, Apr. 16, 1984, *Steve Wynn on a Roll*, Jonathan Z. Larsen.

New York Magazine, Mar. 27, 1995, *Intelligencer*, Pat Wechsler and Roger D. Friedman.

New York Times Magazine, Dec. 8, 1957, *Bingo Binge is Big Business*, Robert Daley.

New York Times Magazine, Feb. 5, 1978, *The Mob Gambles on Atlantic City*, Howard Blum and Jeff Gerth.

Newsweek, Dec. 8, 1980, *A Sword in Atlantic City.*

Newsweek, Feb. 20, 1984, *Gambling's Hot Shooter*, David T. Friendly.

Newsweek, Dec. 28, 1987, *Boesky's Sentence—Who Will Be Next?*

Newsweek, Jan. 2, 1989, *Nailing the Junk Kings.*

Newsweek, Apr. 11, 1989, *Hitting Milken Where it Hurts*, Carolyn Friday and David Pauly.

Newsweek, Oct. 22, 1990, *How Crooked Was Milken?*

Overdrive, February 1974, *The Intricate Financial Web of Allen Dorfman.*
Overdrive, June 1974, *Central States Pension Fund Loans Help Tell Tale of Teamsters Officials, Organized Crime and the Attorney General of the United States.*
Penthouse, May 1985, *Meshulam Riklis Interview.*
Spirit Magazine, Jan. 1994, *Hot For The Game,* Mark Seal.
Time, Mar. 21, 1988, *Stop! In the Name of Money!*
Time, Sep. 19, 1988, *Throwing the Book at Drexel,* Stephen Koepp.
Time, Jan. 16, 1989, *Flashy Symbol of An Acquisitive Age,* Otto Friedrich.
Time, Jan. 10, 1994, *Las Vegas, The All-American City,* Kurt Andersen.
U.S. News and World Report, Sep. 24, 1990, *Michael Milken.*

DOCUMENTS

Adams, et al. v. Sindler, et al., Case No. 89-CV-1422, U.S. District Court, Southern District of California (San Diego), Docket.
The American Gaming Summit, tape transcript, Dec. 7, 1994. Keynote speaker: Steve Wynn.
Baldwin, Robert H., v. Angela Baldwin, Clark County District Court, Case No. D 124862, 1990.
CBS News—West 57th Transcript, Apr. 2, 1988. Subject: Steve Wynn.
CNN, Atlantic City Gaming Investigation, taped transcript, Joe Trento.
Central States Southeast and Southwest Areas Pension Fund Synopsis of the Pension Fund's Nevada Investment History, May 24, 1985.
Clark County Liquor and Gaming Licensing Board, Clark County, Nevada, Findings of Fact in the Matter of the Disciplinary Action Against the Work Card License of Charles Meyerson, 28 Apr. 1992.
Clark County Sanitation District, Trustee Briefing Report, Oct. 11, 1994. Subject: Cross-town Interceptor and Relief Sewer Project, Schedule G.
Congressional Record, Jan. 5, 1995, *When Gambling Comes to Town,* Stephen J. Simurda.
Executive Retirement Plan Agreement between Golden Nugget, Inc. and Stephen A. Wynn, Dec. 1, 1986.
The Extension of Credit to Members and Associates of Organized Crime, Testimony of Lt. Col. Justin Dintino, Mar. 1, 1983.
Federal Bureau of Investigation, Debriefing Memo of Joseph Vincent Agosto, Aug. 19, 1983.
Gaming Board for Great Britain, Application for Certificate of Consent, Golden Nugget Great Britain, 3 February 1982.
Gaming Board for Great Britain, Consent Application, 19 February 1982. Applicant: Golden Nugget Great Britain.
Golden Nugget Corp. v. Trump, Donald J., Eighth Judicial District Court, Clark County, Case No. 91-A-293915-C, Transcript of Deposition of Dennis Gomes.
Golden Nugget, Inc. Notice of Annual Meeting of Shareholders, 1988.
Golden Nugget, Inc. Notice of Annual Meeting of Shareholders, 1989.
Golden Nugget, Inc., Report to Shareholders for the year 1988.
Golden Nugget, Inc., Report to Shareholders for the year 1987.

IRS Form 990, Return of Organization Exempt from Income Tax for 1990, UNLV Foundation.

IRS Form 990, Return of Organization Exempt from Income Tax for 1991, UNLV Foundation.

International Teamsters Union, 1974, Synopsis of the Central States, Southeast and Southwest Area Pension Fund's Nevada Investments.

Las Vegas Metropolitan Police Department, DR#80-18-55-C, Homicide Report. Victim: Joseph Conlan. Suspect: Louis Cappiello. Location: 3413 Eastern Ave. Date: Jan. 8, 1980.

Letter from Bruce A. Levin, Vice President and General Counsel, Golden Nugget, Inc., Sep. 29, 1982, to Gaming Control Board. Subject: Voluntary submission of information by Golden Nugget, Inc.

Letter from Edward M. Doumani to Steven Wynn, Jan. 19, 1980. Subject: Corporate abuses.

Metropolitan Police New Scotland Yard, Central Officer's Special Report, 14 Feb. 1982. Subject: Golden Nugget Great Britain, Inc.

Metropolitan Police New Scotland Yard, Central Officer's Special Report, 30 March 1982. Subject: Golden Nugget Great Britain, Inc.

Metropolitan Police New Scotland Yard, London, England, Central Officer's Special Report, 9 September 1983. Subject: Golden Nugget Great Britain, Inc.

Mirage Resorts, Inc. Notice of Annual Meeting of Stockholders, 1993.

Mirage Resorts, Inc. Notice of Annual Meeting of Shareholders, 1992.

Mirage Resorts, Inc., et al., v. John Moran, et al., U.S. District Court, District of Nevada, Case No. CV-S-93-OO-369 HDM (RJJ), Complaint.

Mirage Resorts, Inc., USA Capital Management Group, Inc., Initiating Coverage, Aug. 13, 1992, Tom Hantges and Joseph Milanowski.

Nevada Commission on Ethics, In the Matter of the Opinion Request Regarding Roland Massimino and James Weaver, Nov. 15, 1994. Thomas R.C. Wilson.

Nevada Gaming Commission, Transcript, Jun. 2, 1967, Frontier Hotel Licensing Hearing.

Nevada Gaming Commission, Transcript, Jun. 15, 1967, Frontier Hotel Licensing Hearing.

Nevada Gaming Commission, Transcript of Golden Nugget, Inc. Licensing Hearing of Stephen A. Wynn, Apr. 19, 1973.

Nevada Gaming Commission, Transcript, Jun. 16, 1977. Subject: Al Harris.

Nevada Gaming Commission, Jul. 28, 1994, Transcript, Case No. 9304, State Gaming Control Board v. Kenneth Richard Wynn.

Nevada Gaming Control Board, Transcript, Jun. 1, 1967, Frontier Hotel Licensing Hearing.

Nevada Gaming Control Board, Summary submitted by Audit Division, Apr. 3, 1973, regarding Stephen A. Wynn.

Nevada Gaming Control Board, Transcript, Apr. 11, 1973, Licensing Application of Stephen A. Wynn.

Nevada Gaming Control Board, Transcript of Proceedings Regarding Al Harris, Apr. 13, 1977.

Nevada Gaming Control Board, Jun. 12, 1978, Transcript of Hearing, Licensing of Elaine Wynn.

Nevada Gaming Control Board, Memorandum, June 4, 1982. Subject: Golden Nugget, Inc. Insider Trading Investigation.

Nevada Gaming Control Board, Apr. 22, 1982, Transcript, Licensing of Kenneth Wynn.

Nevada Gaming Control Board, Sep. 12, 1984, Transcript of Licensing Hearing of Robert Baldwin.

Nevada Gaming Control Board Minutes. Subject: Key employee licensure hearing, Louis Patrick Cappiello, March 1990.

Nevada Gaming Control Board, Transcript of Key Employee Licensing Investigation of Charles Meyerson, Apr. 14-15, 1993.

New Jersey Casino Control Commission, Sep. 19, 1986, Statement of Chairman Walter Reed. Subject: Golden Nugget Atlantic City.

New Jersey Casino Control Commission, Sep. 19, 1986, Statement of Carl Zeitz. Subject: Golden Nugget Atlantic City.

New Jersey Casino Control Commission, Sep. 19, 1986, Statement of Commissioner Valerie Armstrong. Subject: Golden Nugget Atlantic City.

New Jersey Casino Control Commission, Sep. 19, 1986, Statement of Commissioner E. Kenneth Burdge. Subject: Golden Nugget Atlantic City.

New Jersey Division of Gaming Enforcement, Licensing Application of Stephen A. Wynn, Nov. 24, 1980.

New Jersey Division of Gaming Enforcement, Supplemental Summary Report, Feb. 10, 1981. Subject: Financial Status of Stephen and Elaine Wynn.

New Jersey Division of Gaming Enforcement, Reporter's Transcript of Statement of Anita Kayne Cosby. Feb. 10, 1981.

New Jersey Division of Gaming Enforcement, Aug. 12, 1985, Golden Nugget Atlantic City Licensing.

New Jersey Division of Gaming Enforcement, Aug. 27, 1984, Report to Chairman Walter N. Read regarding Charles Meyerson, Applicant for a Renewal of Casino Key Employee License.

New Jersey Division of Gaming Enforcement, photocopies of personal phone book, Charles Meyerson, 1985.

New Jersey Division of Gaming Enforcement, Jul. 3, 1986, Report to Judge Richard Voliva, Office of Administrative Law, Regarding Charles Meyerson, Applicant for Renewal of Casino Key Employee License.

New Jersey Division of Gaming Enforcement, Feb. 26, 1986, Golden Nugget Atlantic City Licensing Investigation.

New Jersey Division of Gaming Enforcement, Casino Control Commission, Order Placing Respondent Alphonse Malangone on Exclusion List. Aug. 17, 1990.

New Jersey State Commission of Investigation, Statement of Lieutenant Colonel Justin Dintino, Mar. 1, 1983.

Offense Report, Sheriff's Office, Kingman, Arizona. Subject: Nancy E. Mottolla.

President's Commission on Organized Crime, Record of Hearing IV, Nov. 27-29, 1984, Washington, D.C., Organized Crime and Cocaine Trafficking.

President's Commission on Organized Crime, Record of Hearing, VII, Jun. 24-26, 1985, New York. Organized Crime and Gambling.

Securities and Exchange Commission, Form 10-K, Dunes Hotel and Casino, Inc., Fiscal year ending 1984.

Securities and Exchange Commission, Form 10-K, Golden Nugget, Inc., Fiscal year ending 1977.

Securities and Exchange Commission, Form 10-K, Golden Nugget, Inc., Fiscal year ending 1978.

Securities and Exchange Commission, Form 10-K, Golden Nugget, Inc., Fiscal Year 1979.

Securities and Exchange Commission, Form 10-K, Golden Nugget, Inc., Fiscal year ending 1980.

Securities and Exchange Commission, Form 10-K, Golden Nugget, Inc., Fiscal year ending 1982.

Securities and Exchange Commission, Form 10-K, Golden Nugget, Inc., Fiscal year ending 1983.

Securities and Exchange Commission, Form 10-K, Golden Nugget, Inc., Fiscal year ending 1984.

Securities and Exchange Commission, Form 10-K, Golden Nugget, Inc., Fiscal year ending 1985.

Securities and Exchange Commission, Form 10-K, Golden Nugget, Inc., Fiscal year ending 1986.

Securities and Exchange Commission, Form 10-K, Golden Nugget, Inc., Fiscal year ending 1987.

Securities and Exchange Commission, Form 10-K, Golden Nugget, Inc., Fiscal year ending 1988.

Securities and Exchange Commission, Form 10-K, Golden Nugget, Inc., Fiscal year 1989.

Securities and Exchange Commission, Form 10-K, Golden Nugget, Inc., Fiscal year ending 1993.

Securities and Exchange Commission, Litigation Release regarding SEC v. Rapid-American Corporation, Aug. 16, 1979.

State of New York, Report to Governor Nelson A. Rockefeller by the Bingo Control Inquiry, Mar. 1, 1962.

Statement of Shirley Ann Fair to Drug Enforcement Administration, Jul. 21, 1980.

Stipulated Factual Statement With Reference To The License Application of Golden Nugget Atlantic City Corp., 1982.

Stipulations Between Division of Gaming Enforcement and Golden Nugget Atlantic City, Aug. 25, 1986.

The Structure of Organized Crime in New Jersey, Lt. Col. Justin Dintino, prepared for United States Senate Judiciary Committee, Feb. 16, 1983.

U.S. v. Andrew Ira Alkin, Jennifer Lynn Josephs, and Louis Patrick Cappiello, Docket, 1973.

U.S. v. Michael Dennis Jones, Richard Bert Colucci, Louis Patrick Cappiello, and Randy D'Anna, Defendants. U.S. District Court, District of Nevada. Reporter's Transcript on Appeal. September 11 and 12, 1980.

U.S. v. Anthony Salerno, et al., District Court for the Southern District of New York, case no. 85 Cr. 139.

U.S. v. Anthony Salerno, et al., District Court for the Southern District of New York, case no. 86 Cr. 245.

U.S. v. Anthony Salerno, et al., District Court for the Southern District of New York, case no. 86 Cr. 245, Wiretap Transcript, Exhibit 2028-A, Dec. 4, 1984 (conversation between Anthony Salerno and Robby Margolies at the Palma Boy Social Club, 416 E. 115th Street, New York, NY).

U.S. v. Anthony Salerno, et al., District Court for the Southern District of New York, case no. 86 Cr. 245, Wiretap Transcript, Exhibit 2024-A, November 27, 1985 (conversation among Anthony Salerno, Cirino Salerno, Louis Rotundo, Jimmy Cashin, John Tronolone and Willie Cohn at the Palma Boy Social Club, 416 E. 115th Street, New York, NY).

U.S. v. Anthony Salerno, et al., District Court for the Southern District of New York, case no. 86 Cr. 245, Partial Transcript.

U.S. Senate Permanent Subcommittee on Investigations, Hearings on Organized Crime: 25 Years after Vilachi, April 1988.

U.S. v. Michael R. Milken, Lowell J. Milken and Bruce L. Newberg, United States District Court Southern District of New York, Indictment.

Wynn, Stephen A. v. Casino News, Inc., et al., Case No. A337527, District Court, Clark County, Nevada, Summons and Complaint, Sep. 14, 1994.

Wynn, Stephen A. v. Casino News, Inc., et al., Case No. A337527, District Court, Clark County, Nevada, Answer, Oct. 7, 1994.

NOTES

PROLOGUE: Having been born in nearby Henderson and raised in Las Vegas, I had become somewhat blasé about the endless hucksterism that takes place on the Strip. After all, if you've seen one hyperbolic hotel grand opening replete with fireworks, political speeches, television celebrities, heavyweight champions, and jumbo shrimp, you've seen them all, right? Or so I thought.

That all changed on the night of October 27, 1993. Standing amid the incredible horde of humanity present to watch the implosion of the Dunes was like taking a ringside seat at the Apocalypse. Gazing through the crowd, I expected to see a platoon of science fiction and horror writers scribbling notes for the next generation of end–of–the–world epics.

Instead, it was mostly stunned tourists, drunken teenagers, and police officers. An interview with Elaine and Steve Wynn by Janie Greenspun Gale for the *Las Vegas Life* public television program was helpful in capturing the Mirage Resorts king's view of himself.

CHAPTER 1: Steve Wynn, in 1994, on Anthony Salerno: "My father was a baggy–pants bingo operator who died broke. My father never lived in New York City. He lived in Utica, New York. My dad spent the last two years of his life in a hospital with congenital heart failure and aortic stenosis because of rheumatic fever. My father wouldn't even know who Anthony J. Salerno was.

"Anybody who would have said that would have in and of itself indicated such abysmal ignorance of anything associated with my family. ... No one in the history of the world has ever said that Anthony J. Salerno had anything to do with me or my father, ever."

Wynn has recounted his first trip to Las Vegas for many interviewers, always with the cow–skull–in–the–desert image. Interviews with former Wynn professional companion Ron Tucky, retired Hughes executive Robert Maheu, and veteran Southern Nevada deli operator Max Corsun filled in the gaps.

A word on Tucky: In all the hours we spoke on tape and off the record, Tucky avoided making a single deeply embittered remark about his former employer. Tucky, himself the son of a bookmaker, and who had been a boon companion to multiple millionaires for many years before joining Wynn, appeared more hurt than spiteful of the man who, he claims, once told him he would be in his last will.

Nevada Gaming Control Board transcripts and the March 1, 1962, report to New York Gov. Nelson Rockefeller by the state's Moreland Act Commission on bingo also were useful. Nowhere in print to my knowledge has Steve Wynn ever fully described the scope of his father's bingo operations, which spanned as many as seven states.

The "302" FBI interview of Joseph Vincent Agosto not only raised the issue of Mike Wynn's mob contacts, it was incorporated in the information supplied by law enforcement authorities to New Scotland Yard investigators. Agosto provided information to his contact agent with an understanding that the material was learned from another source. Agosto, an integral part of the government's skimming case against Tropicana Hotel officers and members of the Kansas City mob, died of a heart attack in 1983.

Legendary organized crime writer Hank Messick's *Syndicate Abroad* and Wallace Turner's *Gambler's Money* were valuable in providing a view of gambling from a Kefauver slant. Perhaps one of the best magazine profiles ever written about Wynn was a 1986 piece in *LV* magazine by Scott A. Zamost. A profile on Elaine Wynn in *The Nevadan Today* and a short but insightful feature on Zelma Wynn by *Man of Honor* author Sergio Lalli in the *Nevada Casino Journal* proved useful.

The Utica Public Library reference department was also a great help. Among the newspapers whose articles contributed to this chapter: *Annapolis Capital–Gazette*, *Las Vegas Review–Journal*, *Las Vegas Sun*, *New York Times*, and *Utica Observer –Dispatch*.

CHAPTER 2: Maurice Friedman ranks as one of the great Las Vegas hucksters. Although his name appears in many books and magazine articles, as well as in the transcripts of the federal case against the mobbed–up owners of the Frontier circa 1967, the best information available on him undoubtedly is found in Ed Becker and Charlie Rappleye's book, *All–American Mafioso: The Johnny Rosselli Story* (1995, Barricade Books). Rappleye is an excellent investigative reporter, and Becker is one of the last great Las Vegas mob experts.

Transcripts from the Nevada Gaming Commission and Gaming Control Board were helpful in understanding the Frontier purchase and in comprehending just how much the authorities knew about the mobbed–up takeover team. Interviews with Claudine Williams and Maheu also are appreciated.

The offense report from the Mohave County Sheriff's Office was essential in learning more about the death of Nancy Mottola. Articles from the *Las Vegas Review–Journal* and *Sun* offered background on Niggy Devine, one of the great Southern Nevada enigmas.

CHAPTER 3: If Las Vegas ever gets around to erecting statues of its founding fathers, perhaps banker E. Parry Thomas will be one of the first to be honored. He is that important to the growth of Las Vegas and to the grooming of young Steve Wynn's career. For all his importance, a relatively small amount of information has been published about Thomas. Perhaps the best article on his role in the growth of Las Vegas was "Just Don't Touch the Dice," in *Utah Holiday* magazine.

No story that analyzes the Teamsters Central States Pension Fund is possible without the pioneering journalism of Jim Drinkhall. From *Overdrive*, the Teamsters magazine, came articles titled "The Intricate Financial Web of Allen Dorfman" and "Central States Pension Fund Loans Help Tell Tale of Teamsters Officials, Organized Crime and the Attorney General of the United States."

Documents from the Securities and Exchange Commission and Messick's *Syndicate Abroad* aided in understanding Morris Shenker's incredibly complex career. The Lewis Rosenstiel material was gathered in part from Robert Lacey's *Little Man: Meyer Lansky and the Gangster Life* and from Anthony Summers's *Official and Confidential: The Secret Life of J. Edgar Hoover.*

CHAPTER 4: Documents from the Securities and Exchange Commission and transcripts from the Nevada Gaming Commission and State Gaming Control Board provided the foundation for understanding Wynn's takeover of the Golden Nugget.

Dan Moldea's *Interference: How Organized Crime Influences Professional Football* contributed to the Jerry Zarowitz story, as did interviews with several Las Vegans, who requested anonymity.

Lee Solkey's *Dummy Up and Deal* is a slender book that provided perhaps the first insight into the life of Las Vegas blackjack dealers. The *Las Vegas Sun, Review–Journal,* and *Valley Times* helped flesh out this chapter, as did interviews with more than a dozen casino executives, whose request not to be identified will be honored.

CHAPTER 5: Drug Enforcement Administration affidavits and Golden Nugget Inc.'s SEC Form 10-Ks as well as the 1980 and 1986 licensing background investigations of Steve Wynn helped detail his relationship with Louis Patrick Cappiello. The shooting case of Joseph Conlan and Philip Taft was gathered from police records, which are now under seal.

An excerpt from the affidavit of Dennis Gomes also proved a valuable resource. Cappiello continues to make his home in Las Vegas, where he has been employed by a sanitation company, sausage distributor, and Chinese restaurant. Neil Azzinaro has returned to the gaming industry and is employed at a local resort. Articles in the *Las Vegas Review–Journal* and interviews with current and former law enforcement officials also came in handy.

CHAPTER 6: *Atlantic City: 125 Years of Ocean Madness* by Vicki Gold and Lee Eisenberg and *Boardwalk Jungle* by Ovid Demaris were two books among many that provided background for this chapter.

Interviews with current and former investigators with the New Jersey Division of Gaming Enforcement helped temper the findings of their at–times–devastating inquiries. "The Mob Gambles on Atlantic City" by Jeff Gerth and Howard Blum in the *New York Times Magazine* and "The Invisible Enterprise" by the James Cook and Jane Carmichael in *Forbes* were of great assistance in capturing the scope of La Cosa Nostra's grip on the Boardwalk.

The Gaming Control Board's investigation into suspected insider trading within the Golden Nugget provided the motivation for the Federal Organized Crime Strike Force to investigate. For the record, letters and documents related to the confidential control board investigation were gathered from private, not state, sources.

CHAPTER 7: Gaming Control Board transcripts proved invaluable in writing this chapter, as did Connie Bruck's *Master of the Game* and the investigative journalism of Daniel Heneghan of the *Press* of Atlantic City. Public statements by former Casino

Control Commissioner Walter Read and the background investigations of Meyerson and Wynn contributed a great deal. Articles from the *Las Vegas Review–Journal* and *New York Times* also helped.

CHAPTER 8: The New Jersey Division of Gaming Enforcement's public statements on money laundering and casino gambling, especially the findings of Lt. Col. Justin Dintino of the state police, were important contributors to this chapter. No discussion of Anthony Castelbuono's money–laundering foray in Atlantic City would be complete without the transcript on the subject from the President's Commission on Organized Crime and New Jersey gaming authorities' investigation of the matter. An interview with Drug Enforcement Administration official Joel Gutensohn is greatly appreciated, and Steve Wynn has had much to say on this subject.

CHAPTER 9: Mel Edward Harris, son of mob bookmaker Al Harris, met twice with Anthony Salerno at the Palma Boy Social Club. Salerno, however, discussed Harris—and the jobs he might provide friends of the mob—on a number of other occasions.

Interviews with several organized crime associates who were acquainted with Salerno for nearly thirty years were a big help. FBI tape surveillance transcripts, the transcript of Anthony Salerno's federal racketeering trial, and documents from the Victor Palmieri–Golden Nugget federal lawsuit helped form this chapter. Public statements by New Jersey gaming regulators and the transcript of the April 1988 CBS *West 57th* television news program also provided insight.

CHAPTER 10: The New Scotland Yard background investigation of Steve Wynn and Golden Nugget produced the most controversial document in Wynn's often–controversial life. Where several American law enforcement agencies were content with leaving suspicions unwritten, the Yard's investigators poured on damaging material. It should be noted that, although much of the information is gleaned from intelligence files, those files were opened at the offices of the FBI, IRS, New Jersey Division of Gaming Enforcement, and Nevada Gaming Control Board.

Boardwalk Jungle by Demaris was useful in balancing the political perspective on the movement of American casino corporations to Great Britain. Scotland Yard has declined to comment on its investigation. Interviews with Wynn and Bob Maxey were helpful in understanding both sides of this issue.

CHAPTER 11: The opening scene of this chapter comes from a personal experience. I was seated at the Gourmet Cafe drinking a cup of coffee with Las Vegas attorney George Ogilvie when Wynn pressed his face up to the restaurant's window. In a brief interview on the sidewalk after Milken checked in with federal parole and probation officials, he was guarded but gracious. Wynn made a special point of noting that his friend, "Milken– Schmilken," was personally responsible for providing 100,000 jobs to the Southern Nevada market.

Several books on Milken were used to flesh out this complex individual. On the pro–Michael side: Fenton Bailey's *Fall From Grace* and Jesse Kornbluth's *Highly Confident*. On the anti–Michael side: James B. Stewart's *Den of Thieves*, Connie Bruck's *The Predator's Ball*, and Benjamin J. Stein's *A License to Steal*. Magazine articles from

Forbes, Business Week, Fortune, Insight, New Republic, Newsweek, and *Time,* and newspaper stories from the *Las Vegas Review–Journal, Las Vegas Sun, New York Times,* and *Wall Street Journal* added much to this chapter.

Interviews with Wynn and other Las Vegas casino operators acquainted with Milken also were helpful.

CHAPTER 12: Nevada Gaming Control Board transcripts were used in researching this chapter as were articles in the *Las Vegas Review–Journal* and *Las Vegas Sun.* Interviews with Charlie Meyerson, Steve Wynn, Frank Schreck, and C. Stanley Hunterton also were conducted.

In June 1995, Genovese capo Alphonse "Allie Shades" Malangone was indicted in the largest investigation into the New York garbage–carting industry in history. Genovese soldier Carmine "Baby Carmine" Russo and his running mate Elia "Chinatown" Albanese were arrested days earlier for allegedly hauling 7,000 pounds of illegal fireworks through the Holland Tunnel into New York for sale before July Fourth. Albanese has been arrested twenty–seven times on fireworks violations since 1972. Albanese, Russo, Gerard Guadagno, and Frank Carbonaro also were indicted in two bank robberies, the largest a $1.4 million Chemical Bank heist.

CHAPTER 13: Interviews with Ron Tucky and Las Vegans who asked not to be identified contributed to this chapter. David Spanier's *All Right, Okay, You Win,* David Johnston's *Temples of Chance,* and *Boardwalk Jungle* were helpful, too.

Documents from the Nevada Gaming Control Board, Securities and Exchange Commission, Clark County Business Licensing, Clark County Commission were essential, as were articles from *Newsweek, Forbes,* and *New York* magazines and newspaper stories by Las Vegas columnist Don Digilio and syndicated television columnist Tom Shales. Other *newspapers: New York Times, Boston Globe, Los Angeles Times, Las Vegas Review–Journal, Las Vegas Sun.*

CHAPTER 14: Guests are allowed to visit Shadow Creek by invitation only. Under the potential threat of an inquiry by the Internal Revenue Service, Wynn has begun allowing a slightly wider array of Mirage resorts employees to play the course.

Interviews with Ron Tucky and several Las Vegans who have played Shadow Creek more than once helped capture the spirit of the course. An interview with former Ben Siegel attorney Lou Wiener, Jr., was valuable in understanding the evolution of the golf course as a marketing tool in Las Vegas. Articles in *Cigar Aficionado, Forbes, Golf, Spy, Golf Digest,* the *Las Vegas Review– Journal,* and *Las Vegas Sun* were of assistance. In particular was Sun columnist Dean Juipe's humorous and insightful story on life inside Shadow Creek's cyclone fence.

CHAPTER 15: *Philadelphia Inquirer* reporter Fen Montaigne's profile briefly mentioned Wynn's backyard dolphin idea, and Ron Tucky recalled Wynn's fascination with the creatures after the boss had returned from visiting hotel developer Chris Hemmeter in Hawaii. Officials at the National Marine Fisheries Service took time away from their daunting tasks to render assistance.

Articles from the *Las Vegas Review–Journal* and *Las Vegas Sun*, including an especially well–done story by Lynn Waddell, helped to capture the essence of the controversy.

CHAPTER 16: Interviews with Tucky, Mike Flores, and Steve Miller, Nevada and New Jersey gaming officials, and press conference appearances by Steve Wynn and John Wilhelm came into play in this chapter. The Trump–Wynn lawsuit hearings and the Dennis Gomes deposition also were incorporated. *Trump: The Art of the Deal* by Donald Trump and Tony Schwartz was useful as well.

The magazines: *Forbes, Business Week, GQ.* Newspapers: *Las Vegas Review–Journal, Las Vegas Sun, Salt Lake Tribune,* and *Press* of Atlantic City, especially articles by Carri Geer, Daniel Heneghan, Dave Palermo, Howard Stutz, and Al Tobin. Kim Eisler's particularly insightful profile of Wynn in *M. Inc.* magazine remains one of the few investigative stories ever written on the subject.

CHAPTER 17: Interviews with Michael Gaughan of the Barbary Coast and Gold Coast, Mike Sloan of Circus Circus, Bruce MacDonald of Foxwoods, and an array of Las Vegas casino executives who agreed to speak only if their names were not revealed, were used in researching this chapter.

Among the newspapers: S*t. Petersburg Post, Orlando Sun– Sentinel, Vancouver Sun, Chicago Tribune, New York Times, Miami Herald, Boston Globe, Connecticut Post, Hartford Courant, Detroit News, Detroit Free Press, Kansas City Star, New Orleans Times–Picayune.*

CHAPTER 18: A variety of sources at the Clark County School District, Clark County Commission, University of Nevada–Las Vegas, and State Gaming Control Board agreed to share information if their names were not revealed. One person who had no such qualms about conducting an interview was University Regent Shelley Berkley, who graduated from UNLV and went on to become a driving force behind the Sands Hotel and the fundraising and lobbying arms of the Jewish communities in Southern Nevada and throughout the country. Her candor in the face of the potential political repercussions is greatly appreciated.

Shark Attack author Don Yaeger shared his insights and his manuscript. Articles from the following publications were used in this chapter: *Forbes, Las Vegas Review–Journal, Las Vegas Sun, Salt Lake Tribune, USA Today.* Journalists whose work was particularly helpful include Warren Bates, Jeff German, A.D. Hopkins, Mary Hynes, former Nevada Governor Mike O'Callaghan, and Danny Robbins.

EPILOGUE: Interviews with Michael Gaughan, Mike Sloan, Claudine Williams, and a host of Wynn's colleagues and casino industry allies contributed much to this epilogue. Press conference statements by Steve Wynn, Culinary International official John Wilhelm, and Nevada Governor Bob Miller also were used. SEC Form 10–Ks and annual reports to Mirage Resorts stockholders were incorporated as well.

The epilogue includes a brief excerpt from Budd Schulberg's *What Makes Sammy Run?* The work of journalists John Gallant, Marian Green, and Dave Palermo also contributed.

INDEX